To Anne

CONTENTS

Acknowledgments   ix

Introduction   1

1. The Long Tail   15

2. The Rise and Fall of the Hit   27

3. A Short History of the Long Tail   41

4. The Three Forces of the Long Tail   52

5. The New Producers   58

6. The New Markets   85

7. The New Tastemakers   98

8. Long Tail Economics   125

9. The Short Head   147

10. The Paradise of Choice   168

11. Niche Culture   177

12. The Infinite Screen   192

13. Beyond Entertainment   201

14. Long Tail Rules   217

Coda: Tomorrow's Tail   225

Notes on Sources and Further Reading   227

Index   231

THE LONG TAIL

THE
LONG TAIL

How Endless Choice is
Creating Unlimited Demand

CHRIS ANDERSON

BUSINESS
BOOKS

Published by Random House Business Books in 2006

First published in the United Kingdom in 2006
by Random House Business Books
First published in the United States in 2006
by Hyperion

Random House Business Books
The Random House Group Limited
20 Vauxhall Bridge Road, London, SW1V 2SA

Random House Australia (Pty) Limited
20 Alfred Street, Milsons Point, Sydney
New South Wales 2061, Australia

Random House New Zealand Limited
18 Poland Road, Glenfield
Auckland 10, New Zealand

Random House (Pty) Limited
Isle of Houghton, Corner of Boundary Road & Carse O'Gowrie
Houghton 2198, South Africa

Random House Publishers India Private Limited
301 World Trade Tower, Hotel Intercontinental Grand Complex,
Barakhamba Lane, New Delhi 110 001, India

The Random House Group Limited Reg. No. 954009

www.randomhouse.co.uk

A CIP catalogue record for this book
is available from the British Library

Papers used by Random House are natural, recyclable products
made from wood grown in sustainable forests. The manufacturing
processes conform to the environmental regulations of the country of origin

ISBN 9781844138500 (from January 2007)
ISBN 184413850X

Design by Victoria Hartman
Printed and bound in Great Britain by
Mackays of Chatham plc, Chatham, Kent

ACKNOWLEDGMENTS

This book has benefited from the help and collaboration of literally thousands of people, thanks to the relatively open process of having it start as a widely read article and continue in public as a blog of work in progress. The result is that there are many people to thank, both here and in the chapter notes at the end of the book.

First, the person other than me who worked the hardest, my wife, Anne. No project like this could be done without a strong partner. Anne was all that and more. Her constant support and understanding made this possible, and the price was significant, from all the Sundays taking care of the kids while I worked at Starbucks to the lost evenings, absent vacations, nights out not taken, and other costs of an all-consuming project. But more than that, she was my sounding board, my first reader, my counsel, confidante, and an endless source of encouragement and advice. (Our young children—Daniel, Erin, Toby, and Isabel—also spent a year without seeing much of their father, and I thank them for rising to the occasion with sterling behavior and, one hopes, no permanent scars.)

In the research and outlining phase of the book, I was fortunate to have had the use of perhaps two of the best working and thinking spaces on the planet. Louis Rossetto and Jane Metcalfe, our friends, neighbors, and the founders of *Wired*, graciously lent me their beautiful Berkeley offices for several months in the summer of 2005. (I was a "scholar in residence," a title that made me feel smarter all by itself.) And another dear friend, Peter Schwartz, gave me space in the equally beautiful Emeryville offices of his Global Business Network, where I did much of my later-stage brainstorming and whiteboarding with my crack writing assistant, Steven Leckart.

My other invaluable partners were my team at *Wired*, particularly Bob Cohn and Thomas Goetz, the executive and deputy editors, respectively. They rose to the occasion brilliantly, managing to both encourage me and cover for me as the book consumed more and more of my time. Bob also edited the original Long Tail article, helping me refine the arguments and phrasing, a contribution that continues to pay dividends. Melanie Cornwell's comments on the manuscript caught many pop culture errors and otherwise made it smarter. Also thanks to Blaise Zerega, who as managing editor kept the wheels from falling off while I was only semi-present, and Joanna Pearlstein, our research director, who helped with many of the early infographics. And special thanks to Si Newhouse for entrusting me with his remarkable platform for ideas in the first place and generously allowing me to take the time off to expand one into a book.

Many academics contributed in important ways to quantifying Long Tail effects and exploring their implications. Erik Brynjolfsson from MIT's Sloan School of Management and Jeffrey Hu from Purdue's Krannert School of Management did some of the early work on estimating Amazon's Long Tail, which gave me both an analytical framework on which to build the theory and the confidence to know that it could be done. Their continuing research in this area is fascinating, and their support for my work is greatly appreciated. At Harvard Business School, Anita Elberse's work on the Long Tail of Netflix and DVDs has been very helpful, and I look forward to both its publication and future work with her.

At Stanford Business School, Professor Haim Mendelson allowed me to present to one of his classes and make the Long Tail a research subject. As a result, I was fortunate to work with his students Angie Shelton, Natalie Kim, Saloni Saraiya, and Bethany Poole, who wrote case studies of Yahoo! Music and eBay. On the eBay research we also had the help of Terapeak, which provided invaluable data on the Long Tail of buyers and sellers on that marketplace. And at the University of California, Berkeley, economist Hal Varian has been a font of ideas and advice, along with inspiring me to consider new angles and aspire to greater rigor.

One of the early sources of data and a continuing best-practice Long Tail example was RealNetworks' Rhapsody. Rob Glaser and Matt Graves there were a source of constant help and encouragement, for which I am eternally grateful. Reed Hastings, the CEO of Netflix, was not only an early supporter and data provider, but also the one who advised me that my "Long Tail" phrase might have legs, which turned out to be wise indeed. Dave Goldberg at Yahoo! helped with insight into the music industry, and Bill Fisher of DVDStation provided both data and wisdom into the changing DVD economy. And Robbie Vann-Adibé, formerly of Ecast, deserves a special thanks for getting me started on this.

Thinkers and writers who contributed to this book in both words and ideas include Umair Haque, who helped tremendously with the House Music section; Glenn Fleishman, who contributed hugely to the Amazon sections; Andrew Blau of GBN, who helped me think through the Long Tail from an incentives perspective; Rob Reid, whose long and brilliant emails on the changing entertainment economy I've quoted at length; and Kevin Laws, whose early insights into the power of a mass of niches influenced the original article.

My agent, John Brockman, not only was a great sounding board and advisor, but also invited me into his extraordinary world of thinkers and scientists, and I count the many dinners and meetings I've had at his invitation as among some of the most interesting of my life. My editor at Hyperion, Will Schwalbe, helped me tremendously in focusing the book; its current structure is largely due to his wise advice and its completion is due to his constant enthusiasm and gentle guidance.

My parents deserve special thanks. To my father, Jim Anderson, for showing me the importance of a global view and intellectual honesty. And to my mother, Carlotta Anderson, for inspiring me with rhetorical rigor and boundless curiosity.

The research on the book industry was among the most difficult, since the ideal source data (Amazon's sales records) was unavailable and we were forced to reverse-engineer much of it from third-party data. For that, I owe special thanks to Morris Rosenthal and Tim O'Reilly. Finally, thanks to John Battelle, the author of *The Search*, whose example of blogging a book in progress inspired me to start thelongtail.com, which has been the source of incalculable other good ideas, advice, data, and wisdom from my thousands of smart readers, who deserve the last, and heartfelt, thanks.

THE LONG TAIL

INTRODUCTION

The tracking of top-seller lists is a national obsession. Our culture is a massive popularity contest. We are consumed by hits—making them, choosing them, talking about them, and following their rise and fall. Every weekend is a box-office horse race, and every Thursday night is a Darwinian struggle to find the fittest TV show and let it live to see another week. A few hit songs play in heavy rotation on the radio dials, while entertainment executives in all these industries sweat as they search for the next big thing.

This is the world the blockbuster built. The massive media and entertainment industries grew up over the past half century on the back of box-office rockets, gold records, and double-digit TV ratings. No surprise that hits have become the lens through which we observe our own culture. We define our age by our celebrities and mass-market products—they are the connective tissue of our common experience. The star-making system that Hollywood began eight decades ago has now spun out into every corner of commerce, from shoes to chefs. Our media is obsessed with what's hot and what's not. Hits, in short, *rule*.

Yet look a little closer and you'll see that this picture, which first emerged with the postwar broadcast era of radio and television, is now starting to tatter at the edges. Hits are starting to, gasp, *rule less*. Number one is still number one, but the sales that go with that are not what they once were.

Most of the top fifty best-selling albums of all time were recorded in the seventies and eighties (the Eagles, Michael Jackson), and none of them were made in the past five years. Hollywood box-office revenue was down by more than 6 percent in 2005, reflecting the reality that the theatergoing audience is falling even as the population grows.

Every year network TV loses more of its audience to hundreds of niche cable channels. Males age eighteen to thirty-four, the most desirable audience for advertisers, are starting to turn off the TV altogether, shifting more and more of their screen time to the Internet and video games. The ratings of top TV shows have been falling for decades, and the number one show today wouldn't have made the top ten in 1970.

In short, although we still obsess over hits, they are not quite the economic force they once were. Where are those fickle consumers going instead? No single place. They are scattered to the winds as markets fragment into countless niches. The one big growth area is the Web, but it is an uncategorizable sea of a million destinations, each defying in its own way the conventional logic of media and marketing.

ITUNES KILLED THE RADIO STAR

I came of age in the peak of the mass-culture era—the seventies and eighties. The average teenager then had access to a half dozen TV channels, and virtually everyone watched a few or more of the same handful of TV shows. There were three or four rock radio stations in any town that largely dictated what music people listened to; only a few lucky kids with money built record collections that ventured farther afield.

We all saw the same summer blockbusters in the theater and got our news from the same papers and broadcasts. About the only places you could explore outside the mainstream were the library and the comic book shop. As best I can recall, the only culture I was exposed to other than mass culture was books and whatever my friends and I made up, and that traveled no farther than our own backyards.

Contrast my adolescence with that of Ben, a sixteen-year-old who grew up with the Internet. He's the single child of affluent parents in the tony North Berkeley Hills, so he's got a Mac in his bedroom, a fully stocked iPod (and a weekly iTunes allowance), and a posse of friends with the same. Like the rest of his teenage friends, Ben has never known a world without broadband, cell phones, MP3s, TiVo, and on-line shopping.

The main effect of all this connectivity is unlimited and unfiltered access to culture and content of all sorts, from the mainstream to the farthest fringe of the underground. Ben is growing up in a different world from the one I grew up in, a world far less dominated by any of the traditional media and entertainment industries. If you don't recognize yourself in the pages to come in this book, imagine Ben instead. His reality is the leading edge of all of our futures.

From Ben's perspective, the cultural landscape is a seamless continuum from high to low, with commercial and amateur content competing equally for his attention. He simply doesn't distinguish between mainstream hits and underground niches—he picks what he likes from an infinite menu where Hollywood movies and player-created video-game stunt videos are listed side by side.

Ben watches just two hours or so a week of regular TV, mostly *West Wing* (time shifted, of course) and *Firefly,* a canceled space serial he has stored on his TiVo. He also counts as TV the anime he downloads with BitTorrent, a peer-to-peer file-sharing technology, because it was originally broadcast on Japanese television (the English subtitles are often edited in by fans).

When it comes to movies, he's a sci-fi fan, so he's pretty mainstream. *Star Wars* is a passion, as was the *Matrix* series. But he also watches movies he downloads, such as amateur machinima (movies made by controlling characters in video games) and independent productions such as *Star Wars Revelations,* a fan-created tribute film with special effects that rival the Lucas originals.

Some of the music on his iPod is downloaded from iTunes, but most comes from his friends. When one of the group buys a CD, he or she typically makes copies for everyone else. Ben's taste is mostly classic rock—Led Zeppelin and Pink Floyd—with a smattering of video-game soundtracks. The only radio he listens to is when his parents turn on NPR in the car.

Ben's reading ranges from *Star Wars* novels to Japanese manga, with a large helping of Web comics. He, like a few of his friends, is so into Japanese subculture that he's studying Japanese in school. When I was in school, kids studied Japanese because Japan was a dominant economic power and language skills were thought to open up career opportunities. But now kids study Japanese so they can create their own anime subtitles and dig deeper into manga than the relatively mainstream translated stuff.

Most of Ben's free time is spent online, both randomly surfing and participating in user forums such as Halo and *Star Wars* discussion sites. He's not interested in news—he reads no newspapers and watches no TV news—but follows the latest tech and subculture chatter on sites such as Slashdot (geek news) and Fark (weird news). He instant messages constantly all day with his ten closest friends. He doesn't text much on his cell phone, but he has friends that do. (Texting is preferred by those who are out and about a lot; IM is the chat channel of choice for those who tend to spend more time in their own rooms.) He plays video games with friends, mostly online. He thinks Halo 2 rocks, especially the user-modified levels.

I suspect that had I been born twenty-five years later, my teenage years would have been quite similar. The main difference between Ben's adolescence and my own is simply choice. I was limited to what was broadcast over the airwaves. He's got the Internet. I didn't have TiVo (or even cable); he has all that and BitTorrent, too. I had no idea there was even such a thing as manga, much less how to get it. Ben has access to it all. Would I have watched *Gilligan's Island* reruns if I'd been able to build a clan with friends in World of Warcraft online instead? I doubt it.

TV shows were more popular in the seventies than they are now not because they were better, but because we had fewer alternatives to compete for our screen attention. What we thought was the rising tide of common culture actually turned out to be less about the triumph of

Hollywood talent and more to do with the sheepherding effect of broadcast distribution.

The great thing about broadcast is that it can bring one show to millions of people with unmatchable efficiency. But it can't do the opposite—bring a million shows to one person each. Yet that is exactly what the Internet does so well. The economics of the broadcast era required hit shows—big buckets—to catch huge audiences. The economics of the broadband era are reversed. Serving the same stream to millions of people at the same time is hugely expensive and wasteful for a distribution network optimized for point-to-point communications.

There's still demand for big cultural buckets, but they're no longer the only market. The hits now compete with an infinite number of niche markets, of any size. And consumers are increasingly favoring the one with the most choice. The era of one-size-fits-all is ending, and in its place is something new, a market of multitudes.

This book is about that market.

This shattering of the mainstream into a zillion different cultural shards is something that upsets traditional media and entertainment no end. After decades of executives refining their skill in creating, picking, and promoting hits, those hits are suddenly not enough. The audience is shifting to something else, a muddy and indistinct proliferation of . . . Well, we don't have a good term for such non-hits. They're certainly not "misses," because most weren't aimed at world domination in the first place. They're "everything else."

It's odd that this should be an overlooked category. We are, after all, talking about the vast majority of everything. Most movies aren't hits, most music recordings don't make the top 100, most books aren't best-sellers, and most video programs don't even get measured by Nielsen, much less clean up in prime time. Many of them nevertheless record audiences in the millions worldwide. They just don't count as hits, and are therefore not counted.

But they're where the formerly compliant mass market is scattering to. The simple picture of the few hits that mattered and the everything else that didn't is now becoming a confusing mosaic of a million mini-markets and micro-stars. Increasingly, the mass market is turning into a mass of niches.

That mass of niches has always existed, but as the cost of reaching it falls—consumers finding niche products, and niche products finding consumers—it's suddenly becoming a cultural and economic force to be reckoned with.

The new niche market is not replacing the traditional market of hits, just sharing the stage with it for the first time. For a century we have winnowed out all but the best-sellers to make the most efficient use of costly shelf space, screens, channels, and attention. Now, in a new era of networked consumers and digital everything, the economics of such distribution are changing radically as the Internet absorbs each industry it touches, becoming store, theater, and broadcaster at a fraction of the traditional cost.

Think of these falling distribution costs as a dropping waterline or a receding tide. As they fall, they reveal a new land that has been there all along, just underwater. These niches are a great uncharted expanse of products that were previously uneconomic to offer. Many of these kinds of products have always been there, just not visible or easy to find. They are the movies that didn't make it to your local theater, the music not played on the local rock radio station, the sports equipment not sold at Wal-Mart. Now they're available, via Netflix, iTunes, Amazon, or just some random place Google turned up. The invisible market has turned visible.

Other niche products are new, created by an emerging industry at the intersection between the commercial and noncommercial worlds, where it's hard to tell when the professionals leave off and the amateurs take over. This is the world of bloggers, video-makers, and garage bands, all suddenly able to find an audience thanks to those same enviable economics of digital distribution.

THE 98 PERCENT RULE

This book began with a quiz I got wrong. One of the things I do as the editor of *Wired* is give speeches about technology trends. Because I started my career in the science world and then learned economics at *The Economist,* I look for those trends first in hard data. And, fortunately enough, there has never been more data available. The secrets of twenty-first-century economics lie in the servers of the companies that are all around us, from eBay to Wal-Mart. Although it's not always easy to get the raw numbers, the executives at those companies swim in that data every day and have a great intuitive feel for what's meaningful and what isn't. So the trick to trend-spotting is to ask them.

Which is what I was doing in January 2004, in the offices of Robbie Vann-Adibé, the CEO of Ecast, a "digital jukebox" company. Digital jukeboxes are just like regular jukeboxes—a big enclosure with speakers and blinking lights, often found in bars—with the difference that rather than a hundred CDs, they have a broadband connection to the Internet and patrons can choose from thousands of tracks that are downloaded and stored on a local hard drive.

During the course of our conversation, Vann-Adibé asked me to guess what percentage of the 10,000 albums available on the jukeboxes sold at least one track per quarter.

I knew, of course, that Vann-Adibé was asking me a trick question. The normal answer would be 20 percent because of the 80/20 Rule, which experience tells us applies practically everywhere. That is: 20 percent of products account for 80 percent of sales (and usually 100 percent of the profits).

But Vann-Adibé was in the digital content business, which is different. So I thought I'd go way out on a limb and venture that a whopping 50 percent of those 10,000 albums sold at least one track a quarter.

Now, on the face of it, that's absurdly high. Half of the top 10,000 books in a typical book superstore don't sell once a quarter. Half of the top 10,000 CDs at Wal-Mart don't sell once a quarter; indeed, Wal-Mart doesn't even carry half that many CDs. It's hard to think of any market where such a high fraction of such a large inventory sells. But my sense was that digital was different, so I took a chance on a big number.

I was, needless to say, way, way off. The answer was 98 percent.

"It's amazing, isn't it?" Vann-Adibé said. "Everyone gets that wrong." Even he had been stunned: As the company added more titles to its collections, far beyond the inventory of most record stores and into the world of niches and subcultures, they continued to sell. And the more the company added, the more they sold. The demand for music beyond the hits seemed to be limitless. True, the songs didn't sell in big numbers, but nearly all of them sold something. And because these were just bits in a database that cost nearly nothing to store and deliver, all those onesies and twosies started to add up.

What Vann-Adibé had discovered was that the aggregate market for niche music was huge, and effectively unbounded. He called this the "98 Percent Rule." As he later put it to me, "In a world of almost zero packaging cost and instant access to almost all content in this format, consumers exhibit consistent behavior: They look at almost everything. I believe that this requires major changes by the content producers—I'm just not sure what changes!"

I set out to answer that question. I realized that his counterintuitive statistic contained a powerful truth about the new economics of entertainment in the digital age. With unlimited supply, our assumptions about the relative roles of hits and niches were all wrong. Scarcity requires hits—if there are only a few slots on the shelves or the airwaves, it's only sensible to fill them with the titles that will sell best. And if that's all that's available, that's all people will buy.

But what if there are infinite slots? Maybe hits are the wrong way to look at the business. There are, after all, a lot more non-hits than hits, and now both are equally available. What if the non-hits—from healthy niche product to outright misses—all together added up to a market as big as, if not bigger than, the hits themselves? The answer to that was clear: It would radically transform some of the largest markets in the world.

And so I embarked on a research project that was to take me to all the leaders in the emerging digital entertainment industry, from Amazon to iTunes. Everywhere I went the story was the same: Hits are great, but niches are emerging as the big new market. The 98 Percent Rule turned out to be nearly universal. Apple said that every one of the then 1 million tracks in iTunes had sold at least once (now its inventory is twice that). Netflix reckoned that 95 percent of its 25,000 DVDs (that's now 55,000) rented at least once a quarter. Amazon didn't give out an exact number, but independent academic research on its book sales suggested that 98 percent of its top 100,000 books sold at least once a quarter, too. And so it went, from company to company.

Each company was impressed by the demand they were seeing in categories that had been previously dismissed as beneath the economic fringe, from the British television series DVDs that are proving surprisingly popular at Netflix to the back-catalog music that's big on iTunes. I realized that, for the first time, I was looking at the true shape of demand in our culture, unfiltered by the economics of scarcity.

That shape is, to be clear, really, really weird. To think that basically everything you put out there finds demand is just odd. The reason it's odd is that we don't typically think in terms of one unit per quarter. When we think about traditional retail, we think about what's going to sell a lot. You're not much interested in the occasional sale, because in traditional retail a CD that sells only one unit a quarter consumes exactly the same half-inch of shelf space as a CD that sells 1,000 units a quarter. There's a value to that space—rent, overhead, staffing costs, etc.—that has to be paid back by a certain number of inventory turns per month. In other words, the onesies and twosies waste space.

However, when that space doesn't cost anything, suddenly you can look at those infrequent sellers again, and they begin to have value. This was the insight that led to Amazon, Netflix, and all the other companies I was talking to. All of them realized that where the economics of traditional retail ran out of steam, the economics of online retail kept going. The onesies and twosies were still only selling in small numbers, but there were so, so *many* of them that in aggregate they added up to a big business.

Throughout the first half of 2004 I fleshed out this research in speeches, the thesis advancing with each talk. Originally the speech was called "The 98 Percent Rule." Then it was "New Rules for the New Entertainment Economy" (not one of my better naming moments).

But by then I had some hard data, thanks to Rhapsody, which is one of the online music companies. They had given me a month's worth of customer usage data, and when I graphed it out, I realized that the curve was unlike anything I'd seen before.

It started like any other demand curve, ranked by popularity. A few hits were downloaded a huge number of times at the head of the curve, and then it fell off steeply with less popular tracks. But the interesting thing was that it never fell to zero. I'd go to the 100,000th track, zoom in, and the downloads per month were still in the thousands. And the curve just kept going: 200,000, 300,000, 400,000 tracks—no store could ever carry this much music. Yet as far as I looked, there was still demand. Way out at the end of the curve, tracks were being downloaded just four or five times a month, but the curve still wasn't at zero.

In statistics, curves like that are called "long-tailed distributions," because the tail of the curve is very long relative to the head. So all I did was focus on the tail itself, turn it into a proper noun, and "The Long Tail" was born. It started life as slide 20 of one of my "New Rules" presentations. I think it was Reed Hastings, the CEO of Netflix, who convinced me that I was burying my lead. By the summer of 2004 "The Long Tail" was not just the title of my speeches; I was nearly finished with an article of the same name for my own magazine.

When "The Long Tail" was published in *Wired* in October 2004, it quickly became the most cited article the magazine had ever run. The three main observations—(1) the tail of available variety is far longer than we realize; (2) it's now within reach economically; (3) all those niches, when aggregated, can make up a significant market—seemed indisputable, especially backed up with heretofore unseen data.

TAILS EVERYWHERE

One of the most encouraging aspects of the overwhelming response to the original article was the breadth of industries in which it resonated. The article originated as an analysis of the new economics of the entertainment and media industries, and I only expanded it a bit to mention in passing that companies such as eBay (with used goods) and Google (with small advertisers) were also Long Tail businesses. Readers, however, saw the Long Tail everywhere, from politics to public relations, and from sheet music to college sports.

What people intuitively grasped was that new efficiencies in distribution, manufacturing, and marketing were changing the definition of what was commercially viable across the board. The best way to describe these forces is that they are turning unprofitable customers, products, and markets into profitable ones. Although this phenomenon is most obvious in entertainment and media, it's an easy leap to eBay to see it at work more broadly, from cars to crafts.

Seen broadly, it's clear that the story of the Long Tail is really about the economics of abundance—what happens when the bottlenecks that stand between supply and demand in our culture start to disappear and everything becomes available to everyone.

People often ask me to name some product category that does not lend itself to Long Tail economics. My usual answer is that it would be in some undifferentiated commodity, where variety is not only absent but unwanted. Like, for instance, flour, which I remembered being sold in the supermarket in a big bag labeled "Flour." Then I happened to step inside our local Whole Foods grocery and realized how wrong I was: Today the grocery carries more than twenty different types of flour, ranging from such basics as whole wheat and organic varieties to exotics such as amaranth and blue cornmeal. There is, amazingly enough, already a Long Tail in flour.

Our growing affluence has allowed us to shift from being bargain shoppers buying branded (or even unbranded) commodities to becoming mini-connoisseurs, flexing our taste with a thousand little indulgences that set us apart from others. We now engage in a host of new consumer behaviors that are described with intentionally oxymoronic terms: "massclusivity," "slivercasting," "mass customization." They all point in the same direction: more Long Tails.

A PREVIEW OF TWENTY-FIRST-CENTURY ECONOMICS

This book is partly an economic research project, with the help and involvement of students and professors from the Stanford, MIT, and Harvard business schools. It's partly the fruit of more than a hundred speeches, brainstorming sessions, and site visits with companies and industry groups that see the Long Tail changing their world. And it's partly a collaboration with the dozens of companies and executives who shared many megabytes of internal data, giving me an unprecedented view on the emerging micro-economics of markets in the online age.

What's fascinating about this moment is that the economics of the twenty-first century are already evident in outline form in the databases of the Googles, Amazons, Netflixes, and iTunes of the world. In those many terabytes of user behavior data is a clue to how consumers will behave in markets of infinite choice, a question that hadn't been meaningful until recently but has now become essential to understand.

Surprisingly, very few economists are looking at this data, mostly because they haven't asked (most of the academics I worked with are in business schools, only a few of them are economists). There are some exceptions—University of California Berkeley economist Hal Varian works part-time at Google, and auction-theory economists unsurprisingly love eBay—but they're rare. Some of the data in this book has never before seen the light of day.

Given the uncharted waters, I solicited a lot of help from experts in all corners. As an experiment, I worked through many of the trickier conceptual and articulation issues in public, on my blog at thelongtail.com. The usual process would go like this: I'd post a half-baked effort at explaining how the 80/20 Rule is changing, for instance, and then dozens of smart readers would write comments, emails, or their own blog posts to suggest ways to improve it. Somehow this wonky public brainstorming managed to attract an average of more than 5,000 readers a day.

In software, developers release early ("beta") versions of their code to their most avid users. In exchange for the privileged early look at the program, these users test it on their own machines, in their own way, and find errors that the developer missed. Such beta-testing is essential to creating robust software applications. My hope is that the same process—stress-testing many of my ideas in public—has led to a better, or at least sounder, book.

I should note here the difference between beta-testing ideas in public and actually writing a book in public. Although many have tried to do the latter—posting draft chapters online and sometimes even opening the text to collective editing—I chose to use the blog mostly as a public diary of my research in progress. The actual writing of the book, and most of the words in the following pages, I did offline.

Finally, one more note on parentage. Although I coined the term "The Long Tail," I can't claim any credit for creating the concept of using the efficient economics of online retail to aggregate a large inventory of relatively low sellers. That would be Amazon's Jeff Bezos, circa 1994. Most of what I've learned has come from talking to him, his counterparts at Netflix and Rhapsody, and others who have all been acting on this for years.

Those entrepreneurs are the real inventors here. What I've tried to do is synthesize the results into a framework. That is, of course, what economics does: It seeks to find neat, easily understood frameworks that describe real-world phenomena. Coming up with the framework is an advance in itself, but it pales next to the original inventions of all those who discovered and acted on the phenomena in the first place.

1

THE LONG TAIL

HOW TECHNOLOGY IS TURNING MASS MARKETS INTO MILLIONS OF NICHES

In 1988, a British mountain climber named Joe Simpson wrote a book called *Touching the Void*, a harrowing account of near death in the Peruvian Andes. Though reviews for the book were good, it was only a modest success, and soon was largely forgotten. Then, a decade later, a strange thing happened. Jon Krakauer's *Into Thin Air,* another book about a mountain-climbing tragedy, became a publishing sensation. Suddenly, *Touching the Void* started to sell again.

Booksellers began promoting it next to their *Into Thin Air* displays, and sales continued to rise. In early 2004, IFC Films released a docudrama of the story, to good reviews. Shortly thereafter, HarperCollins released a revised paperback, which spent fourteen weeks on the *New York Times* best-seller list. By mid-2004, *Touching the Void* was outselling *Into Thin Air* more than two to one.

What happened? Online word of mouth. When *Into Thin Air* first came out, a few readers wrote reviews on Amazon.com that pointed out the similarities with the then lesser-known *Touching the Void,* which they praised effusively. Other shoppers read those reviews, checked out the older book, and added it to their shopping carts. Pretty soon the online bookseller's software noted the patterns in buying behavior—"Readers who bought *Into Thin Air* also bought *Touching the Void*"—and started recommending the two as a pair. People took the suggestion, agreed wholeheartedly, wrote more rhapsodic reviews. More sales, more algorithm-fueled recommendations—and a powerful positive feedback loop kicked in.

Particularly notable is that when Krakauer's book hit shelves, Simpson's was nearly out of print. A decade ago readers of Krakauer would never even have learned about Simpson's book—and if they had, they wouldn't have been able to find it. Online booksellers changed that. By combining infinite shelf space with real-time information about buying trends and public opinion, they created the entire *Touching the Void* phenomenon. The result: rising demand for an obscure book.

This is not just a virtue of online booksellers; it is an example of an entirely new economic model for the media and entertainment industries, one just beginning to show its power. Unlimited selection is revealing truths about *what* consumers want and *how* they want to get it in service after service—from DVDs at the rental-by-mail firm Netflix to songs in the iTunes Music Store and Rhapsody. People are going deep into the catalog, down the long, long list of available titles, far past what's available at Blockbuster Video and Tower Records. And the more they find, the more they like. As they wander farther from the beaten path, they discover their taste is not as mainstream as they thought (or as they had been led to believe by marketing, a hit-centric culture, and simply a lack of alternatives).

The sales data and trends from these services and others like them show that the emerging digital entertainment economy is going to be radically different from today's mass market. If the twentieth-century entertainment industry was about *hits*, the twenty-first will be equally about *niches*.

For too long we've been suffering the tyranny of lowest-common-denominator fare, subjected to brain-dead summer blockbusters and manufactured pop. Why? Economics. Many of our assumptions about popular taste are actually artifacts of poor supply-and-demand matching—a market response to inefficient distribution.

The main problem, if that's the word, is that we live in the physical world, and until recently, most of our entertainment media did, too. That world puts dramatic limitations on our entertainment.

THE TYRANNY OF LOCALITY

The curse of traditional retail is the need to find local audiences. An average movie theater will not show a film unless it can attract at least 1,500 people over a two-week run. That's essentially the rent for a screen. An average record store needs to sell at least four copies of a CD per year to make it worth carrying; that's the rent for a half inch of shelf space. And so on, for DVD rental shops, video-game stores, booksellers, and newsstands.

In each case, retailers will carry only content that can generate sufficient demand to earn its keep. However, each can pull from only a limited local population—perhaps a ten-mile radius for a typical movie theater, less than that for music and bookstores, and even less (just a mile or two) for video rental shops. It's not enough for a great documentary to have a potential national audience of half a million; what matters is how much of an audience it has in the northern part of Rockville, Maryland, or among the mall shoppers of Walnut Creek, California.

There is plenty of great entertainment with potentially large, even rapturous, national audiences that cannot clear the local retailer bar. For instance, *The Triplets of Belleville*, a critically acclaimed film that was nominated for the best animated feature Oscar in 2004, opened on just six screens nationwide. An even more striking example is the plight of Bollywood in America. Each year, India's film industry produces more than eight hundred feature films. There are an estimated 1.7 million Indians living in the United States. Yet the top-rated Hindi-language film, *Lagaan: Once Upon a Time in India*, opened on just two screens in the States. Moreover, it was one of only a handful of Indian films that managed to get *any* U.S. distribution at all that year. In the tyranny of geography, an audience spread too thinly is the same as no audience at all.

Another constraint of the physical world is physics itself. The radio spectrum can carry only so many stations, and a coaxial cable only so many TV channels. And, of course, there are only twenty-four hours of programming a day. The curse of broadcast technologies is that they are profligate users of limited resources. The result is yet another instance of having to aggregate large audiences in one geographic area—another high bar above which only a fraction of potential content rises.

For the past century, entertainment has offered an easy solution to these constraints: a focus on releasing *hits*. After all, hits fill theaters, fly off shelves, and keep listeners and viewers from touching their dials and remotes. There's nothing inherently wrong with that. Sociologists will tell you that hits are hardwired into human psychology—that they're the effect of a combination of conformity and word of mouth. And certainly, a healthy share of hits do earn their place: Catchy songs, inspiring movies, and thought-provoking books can attract big, broad audiences.

However, most of us want more than just the hits. Everyone's taste departs from the mainstream somewhere. The more we explore alternatives, the more we're drawn to them. Unfortunately, in recent decades, such alternatives have been relegated to the fringes by pumped-up marketing vehicles built to order by industries that desperately needed them.

Hit-driven economics, which I'll discuss in more depth in later chapters, is a creation of an age in which there just wasn't enough room to carry everything for everybody: not enough shelf space for all the CDs, DVDs, and video games produced; not enough screens to show all the available movies; not enough channels to broadcast all the TV programs; not enough radio waves to play all the music created; and nowhere near enough hours in the day to squeeze everything through any of these slots.

This is the world of *scarcity*. Now, with online distribution and retail, we are entering a world of *abundance*. The differences are profound.

MARKETS WITHOUT END

For a better look at the world of abundance, let's return to online music retailer Rhapsody. A subscription-based streaming service owned by RealNetworks, Rhapsody currently offers more than 1.5 million tracks.

Chart Rhapsody's monthly statistics and you get a demand curve that looks much like any record store's: huge appeal for the top tracks, tailing off quickly for less popular ones. Below is a graph representing the top 25,000 tracks downloaded via Rhapsody in December 2005.

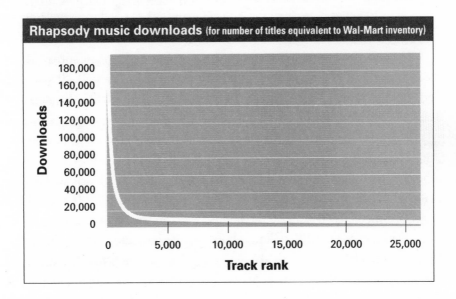

The first thing you might notice is that all the action appears to be in a tiny number of tracks on the left-hand side. No surprise there. Those are the hits. If you were running a music store and had a finite amount of space on your shelves, you'd naturally be looking for a cutoff point that's not too far from that peak.

So although there are millions of tracks in the collective catalogs of all the labels, America's largest music retailer, Wal-Mart, cuts off its inventory pretty close to the Head. It carries about 4,500 unique CD titles. On Rhapsody, the top 4,500 albums account for the top 25,000 tracks, which is why I cut the chart off right there. What you're looking at is Wal-Mart's inventory, in which the top 200 albums account for more than 90 percent of the sales.

Focusing on the hits certainly seems to make sense. That's the lion's share of the market, after all. Anything after the top 5,000 or 10,000 tracks appears to rank pretty close to zero. Why bother with those losers at the bottom?

That, in a nutshell, is the way we've been looking at markets for the last century. Every retailer has its own economic threshold, but they all cut off what they carry somewhere. Things that are likely to sell in the necessary numbers get carried; things that aren't, don't. In our hit-driven culture, people get ahead by focusing obsessively on the left side of the curve and trying to guess what will make it there.

But let's do something different for a change. After a century of staring at the left of this curve, let's turn our heads to the right. It's disorienting, I know. There appears to be nothing there, right? Wrong—look closer. Now closer. You'll notice two things.

First, that line isn't quite at zero. It just looks that way because the hits have compressed the vertical scale. To get a better view of the niches, let's zoom in and look past the top sellers. This next chart continues the curve from the 25,000th track to the 100,000th. I've changed the vertical scale so the line isn't lost in the horizontal axis. As you can see, we're still talking about significant numbers of downloads. Down here in the weeds, where we'd always assumed there was essentially no meaningful demand, the songs are still being downloaded an average of 250 times a month. And because there are so many of these non-hits, their sales, while individually small, quickly add up. The area under the curve down here where the curve appears from a distance to bump along the bottom actually accounts for some 22 million downloads a month, nearly a quarter of Rhapsody's total business.

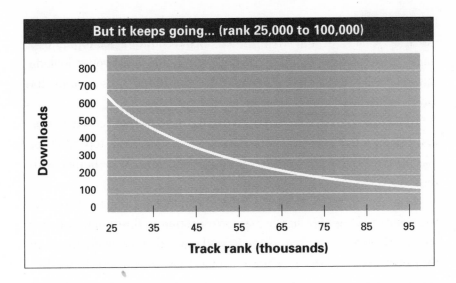

And it doesn't stop there. Let's zoom and pan again. This time it's the far end of the Tail: rank 100,000 to 800,000, the land of songs that can't be found in any but the most specialized record stores.

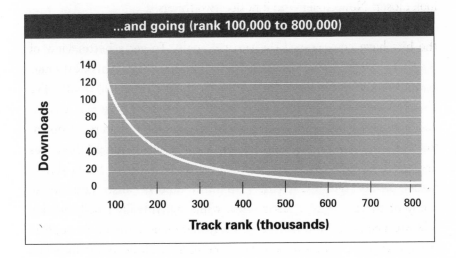

As you can see, the demand way out here is still not zero. Indeed, the area under this curve is still another 16 million downloads a month, or more than 15 percent of Rhapsody's total. Individually, none of those songs is popular, but there are just so *many* of them that collectively they represent a substantial market. Today, Rhapsody runs out of inventory at around 1.5 million tracks, but a year from now the number will probably be more than 2 million. A year after that it could be 4 million.

What's extraordinary is that virtually every single one of those tracks will sell. From the perspective of a store like Wal-Mart, the music industry stops at less than 60,000 tracks. However, for online retailers like Rhapsody the market is seemingly never-ending. Not only is every one of Rhapsody's top 60,000 tracks streamed at least once each month, but the same is true for its top 100,000, top 200,000, and top 400,000—even its top 600,000, top 900,000, and beyond. As fast as Rhapsody adds tracks to its library, those songs find an audience, even if it's just a handful of people every month, somewhere in the world.

This is the Long Tail.

You can find *everything* out here in the Long Tail. There's the back catalog, older albums still fondly remembered by longtime fans or rediscovered by new ones. There are live tracks, B-sides, remixes, even (gasp) covers. There are niches by the thousands, genres within genres within genres (imagine an entire Tower Records store devoted to eighties hair bands or ambient dub). There are foreign bands, once priced out of reach on a shelf in the import aisle, and obscure bands on even more obscure labels—many of which don't have the distribution clout to get into Tower at all.

Oh sure, there's also a lot of crap here in the Long Tail. But then again, there's an awful lot of crap hiding between the radio tracks on hit albums, too. People have to skip over it on CDs, but they can more easily avoid it online, where the best individual songs can be cherry-picked (with the help of personalized recommendations) from those whole albums. So, unlike the CD—where each crap track costs perhaps one-twelfth of a $15 album price—all of the crap tracks online just sit harmlessly on some server, ignored by a marketplace that evaluates songs on their own merit.

What's truly amazing about the Long Tail is the sheer size of it. Again, if you combine enough of the non-hits, you've actually established a market that rivals the hits. Take books: The average Borders carries around 100,000 titles. Yet about a quarter of Amazon's book sales come from *outside* its top 100,000 titles. Consider the implication: If the Amazon statistics are any guide, the market for books that are not even sold in the average bookstore is already a third the size of the existing market—and what's more, it's growing quickly. If these growth trends continue, the potential book market may actually be half again as big as it appears to be, if only we can get over the economics of scarcity. Venture capitalist and former music industry consultant Kevin Laws puts it this way: "The biggest money is in the smallest sales."

The same is true for the other Long Tail markets we've looked at:

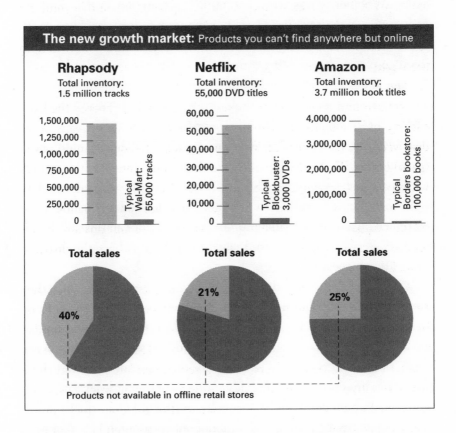

The new growth market: Products you can't find anywhere but online

Rhapsody
Total inventory:
1.5 million tracks

Typical Wal-Mart: 55,000 tracks

Netflix
Total inventory:
55,000 DVD titles

Typical Blockbuster: 3,000 DVDs

Amazon
Total inventory:
3.7 million book titles

Typical Borders bookstore: 100,000 books

Total sales: 40%

Total sales: 21%

Total sales: 25%

Products not available in offline retail stores

When you think about it, most successful Internet businesses are capitalizing on the Long Tail in one way or another. Google, for instance, makes most of its money not from huge corporate advertisers, but from small ones (the Long Tail of advertising). EBay is mostly Tail as well—niche products from collector cars to tricked-out golf clubs. By overcoming the limitations of geography and scale, companies like these have not only expanded existing markets, but more important, they've also discovered entirely new ones. Moreover, in each case those new markets that lie *outside* the reach of the physical retailer have proven to be far bigger than anyone expected—and they're only getting bigger.

In fact, as these companies offered more and more (simply because they *could*), they found that demand actually followed supply. The act of vastly increasing choice seemed to unlock demand for that choice. Whether it was latent demand for niche goods that was already there or the creation of new demand, we don't yet know. But what we do know is that with the companies for which we have the most complete data—Netflix, Amazon, and Rhapsody—sales of products *not offered* by their bricks-and-mortar competitors amounted to between a quarter and nearly half of total revenues—and that percentage is rising each year. In other words, the *fastest-growing* part of their businesses is sales of products that aren't available in traditional, physical retail stores at all.

These infinite-shelf-space businesses have effectively learned a lesson in new math: A very, very big number (the products in the Tail) multiplied by a relatively small number (the sales of each) is still equal to a very, very big number. And, again, that very, very big number is only getting bigger.

What's more, these millions of fringe sales are an efficient, cost-effective business. With no shelf space to pay for—and in the case of purely digital services like iTunes, no manufacturing costs and hardly any distribution fees—a niche product sold is just another sale, with the same (or better) margins as a hit. For the first time in history, hits and niches are on equal economic footing, both just entries in a database called up on demand, both equally worthy of being carried. Suddenly, popularity no longer has a monopoly on profitability. The new shape of culture and commerce looks like this:

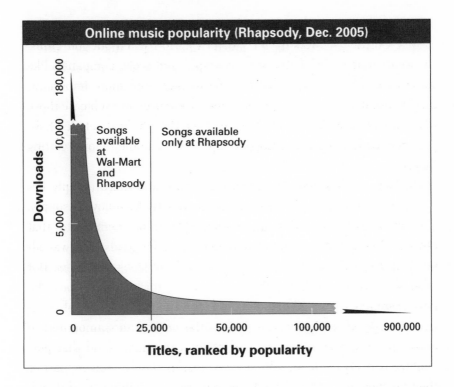

Online music popularity (Rhapsody, Dec. 2005)

Songs available at Wal-Mart and Rhapsody

Songs available only at Rhapsody

Downloads

Titles, ranked by popularity

THE HIDDEN MAJORITY

One way to think of the difference between yesterday's limited choice and today's abundance is as if our culture were an ocean and the only features above the surface were islands of hits. There's a music island composed of hit albums, a movie island of blockbusters, an archipelago of popular TV shows, and so on.

Think of the waterline as being the economic threshold for that category, the amount of sales necessary to satisfy the distribution channels. The islands represent the products that are popular enough to be above that line, and thus profitable enough to be offered through distribution channels with scarce capacity, which is to say the shelf space demands of most major retailers. Scan the cultural horizon and what stands out are these peaks of popularity rising above the waves.

However, islands are, of course, just the tips of vast undersea mountains. When the cost of distribution falls, it's like the water level falling in the ocean. All of a sudden things are revealed that were previously hidden. And there's much, much more under the current waterline than above it. What we're now starting to see, as online retailers begin to capitalize on their extraordinary economic efficiencies, is the shape of a massive mountain of choice emerging where before there was just a peak.

More than 99 percent of music albums on the market today are not available in Wal-Mart. Of the more than 200,000 films, TV shows, documentaries, and other video that have been released commercially, the average Blockbuster carries just 3,000. Same for any other leading retailer and practically any other commodity—from books to kitchen fittings. The vast majority of products are *not* available at a store near you. By necessity, the economics of traditional, hit-driven retail limit choice.

When you can dramatically lower the costs of connecting supply and demand, it changes not just the numbers, but the entire nature of the market. This is not just a quantitative change, but a qualitative one, too. Bringing niches within reach reveals latent demand for non-commercial content. Then, as demand shifts toward the niches, the economics of providing them improve further, and so on, creating a positive feedback loop that will transform entire industries—and the culture—for decades to come.

2

THE RISE AND FALL OF THE HIT

LOCKSTEP CULTURE IS THE EXCEPTION, NOT THE RULE

Before the Industrial Revolution, most culture was local. The economy was agrarian, which distributed populations as broadly as the land, and distance divided people. Culture was fragmented, creating everything from regional accents to folk music. The lack of rapid transportation and communications limited cultural mixing and the propagation of new ideas and trends. It was an earlier era of niche culture, one determined more by geography than affinity.

Influences varied from town to town because the vehicles for carrying common culture were so limited. Aside from traveling theatrical acts and a small number of books available to the literate, most culture spread no faster than people themselves. There was a reason the Church was the main mass cultural unifier in Western Europe; it had the best distribution infrastructure and, thanks to Gutenberg's press, the most mass-produced media (the Bible).

But in the early nineteenth century, the era of modern industry and the growth of the railroad system led to massive waves of urbanization and the rise of the great cities of Europe. These new hives of commerce and hubs of transportation mixed people like never before, creating a powerful engine of new culture. All it needed was mass media to give it wing.

In the mid to late nineteenth century, several technologies emerged to do just that. First, commercial printing technology improved and went mainstream, then the new "wet plate" technique made photography popular. Finally, in 1877, Edison invented the phonograph. These technologies led to the first great wave of pop culture, carried on such media as illustrated newspapers and magazines, novels, printed sheet music, political pamphlets, postcards, greeting cards, children's books, and commercial catalogs.

Along with news, newspapers spread word of the latest fashions from the urban style centers of New York, London, and Paris. Then, in the beginning of the twentieth century, Edison created yet another mass market with the moving picture, which gave the stars of stage a new, recorded medium to reach bigger audiences and "play" many towns simultaneously.

We are a gregarious species, highly influenced by what others do. And now, with film, there was a medium that could not only show us what other people were doing, but could also endow it with such an intoxicating glamour that it was hard to resist. It was the dawn of the celebrity age.

These potent carriers of culture had the effect of linking people across time and space, synchronizing society. For the first time in history, it was a safe bet that not only had your neighbor read the same news you had in the paper this morning, and gleaned knowledge of the same music and movies, but that the same was true for people across the country.

The rise of such powerful technologies of mass culture was not greeted with universal acclaim. In 1936, Marxist philosopher Walter Benjamin expressed his concern for the loss of "aura" (the transcendent qualities of art) in an age of mechanical reproduction. Emphasizing the examples of photography and film, along with recorded rather than performed music, Benjamin worried that "mechanical reproduction of art changes the reaction of the masses toward art. The reactionary attitude toward a Picasso painting changes into the progressive reaction toward a Chaplin movie. . . . The conventional is uncritically enjoyed, and the truly new is criticized with aversion."

But he hadn't seen anything yet. The impending explosion of the broadcast mediums of radio and television would eventually change the game completely. The power of electromagnetic waves is that they spread in all directions essentially for *free,* a trait that made them as mind-blowing when they were first introduced as the Internet would be some fifty years later. The ability to reach everyone within dozens of miles for the price of a single broadcast was so economically compelling that broadcaster RCA even got into the radio-set manufacturing business in the early 1920s to subsidize and thus accelerate the adoption of receivers that could pick up its programming.

But local and regional broadcasts still only reached local and regional audiences, which often weren't big enough for national advertisers. Going national would require another technology. In 1922, AT&T's long-distance and local Bell operating divisions developed technologies for transmitting voice- and music-grade audio on the then-new long-distance phone networks. New York's WEAF station, which had long been a technology test bed, put together a regular schedule of programs and created some of the first broadcasts to incorporate commercial endorsements or sponsorships. They were redistributed to stations beyond New York on long-distance phone lines. This was an immediate success, and created links with other stations that could go both ways, taking national what was once local coverage of sports or political events.

This was the beginning of what would become known first as "chain" or "network" broadcasting. It was also the start of a shared national culture, synchronized to the three-note NBC chimes, which were originally a system cue to network engineers to switch between the news and entertainment feeds.

Between 1935 and the 1950s, the Golden Age of Radio led to the rise of national stars, from Edward R. Murrow to Bing Crosby. Then television took over, birthing the ultimate in lockstep culture. By 1954, an astounding 74 percent of TV households were watching *I Love Lucy* every Sunday night.

The Golden Age of Television marked the peak of the so-called watercooler effect, the phrase describing the buzz in the office around a shared cultural event. In the 1950s and 1960s, it was a safe assumption that nearly everyone in your office had watched the same thing the previous night. Most folks had probably seen Walter Cronkite read the evening news, and then tuned in to whatever the top show was that night: *The Beverly Hillbillies, Gunsmoke,* or *The Andy Griffith Show.*

Throughout the eighties, nineties, and even into the twenty-first century, television continued to be the great American unifier. Peak sewage usage was routinely measured at halftime of the Super Bowl. Telephone network capacity records were set for call-in voting during the first season of *American Idol.* Each year, TV advertising set a new record as companies paid more and more for prime time. And why not? TV defined the mainstream. Prime time may not have been the only time, but it was the only one that really mattered.

But even as the nineties drew to a close, with the networks basking in their commercial success, the cultural ground was shifting beneath them. The first cracks were to appear in the usual battleground of youth rebellion: music.

Although music was first made more than just performance by the phonograph, it was radio that created the pop idol. In the 1940s and '50s, *Your Hit Parade* became a fixture of Saturday night, billing itself as "an accurate, authentic tabulation of America's taste in popular music." Then, with the rise and youth appeal of rock and roll and R&B, came personality-driven playlists and the celebrity radio DJ. In the 1950s, Alan Freed and Murray "the K" Kaufman helped turn radio into the most powerful hit-making machine the world had ever known.

The machine hit its peak in the form of *American Top 40,* a syndicated weekly radio show started by Casey Kasem in 1970. It began as a three-hour program that counted down the top forty songs on *Billboard*'s Hot 100 singles chart. By the early 1980s, the show was four hours long and could be heard every Sunday on more than 500 stations in the United States alone. For a generation of kids who grew up in the seventies and eighties, this was the carrier signal of pop culture. Every week millions of them synchronized themselves to the rest of the nation, obsessively tracking which bands were up and which were down in a list of songs that wouldn't fill a single rack in a record store.

THE END OF THE HIT PARADE

As the twenty-first century opened, the music industry—the ultimate hit machine—basked in its power. The resounding commercial success of teen pop—from Britney Spears to the Backstreet Boys—showed that the business had its finger firmly on the pulse of American youth culture. The labels had finally perfected the process of manufacturing blockbusters, and their marketing departments could now both predict and create demand with scientific precision.

On March 21, 2000, Jive Records demonstrated that clout by releasing *No Strings Attached,* the second album by *NSYNC, the latest and greatest of the boy bands. *NSYNC had been developed at an even larger label, BMG, but on the advice of its marketing gurus had switched to the urban-oriented Jive to get more street cred (and counter a slightly fey image). It worked. The album sold 2.4 million copies in its first week, making it the fastest-selling album ever. It went on to top the charts for eight weeks, selling 11 million copies by the end of the year.

The industry had cracked the commercial code. They had found the elusive formula to the hit, and in retrospect it was so obvious: Sell virile young men to young women. What worked for Elvis could now be replicated on an industrial scale. It was all about looks and scripted personalities. The music itself, which was outsourced to a small army of professionals (there are fifty-two people credited with creating *No Strings Attached*), hardly mattered.

Labels had good reason for feeling confident. Fans were flocking to record stores. Between 1990 and 2000, album sales had doubled, the fastest growth rate in the industry's history. The business trailed only Hollywood in the entertainment industry ranks.

But even as *NSYNC was celebrating its huge launch, the ground was shifting beneath the industry. The Nasdaq had crashed the week before the album's release, and continued to fall sickeningly the rest of the year as the dot.com bubble burst. No other albums that year set records, and total music sales fell, for only the third time in two decades.

Over the next few years, even after the overall economy recovered, the economics of the music industry got worse. Something fundamental had changed in 2000. Sales fell 2.5 percent in 2001, 6.8 percent in 2002, and just kept dropping. By the end of 2005 (down another 7 percent), music sales in the United States had dwindled more than a quarter from their peak. Twenty of the all-time top 100 albums had come out in the five-year period between 1996 and 2000. The next five years produced only two—OutKast's *Speakerboxxx/The Love Below* and Norah Jones's *Come Away with Me*—rank 92 and 95, respectively.

It's altogether possible that *NSYNC's first-week record will never be broken. Imagine if this boy band goes down in history not just for launching Justin Timberlake but also for marking the very peak of the hit bubble, the last bit of manufactured pop to use the twentieth century's fine-tuned marketing machine to its fullest, before the gears were stripped and the wheels fell off.

Here's a chart of all the hit albums since 1958: gold (over 500,000 sold), platinum (1 to 2 million), multiplatinum (2 to 10 million), and diamond (10 million and up).

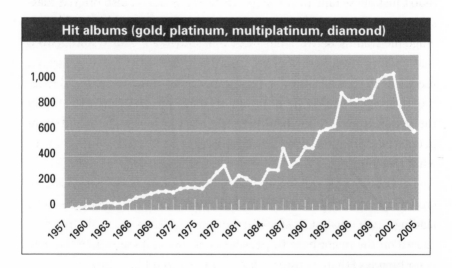

Between 2001 and 2005, the music industry's total sales fell by a quarter. But the number of hit albums fell by nearly half. In 2000, the top five albums—including megahits from Britney Spears and Eminem—sold a combined 38 million copies. In 2005, the top five sold just half that; only 19.7 million copies. In other words, although the music industry is hurting, the hit-making side of it is hurting more. Customers have shifted to less mainstream fare, fragmenting to a thousand different subgenres. For music, at least, this looks like the end of the blockbuster era.

WHO KILLED THE HIT ALBUM?

What caused a generation of the industry's best customers—fans in their teens and twenties—to abandon the record store? The industry's answer was simply "piracy": The combined effects of Napster and other online file trading and CD burning and trading gave rise to an underground economy of any song, anytime, for free. And there's something to that. Despite countless record industry lawsuits, the traffic on the peer-to-peer ("P2P") file-trading networks has continued to grow, with about 10 million users now sharing music files each day.

But while technology was indeed behind the customer flight, it didn't just allow fans to sidestep the cash register. It also offered massive, unprecedented choice in terms of what they could hear. The average file-trading network has more music than any music store. Given that choice, music fans took it. Today, not only have listeners stopped buying as many CDs, they're also losing their taste for the blockbuster hits that used to make them throng those stores on release day. Given the option to pick a boy band or find something new, more and more people are opting for exploration, and are typically more satisfied with what they find.

Peer-to-peer file trading is so massive that a small industry has now grown up around it to measure and learn from the experience. The leading such analyst is BigChampagne, which tracks all the files shared on the major peer-to-peer services. What it's seeing in the data is nothing less than a culture shift from hits to niche artists.

Today, music fans are trading more than 8 million unique tracks, almost all of them far outside the *Billboard* Hot 100. There is a thriving subculture that's into "mashups" (playing a track from one artist over a track from another artist), and another that's into music composed on the eight-bit chips once found in Nintendo video-game machines. Plus, a lot of indie rock of the sort that makes for great shows but no radio play. Notably, boy bands are not particularly popular.

The rise of file-trading networks was not the only tectonic shift in the culture. In 2001 Apple released its first iPod, a simple-looking white MP3 player 4 inches long, 2.5 inches wide, and less than 1 inch thick. It was by no means the first MP3 player on the market, but thanks to its utter simplicity, elegant design, and Apple's highly effective marketing campaign, the iPod became the first must-have portable digital music device. Soon, as people ditched their Walkmans and Discmans, the iPod's white earbuds became ubiquitous and iconic.

What was really disruptive about the iPod was its storage capacity of as much as sixty gigabytes. This allowed users to carry around entire libraries of music, up to ten thousand songs, an inventory equivalent to a small record store. Over the next few years, the iPod became a personal soundtrack for millions of people, as they walked down the street, while they worked, or as they rode public transportation.

But filling an iPod with paid-for tracks is a multithousand-dollar proposition. Compared to that, free is an incredibly tough price to beat. The dorm-room-jukebox case for freely downloading digital songs from the Internet to a PC became an equally compelling case for filling an iPod. Same for ripping, burning, and trading CDs, just as Apple's famous advertising campaign encouraged. The peer-to-peer networks exploded, populated by the combined music inventories of millions of users. The result: a lot of piracy, to be sure, but also massive, unbounded selection—hundreds of times as much variety as in any record store, and all available from basically any laptop.

Of course, these revolutionary methods of acquiring music also provided unmatched ways to *discover* new music. While CD burning and trading between friends is "viral marketing" (buzz that passes from person to person) of the most powerful kind, playlist sharing is word of mouth taken to an industrial scale. And there are even dedicated recommendation services such as Pandora and hundreds of Internet radio stations, businesses that not only thrive on introducing fans to the coolest underground artists, but are also working to match personal tastes with increasing precision.

What if there were 400 Top 40s, one for each narrow music niche? Or 40,000? Or 400,000? Suddenly the concept of the hit gives way to the *micro-hit*. The singular star is joined by a swarm of micro-stars, and a tiny number of mass-market elites become an unlimited number of niche demi-elites. The population of "hits" grows hugely, each one with smaller but presumably more engaged audiences.

This is not a fantasy. It is the emerging state of music today. A good online music service such as Rhapsody will list at least 400 genres and subgenres (breaking genres into new, incredibly specific categories such as "electronica/dance>beats&breaks>cut&paste"), each of which has its own top ten list. This effectively creates 4,000 mini-hits, each far more meaningful for the fans of that genre than Casey Kasem's national playlist ever was. Then there are the infinite number of top ten lists dynamically created for each customer based on his or her listening patterns and particular tastes, no matter how narrow they may be.

BROADCAST BLUES

The troubles in the music industry are not confined to CD sales. Rock radio, long the favored marketing vehicle for the labels, is suffering just as badly. In 1993, Americans spent an average of twenty-three hours and fifteen minutes per week tuned in to the radio. As of spring 2004, that figure had dropped to nineteen hours and forty-five minutes. Listenership is now at a twenty-seven-year low, and it is rock music programming that seems to be suffering the most. In 2005, an average of one U.S. rock radio station went out of business *each week*. Typically, those stations switched to talk radio or Latin formats, which are more "sticky" (they keep audiences listening longer) than rock and pop, which is only as appealing as the current song it's playing. *American Top 40* just doesn't have the pull it once had; Casey Kasem is resting comfortably in retirement.

Experts argue about the primary cause, but here are the main candidates:

- **The rise of the iPod phenomenon:** With the ultimate personal radio, who needs FM?
- **The cell phone:** Commuters stuck in traffic were the salvation of radio in the eighties. Today we're still stuck in traffic, but now we're chatting on the phone.
- **The 1996 Telecommunications Act:** Adding a thousand FM stations to the dial, this legislation increased competition and depressed the economics of the incumbents. The act also relaxed the limits of ownership in each market, leading to . . .
- **Clear Channel:** Often blamed for radio's woes, this corporate media giant is as much a symptom of the industry's brutal economics as it is a cause. As the Telecommunications Act undercut the business of local radio in the late 1990s, Clear Channel was able to do a roll-up of distressed stations. The company now owns more than 1,200 of them, or one out of every ten. Its plan was to lower dramatically the costs of radio by implementing centralized programming and computer-driven local station programming. The result was bland homogenization.
- **The FCC's obscenity crackdown:** It's always been part of the FCC's mandate to police what's said on the airwaves, but it's rarely exercised its duty with as much vigor as in the past five years. The main target was Howard Stern, an earthy radio personality with a taste for the outrageous. After incurring unprecedented fines, Stern finally gave up on terrestrial broadcast. At the end of 2005 he departed for satellite's Sirius Radio, where he debuted—mostly uncensored—to an audience of subscribers in January 2006. Today, broadcasters have more reason to fear that what they say or play could cost them not only money, but also their jobs. The result: further homogenization.

The result of this rock radio meltdown is that the Top 40 era is drawing to a close. Music itself hasn't gone out of favor—just the opposite. It's never been a better time to be an artist or a fan. But it's the

Internet that has become the ultimate discovery vehicle for new music. The traditional model of marketing, selling, and distributing music has gone out of favor. The major label and retail distribution system that grew to titanic size on the back of radio's hit-making machine found itself with a business model dependent on huge, platinum hits—and today there are not nearly enough of those. We're witnessing the end of an era.

Everyone with those white earbuds is listening to what amounts to his or her own commercial-free radio station. Culture has shifted from following the crowd up to the top of the charts to finding your own style and exploring far out beyond the broadcast mainstream, into both relative obscurity and back through time to the classics.

In a 2005 speech, News Corp. chairman Rupert Murdoch showed that he was among the first of the media moguls to grasp the magnitude of today's elite versus amateur divide: "Young people don't want to rely on a Godlike figure from above to tell them what's important," he said. "They want control over their media, instead of being controlled by it."

What's happening in music is paralleled in practically every other sector of mass media and entertainment. Consider these statistics from 2005:

- Hollywood box office fell 7 percent, continuing a decline in attendance that started in 2001 and appears to be accelerating.
- Newspaper readership, which peaked in 1987, fell by 3 percent (its largest single-year drop) and is now at levels not seen since the sixties.
- Magazine newsstand sales are at their lowest level since statistics have been kept, a period of more than thirty years.
- Network TV ratings continue to fall as viewers scatter to cable channels; since 1985, the networks' share of the TV audience has fallen from three-quarters to less than half.

The watercooler effect is losing its power. Today, the top-rated TV show, *CSI*, is watched by just 15 percent of TV households. Those kinds of numbers wouldn't have put it in the top ten in the seventies.

In fact, all but one of the top-rated TV shows of all time are from the late seventies and early eighties (the one newer one is the 1994 Winter Olympics, still more than a decade ago). Collectively, the hundreds of cable-only channels have now passed the networks in total viewership. No single one dominates.

Even the usual must-see TV is no longer anything of the sort. The 2005 World Series had its lowest TV ratings of all time, dropping 30 percent from the previous year. The 2005 NBA playoffs rating reached near-record lows as well, down nearly a quarter from the year before. In 2006 the ratings for the Grammy Awards were off 10 percent. The 2006 Winter Olympics had its lowest ratings in twenty years, down 37 percent from the 2002 Games in Salt Lake City. And the Oscars hit a ratings low not seen since 1987.

As *LA Times* critic Patrick Goldstein puts it, "We are now a nation of niches. There are still blockbuster movies, hit TV shows, and top-selling CDs, but fewer events that capture the communal pop culture spirit. The action is elsewhere, with the country watching cable shows or reading blogs that play to a specific audience."

The arrival of TiVo and other DVRs amplified this dissolution of the watercooler effect by removing the *time* component as well. Today, even if people are watching the same shows, they may not be watching them on the same night or at the same time. Who wants to listen to the morning-after recaps of real-timers, people who will ruin the surprise of shows you've yet to watch?

A HIT-DRIVEN ECONOMY IS A HIT-DRIVEN CULTURE

While the era of the blockbuster hit may have peaked, its effect on our assumptions about media has not. The existing media and entertainment industries are still oriented around finding, funding, and creating blockbusters.

Entertainment products, be they movies, TV shows, or albums, can be expensive to make, market, and distribute. For instance, the average cost of a Hollywood production is now $60 million, with at least that much additionally required for marketing. Yet it is as hard as ever to predict which films will strike a chord with consumers, which is why tried-and-true actors and directors command such high salaries—they bring a little predictability to a woefully unpredictable business. But even stars make flops, so the studios, labels, and networks employ a portfolio approach to spread their risk.

Like venture capitalists, they spread their bets over a number of projects, investing in each one enough money to give it a fighting chance at becoming a hit. They expect that, at best, most of the projects will break even, and a few will flat-out fail. That means that the few that *are* hits must compensate for the drag of the others.

In that sense, these businesses absolutely *need* hits. And not just profitable products—we're talking huge, blow-through-the-numbers megahits. The high costs of production and the uncertainties of success put pressure on the winners not just to win, but to win *big*. And the rest? Well, those would be the misses. Never mind that they may have been critically acclaimed or even heard or seen by millions of people. If those products don't make back their money manyfold, they're just not doing their job to support the rest of the portfolio.

Setting out to make a hit is not exactly the same thing as setting out to make a good movie. There are things you do and don't do in the quest to draw tens of millions of paying viewers. You do pay as much as you can for the biggest-name star you can lure to the project. You don't try to be "too smart." You do have a happy ending. You don't kill off the star. If it's an action movie, more effects are better than fewer. And, all things being equal, it probably *should* be an action movie. Certainly, it's possible to break these rules and still have a hit, but why take chances? After all, you're investing a lot of money.

This hit-driven mind-set has leaked outside of the Hollywood boardrooms and into our national culture. We have been conditioned by the economic demands of a hit machine to expect nothing less. We have internalized the bookkeeping of entertainment risk capital. This is why we follow weekend box office results as we do professional sports—keeping score and separating the clear winners from the seemingly obvious losers.

In our fixation on star power, we cheer the salary inflation of A-listers and follow their absurd public lives with an attention that far exceeds our interest in their work. From superstar athletes to celebrity CEOs, we ascribe disproportionate attention to the very top of the heap. We have been trained, in other words, to see the world through a hit-colored lens.

If it is not a hit, it is a miss. It has failed that economic test and, therefore, never should have been made. With this hit-driven mind-set, history is written by the blockbusters, and the best test of quality is box-office gross. And this doesn't just apply to Hollywood. It's how we assign space on store shelves, fill time slots on television, and build radio playlists. It's all about allocating scarce resources to the most "deserving," which is to say, the most popular.

Ultimately, our response to a hit culture is to reinforce the hit culture. The world of shelf space is a zero-sum game: One product displaces another. Forced to choose, each link in the entertainment industry naturally enough chooses the most popular products, giving them privileged placement. By putting our commercial weight behind the big winners, we actually amplify the gap between them and everything else. Economically, this is the same as saying, "If there can only be a few rich, let them at least be super-rich." The consequence of this is that the steep slope of the demand curve becomes even steeper.

But now that's changing. Instead of the office watercooler, which crosses cultural boundaries as only the random assortment of personalities found in the workplace can, we're increasingly forming our own tribes, groups bound together more by affinity and shared interests than by default broadcast schedules. These days our watercoolers are increasingly virtual—there are many different ones, and the people who gather around them are self-selected. We are turning from a mass market back into a niche nation, defined now not by our geography but by our interests.

3

A SHORT HISTORY OF THE LONG TAIL

FROM THE WISH BOOK TO
THE VIRTUAL SHOPPING CART

While the Long Tail currently manifests itself largely as an Internet phenomenon, its origins predate Amazon and eBay, and even the Web. Instead, it is the culmination of a string of business innovations that date back more than a century—advancements in the ways we make, find, distribute, and sell goods. Think about all the non-Internet elements that enable, for instance, an Amazon purchase: FedEx, standard ISBN numbers, credit cards, relational databases, even bar codes.

It took decades for these innovations to emerge and evolve. What the Internet has done is allow businesses to weave together those types of improvements in a way that amplifies their power and extends their reach. In other words, the Web simply unified the elements of a supply-chain revolution that had been brewing for decades.

Indeed, the true roots of the Long Tail and unlimited shelf space go back to the late nineteenth century and the first giant centralized warehouses—cavernous buildings erected on industrial lots near the junctions of railway lines in the American Midwest, starting in Chicago. Under their immense steel roofs, the era of massive choice and availability arose on towers of wooden pallets, built with the bulk purchasing afforded by then-new mass production. Railway cars delivered this new variety on a network of iron tracks that were transforming the country's economy and culture.

The man who first showed the American consumer just what all of this could mean was a railway agent in North Redwood, Minnesota. His name was Richard Sears. In 1886, a box of watches was mistakenly sent from a Chicago jeweler to a local dealer in North Redwood who didn't want them. Buying them up for himself, Sears sold the watches for a nice profit to other railway agents up and down the line. He then bought more and started a watch distribution company.

By 1887, he'd moved the business to Chicago and placed an advertisement in the *Chicago Daily News* looking for someone who could repair watches (there was no sense, he thought, in scrapping the defective watches that had been returned). Alvah C. Roebuck answered the ad. Six years later, the two partnered up and founded Sears, Roebuck and Co., which used catalogs to sell watches by mail to the rural farmers who were being gouged by local general stores and an army of middlemen.

The promise of Sears, Roebuck and Co. was simple, according to its corporate history: "Thanks to volume buying, to the railroads and post office, and later to rural free delivery and parcel post, it offered a happy alternative to the high-priced rural stores."

What started as watches soon expanded to everything a rural home and business might need. Sears and Roebuck distributed catalogs to farmers, with folksy copy written by Sears himself, and fulfilled their orders from a succession of larger and larger buildings in Chicago. Eventually, the pair constructed a forty-acre, $5 million mail-order plant and office building on Chicago's West Side. When it opened in 1906, with more than 3 million square feet of floor space, the mail-order plant was the largest business building in the world.

What Sears and Roebuck's warehouses and efficient processing operations enabled was nothing less than revolutionary. Imagine being a farmer living deep on the vast Kansas prairie more than a hundred years ago. You are several hours' ride from the nearest general store, and neither the store's products nor the price of gasoline is cheap. Then, one day, the weekly mail delivery brings you the 1897 Sears

"Wish Book"—786 pages of everything under the sun at prices that can hardly be believed.

The 1897 Wish Book was—and still is—astonishing. Even today, in the era of Amazon, it seems impossible that so much variety can exist. Crammed into something the size of a phone book are 200,000 items and variations, all described with tiny type and some 6,000 lithographic illustrations.

Here's a sample of the first ten pages: sixty-seven kinds of tea, thirty-eight kinds of coffee, and twenty-nine kinds of cocoa. Next come several hundred different spices and extracts, and an equal number of canned and dried fruits, followed by a small supermarket's offerings of other foods. By the eleventh page, it is time for more than sixty kinds of soap, and then on for another 770 pages of everything from drugs to guns (including a revolver for sixty-eight cents!) to clothes to buggies to two-dollar violins.

This was mind-blowing stuff for a rural farm family. With the heavy *thunk* of a single mail drop, the choice of available products increased a thousandfold from the typical inventory at the general store. What's more, the catalog also represented a drop of often 50 percent or more in price, even after shipping.

Sears was spreading the word among prospective customers with one of the earliest examples of "viral marketing." In 1905, the company wrote to its best customers in Iowa, asking each to distribute twenty-four catalogs among friends and neighbors. These customers sent Sears the names of people who received the catalogs. When those people placed orders, the original customers, in turn, received premiums for their work: a stove, a bicycle, or a sewing machine.

Likewise, the supply-chain techniques Sears used to achieve its miracle of abundance are not so unfamiliar today: a combination of goods in stock at its warehouses and a "virtual warehouse" network of suppliers who would ship the goods directly from their own factories. Sears even served as an agent for build-on-demand buggy makers.

Within the warehouses themselves, too, the innovations were astounding. Concerned about shipping inefficiencies, Sears managers set up a system in which each order, as it arrived, was allotted a specific time to be shipped. The item(s) had to be in the appropriate bin in the merchandise-assembly room at the assigned time. To meet its deadline the order traveled from bulk storage to the packing room by an intricate system of belts and chutes.

This time-scheduling system brought efficiency to mail order, enabling the Chicago plant to handle ten times as much business. In a short time, the system became known as the "seventh wonder" of the business world. Henry Ford is said to have visited the Chicago plant to study its efficient assembly-line technique.

Ironically, it was Ford's own assembly lines that eventually forced Sears to take the next step in the march to plenty, *the superstore*. With affordable cars and the advent of better modern roads, Sears's rural customers were no longer limited to shopping by catalog. Meanwhile, the great urbanization of America was beginning, and those same customers were abandoning the farm for the factory. In 1900, the rural population still outnumbered the urban population. By 1920, those figures had reversed.

City shoppers preferred stores to catalogs. In 1925, Sears opened one store in its Chicago mail-order plant. The experiment was an immediate success. Before the year was over, Sears had opened seven more retail stores—four in mail-order plants. By the end of 1927, it had twenty-seven stores. Huge selection and low prices appealed to everyone, and the supply-chain efficiencies Sears had developed for mail-order allowed the company to offer unprecedented selection in its retail stores, too (helping to lay the groundwork for what would eventually become the Wal-Mart model).

America was hooked on choice. The superstores offered huge selection at low prices. They preached the religion of economies of scale, a concept (bigger stores are more efficient) that required no more than a price-tag comparison between traditional merchants and superstores to understand. How much farther could it go?

FEEDING THE TAIL

Food was the next frontier. The first supermarket was a King Kullen store that opened in Queens, New York, on August 4, 1930, in the depths of the Great Depression. Comparable to today's no-frills warehouse outlets, this store sold more than one thousand products, serving as the catalyst for a new age in food retailing. Like Sears, King Kullen offered greater variety, lower prices, and one-stop shopping, along with the opportunity for customers to select products directly from shelves.

Along with self-service and abundance came the need to transport and store what had become weekly bulk grocery shopping trips, as opposed to the daily meal shopping of the previous grocer era. Key to the early success of the supermarket was the shopping cart (first introduced in 1937), the automobile, free parking lots, and mechanical refrigerators in the home and store.

In its official history of the industry, the Food Marketing Institute describes the effect:

> The supermarket helped create the Middle Class. Its low prices freed up substantial funds for families to spend on cars, homes, education and other needs and amenities of life. As supermarkets proliferated in the 1950s and 1960s, they played a pivotal role in creating the American middle class. On the supermarket's silver anniversary, President Kennedy said that the supermarket's low-cost mass marketing techniques ". . . have enabled a higher standard of living and have contributed importantly to our economic growth."

> During the Cold War, from 1958 to 1988, some 50,000 Soviet citizens traveled to the U.S., most touring an American supermarket on their trip. The supermarket showcased how a free-market economy could deliver abundant, affordable food and became a metaphor for what capitalism could do and Communism could not. In his autobiography, Boris Yeltsin gave this account of his 1989 visit to a supermarket in Houston: "When I saw those shelves crammed with hundreds, thousands of cans, cartons, and goods of every possible sort, for the first time I felt quite frankly sick with despair for the Soviet people. That such a potentially super-rich country as ours has been brought to a state of such poverty! It is terrible to think of it."

The corner grocery store of the 1920s had carried about 700 items, most sold in bulk, and consumers had to shop elsewhere for meat, produce, baked goods, dairy products, and other items. The supermarket collected all these products under one roof. What's more, the number of unique products it carried climbed: to 6,000 by 1960, 14,000 by 1980, and more than 30,000 today.

THE TOUCHTONE CONSUMER

The next great expansion in variety took place in the home again, with the introduction of toll-free 800 numbers. They started with modest expectations. In 1967, AT&T launched a new product called "interstate inward WATS (Wide Area Telephone Service)," also known as "Automated Collect Calling," which was mostly intended to combat an anticipated shortage of telephone company operators. Operators were becoming overwhelmed by the number of collect calls being accepted by businesses. AT&T thought that the new service might help with that labor shortage but would otherwise have limited appeal. The company never dreamed that by 1992, only twenty-five short years later, 40 percent of the calls on AT&T's long-distance network would be toll-free calls.

What toll-free calling enabled was the return of catalog shopping. The modern automotive age had shifted the population out of the city and into the suburbs, where selection was limited to local shopping centers. An increasingly affluent and materialistic suburban generation was ready to spend again, and by the mid-1970s, they had credit cards to help them act on those desires. The 800 number was the necessary catalyst for a home-shopping boom.

In contrast to the Sears era of massive centralized warehouses containing everything, this later wave of catalogs was more about targeted niches. Color printing technology made it possible for niche retailers to print hundreds of thousands or even millions of catalogs that carpet bombed targeted mailing lists with magazine-quality showcases of their wares. Response rates as low as 1 percent could still be profitable.

Niche products had once again found a way to reach mainstream audiences. Sporting goods, branded apparel, interior design, lingerie, outdoor furniture, hobbies—each month brought a new parade of deep inventory in specialized retail. All it took was a phone call and a credit card, and consumers would have their products in hand in a week or two. But as impressive as this postal cornucopia might have seemed, what the personal computer could offer would soon dwarf it.

THE ULTIMATE CATALOG

The rise of e-commerce on the Web in the early 1990s started by simply building on the catalog model with even more convenient ordering, larger selections, and broader reach at lower cost. The Internet provided a way of offering a catalog to everyone—with no printing and no mailing required. It would clearly work everywhere catalogs worked, and then some.

Of course, some categories were more promising than others. But which?

This was the question Jeff Bezos asked himself as he sat at his desk at the hedge fund D. E. Shaw in New York. It was 1994 and the Internet was starting to take off, growing by 2,300 percent a year from its small existing base. A budding "quant" (math geek), Bezos was asked by his boss to find Internet business opportunities. As he explained, more than ten years later, at an event in Silicon Valley:

> I went to the Direct Marketers Association and got the list of all the things that were sold remotely. Apparel was the number one remote sales category. Gourmet food was number two. Way down at the bottom of the list were books, and the books category was only on there because of things like the Book-of-the-Month Club, because there really are no paper catalogs to speak of that sell books.

The early 1990s were a boom time for the U.S. book industry. Crown Books had already transformed the business with a chain of discount stores, spurring record sales and triggering a wave of similar discounting. Then Barnes & Noble and Borders took it one step further by introducing massive superstores. Sometimes built in converted movie theaters or bowling alleys, these megastores carried as many as

100,000 titles, an inventory five times that of the average local bookstore. It represented an enormous increase in availability and choice, launching an age of abundance for the book buyer.

Books were becoming cheaper and more plentiful—what more could anyone want?

Again, Bezos asked himself that very question:

> I was sorting through these things. If you used the Web in 1994, with the primitive browsers and the technology that was available at the time, it was a pain. The browser was always crashing and things didn't work right and your bandwidth was tiny, even if you had the best modem available at the time.

> I concluded that given the technology at the time if you could do something any other way, that other way would be preferable to doing it on the Web. You didn't want to do apparel on the Web, even though it was the best category, because apparel you could do very effectively through catalogs and through stores. This was my criteria: picking a category where you could substantially improve the customer experience along a dimension that could only be done on the Web.

> It turns out that selection is a very important customer experience driver in the book category. It also turns out that you can't have a big book catalog on paper; it's totally impractical. There are more than 100,000 new books published every year, and even a superstore can't carry them all. The biggest superstores have 175,000 titles and there are only about three that big. So that became the idea: let Amazon.com be the first place where you can easily find and buy a million different books.

What this quant had zeroed in on was an opportunity in what appeared to be a very mature book industry. Although there were lots of publishers, most distribution was handled by just two wholesalers, which had warehouses strategically placed around the country to serve any need.

That suggested a great opportunity for a virtual retailer.

Although 175,000 titles sounds like a lot, Bezos knew the inventory of even the largest superstores was just a tiny fraction of the books available. And being able not only to search for book titles but also to read reviews would clearly make it easier for customers to find what they really wanted.

At the time, there were at least 1.5 million English-language books in print—even the superstores carried just 10 percent of them. Today, the online database Books in Print lists upward of 5.6 million titles. Bezos also knew that more and more publisher catalogs were popping up online, offering academic books, trade books, self-published books, and more. There was no reason why Amazon couldn't offer all of them.

What the Internet presented was a way to eliminate most of the physical barriers to unlimited selection. The bricks-and-mortar super-stores had scale, but they still had to deal with the economics of shelves, walls, staff, locations, working hours, and weather. Because they were bigger and more efficient than the independent booksellers, superstores could offer more selection. However, even their business model hit the wall long before the supply of available titles did.

Today online shopping has passed catalog shopping and now accounts for about 5 percent of American retail spending. It's still growing at a whopping 25 percent a year, and is well on track to fulfill Bezos's original prediction that online retail would eventually reach around 15 percent of total retail, which would give it more than a tenth of the $12 trillion American economy.

One of the largest categories is the online sites of the bricks-and-mortar giants. Bn.com complements Barnes & Noble's brand with a Web site that offers selection on a par with Amazon. Discount cards work equally in both channels, and you can get same-day delivery in Manhattan where B&N has several superstores. If a store doesn't have a book in stock, the clerks are still able to satisfy a customer request by ordering it for them online. Likewise for the online side of Wal-Mart, Best Buy, and innumerable other retailers: The unlimited shelf space of the Web retail allows them to offer their customers more variety and convenience, cementing brand loyalty with existing customers and extending it to new ones who may or may not be near a physical store.

LONG TAILS EVERYWHERE

From purely virtual retailers such as eBay to the online side of traditional retailing, the virtues of unlimited shelf space, abundant information, and smart ways to find what you want—Bezos's original vision—have proven every bit as compelling as he thought. And as a result, there are now Long Tail markets practically everywhere you look.

Just as Google is finding ways to tap the Long Tail of advertising, Microsoft is extending the Tail of video games into small and cheap games that you can download on its Xbox Live network. Open-source software projects such as Linux and Firefox are the Long Tail of programming talent, while offshoring taps the Long Tail of labor. Meanwhile, the Internet has enabled the longest, er, tail of pornography for every possible taste and kink.

More esoteric examples include the proliferation of microbrews as the "Long Tail of beer," the growth of customized T-shirts, shoes, and other clothing as the "Long Tail of fashion," and the growth of online universities as the "Long Tail of education."

Finally, to give an idea of how broadly the theory has been applied, consider this analysis of the "Long Tail of national security" by John Robb, a military analyst who runs the Global Guerrillas Web site:

> Traditionally, warfare (the ability to change society through violence) has been limited to nation-states, except in rare cases. States had a monopoly on violence. The result was a limited, truncated distribution of violence. That monopoly is on the skids due to three trends:
>
> - A democratization of the tools of warfare. Niche producers (for example: gangs) are made possible by the dislocation of globalization. All it takes to participate is a few men, some boxcutters, and a plane (as an example of simple tools combined with leverage from ubiquitous economic infrastructure).
> - An amplification of the damage caused by niche producers of warfare. The magic of global guerrilla systems disruption which turns inexpensive attacks into major economic and social events.

- The acceleration of word of mouth. New groups can more easily find/train recruits, convey their message to a wide audience, and find/coordinate their activities with other groups (allies).

The result: a Long Tail has developed. New niche producers of violence have flourished. Demand for the results these niche suppliers can produce has also radically increased. Big concepts (such as a struggle between Islam and the U.S.), not championed by states, have supercharged niche suppliers like al Qaeda and its clones.

4

THE THREE FORCES OF THE LONG TAIL

MAKE IT, GET IT OUT THERE, AND HELP ME FIND IT

The theory of the Long Tail can be boiled down to this: Our culture and economy are increasingly shifting away from a focus on a relatively small number of hits (mainstream products and markets) at the head of the demand curve, and moving toward a huge number of niches in the tail. In an era without the constraints of physical shelf space and other bottlenecks of distribution, narrowly targeted goods and services can be as economically attractive as mainstream fare.

But that's not enough. Demand must follow this new supply. Otherwise, the Tail will wither. Because the Tail is measured not just in available variety but in the people who gravitate toward it, the true shape of demand is revealed only when consumers are offered infinite choice. It is the aggregate sales, use, or other participation of all those people in the newly available niches that turns the massive expansion of choice into an economic and cultural force. The Long Tail starts with a million niches, but it isn't meaningful until those niches are populated with people who want them.

Collectively, all of this translates into six themes of the Long Tail age:

1. In virtually all markets, **there are far more niche goods than hits.** That ratio is growing exponentially larger as the tools of production become cheaper and more ubiquitous.

2. **The costs of reaching those niches is now falling dramatically.** Thanks to a combination of forces including digital distribution, powerful search technologies, and a critical mass of broadband penetration, online markets are resetting the economics of retail. Thus, in many markets, **it is now possible to offer a massively expanded variety of products.**

3. Simply offering more variety, however, does not shift demand by itself. Consumers must be given ways to find niches that suit their particular needs and interests. A range of tools and techniques—from recommendations to rankings—are effective at doing this. **These "filters" can drive demand down the Tail.**

4. Once there's massively expanded variety and the filters to sort through it, **the demand curve flattens.** There are still hits and niches, but the hits are relatively less popular and the niches relatively more so.

5. All those niches add up. Although none sell in huge numbers, **there are so many niche products that collectively they can comprise a market rivaling the hits.**

6. Once all of this is in place, the **natural shape of demand is revealed,** undistorted by distribution bottlenecks, scarcity of information, and limited choice of shelf space. What's more, that shape is far less hit-driven than we have been led to believe. Instead, it is as diverse as the population itself.

Bottom line: A Long Tail is just culture unfiltered by economic scarcity.

HOW LONG TAILS EMERGE

None of the aforementioned happens without one big economic trigger: reducing the costs of reaching niches. What causes those costs to fall? Although the answer varies from market to market, the explanation usually involves one or more of three powerful forces coming into play.

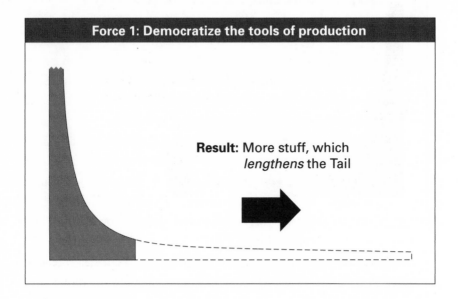

The first force is *democratizing the tools of production*. The best example of this is the personal computer, which has put everything from the printing press to the film and music studios in the hands of anyone. The power of the PC means that the ranks of "producers"—individuals who can now do what just a few years ago only professionals could do—have swelled a thousandfold. Millions of people now have the capacity to make a short film or album, or publish their thoughts to the world—and a surprisingly large number of them do. Talent is not universal, but it's widely spread: Give enough people the capacity to create, and inevitably gems will emerge.

The result is that the available universe of content is now growing faster than ever. This is what extends the tail to the right, increasing the population of available goods manyfold. In music, for instance, the number of new albums released grew a phenomenal 36 percent in 2005, to 60,000 titles (up from 44,000 in 2004), largely due to the ease with which artists can now record and release their own music. At the same time, bands uploaded more than 300,000 free tracks to MySpace, extending the tail even further.

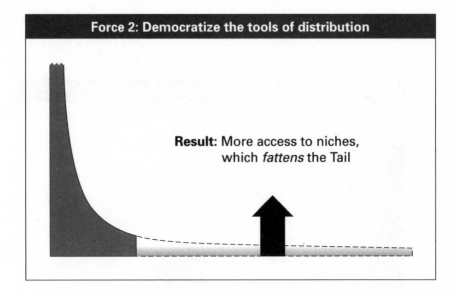

Force 2: Democratize the tools of distribution

Result: More access to niches, which *fattens* the Tail

The second force is *cutting the costs of consumption by democratizing distribution.* The fact that anyone can make content is only meaningful if others can enjoy it. The PC made everyone a producer or publisher, but it was the Internet that made everyone a distributor.

At its most dramatic this is the economics of bits versus atoms, the difference between fractions of pennies to deliver content online and the dollars it takes to do it with trucks, warehouses, and shelves. Still, even for physical goods, the Internet has dramatically lowered the costs of reaching consumers. Over decades and billions of dollars, Wal-Mart set up the world's most sophisticated supply chain to offer massive variety at low prices to tens of millions of customers around the world. Today anybody can reach a market every bit as big with a listing on eBay.

The Internet simply makes it cheaper to reach more people, effectively increasing the liquidity of the market in the Tail. That, in turn, translates to more consumption, effectively raising the sales line and increasing the area under the curve.

The third force is *connecting supply and demand,* introducing consumers to these new and newly available goods and driving demand down the Tail. This can take the form of anything from Google's wisdom-of-crowds search to iTunes' recommendations, along with word-of-mouth, from blogs to customer reviews. The ef-

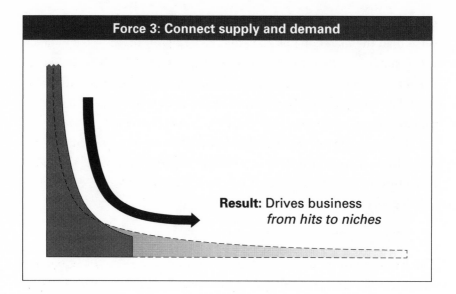

Force 3: Connect supply and demand

Result: Drives business *from hits to niches*

fect of all this for consumers is to lower the "search costs" of finding niche content.

In economics, search costs refer to anything that gets in the way of finding what you want. Some of those costs are non-monetary, such as wasted time, hassle, wrong turns, and confusion. Other costs actually have a dollar figure, such as mistaken purchases or paying too much for something because you couldn't find a cheaper alternative. Anything that makes it easier to find what you want at the price you want lowers your search costs.

We'll go into this more later in the book, but other consumers are often the most useful guides because their incentives are best aligned with our own. Netflix and Google tap consumer wisdom collectively by watching what millions of them do and translating that into relevant search results or recommendations.

Consumers also act as guides individually when they post user reviews or blog about their likes and dislikes. Because it's now so easy to tap this grassroots information when you're looking for something new, you're more likely to find what you want faster than ever. That has the economic effect of encouraging you to search farther outside the world you already know, which drives demand down into the niches.

The other thing that happens when consumers talk amongst themselves is that they discover that, collectively, their tastes are far more diverse than the marketing plans being fired at them suggest. Their interests splinter into narrower and narrower communities of affinity, going deeper and deeper into their chosen subject matter, as is always the case when like minds gather. Encouraged by the company, virtual or not, they explore the unknown together, venturing farther from the beaten path.

The explosion of these technologies that connect consumers is what drives demand from the head to the tail. In other words, the third force further increases demand for the niches and flattens the curve, shifting its center of gravity to the right.

• • •

Think of each of these three forces as representing a new set of opportunities in the emerging Long Tail marketplace. The democratized tools of production are leading to a huge increase in the numbers of producers. Hyperefficient digital economics are leading to new markets and marketplaces. And finally, the ability to tap the distributed intelligence of millions of consumers to match people with the stuff that suits them best is leading to the rise of all sorts of new recommendation and marketing methods, essentially serving as the new tastemakers.

In a nutshell, all of that looks like this:

	Force	Business	Example
1.	Democratize Production	Long Tail *toolmakers, producers*	Digital videocameras, desktop music and video editing software, blogging tools
2.	Democratize Distribution	Long Tail *aggregators*	Amazon, eBay, iTunes, Netflix
3.	Connect Supply and Demand	Long Tail *filters*	Google, blogs, Rhapsody recommendations, and best-seller lists

The next three chapters will explore these new business opportunities in detail.

5

THE NEW PRODUCERS

NEVER UNDERESTIMATE THE POWER OF A MILLION AMATEURS WITH KEYS TO THE FACTORY

On the night of February 23, 1987, the underground Kamiokande II observatory in Japan detected twenty-four neutrinos in a burst lasting thirteen seconds. Although twenty-four neutrinos may not sound like a lot, the observatory usually detects only two or three an hour, and rarely in a pack. So this was something special. But what it actually meant would have to wait a few hours, for other observations to be reported.

Astrophysicists had long theorized that when a star explodes, most of its energy is released as neutrinos—low-mass, subatomic particles that fly through planets like bullets through tissue paper. Part of the theory is that in the early phase of this type of explosion, the only observable evidence is a shower of such particles; it then takes another few hours for the inferno to emerge as visible light. As a result, scientists predicted that when a star went supernova near us, we'd detect the neutrinos about three hours before we'd see the burst in the visible spectrum.

The way to test this correlation between neutrinos and visible light was to make both observations and measure the time difference be-

tween them. But the problem with the optical part of these paired observations was that you had to be looking in the right part of the sky.
This wasn't much of a problem for the neutrino observatories. Because
of its spherical layout, the detector hall of Kamiokande could record
neutrinos penetrating the Earth regardless of which direction they
came from. Yet to see the explosion in visible light, a telescope would
have to be pointed at the exact right spot at the exact right time. And,
needless to say, there was an awful lot of sky to watch.

There just weren't enough professional astronomers who could observe enough of the heavens to have much, if any, chance of spotting
such an event. But there were thousands of amateur astronomers all
too happy to do that job themselves. Armed with relatively inexpensive
computer-guided telescopes with Dobsonian optics, which allow quite
large apertures (twelve inches is not unusual) in telescopes less than
five feet long, and sensitive CCD (charge-coupled device) sensors that
can collect more light than the human eye, contemporary amateur astronomers can photograph the skies better than astronomers with
house-sized telescopes could a century ago.

The first person to see Supernova 1987A was an observer somewhere between the amateurs and the pros. Ian Shelton, a Canadian
grad-school dropout, was housekeeping an observatory in the Chilean
Andes in exchange for time on its twenty-four-inch telescope when academic astronomers weren't using it. One of those free times was the
windy night of February 23. That night Shelton decided to use the telescope to run a three-hour exposure on the Large Magellanic Cloud.

As it happened, exactly 168,000 years earlier and exactly 168,000
light-years away, a star had exploded on the edge of the Tarantula Nebula. From Earth and Shelton's view, however, the explosion looked like
it was happening right then: a splash of light suddenly appearing in
one corner of the Cloud where nothing of note had been before. Shelton stared at the photographic plates for twenty minutes before head-
ing outside to see it with his own eyes. Sure enough, there it was: the
first supernova to be witnessed by the naked eye since 1604.

The connection between Shelton and the Kamiokande II observatory is one of time. The neutrino observatory spotted its burst at 7:35

Universal time. Shelton observed the first bright light around 10:00 Universal time—a little less than three hours after the neutrino shower. So far, right on theory. However, could it have shown up even earlier, before Shelton was watching?

Fortunately, two other dedicated amateur astronomers were at work that night using smaller, nonprofessional telescopes. In New Zealand, Albert Jones, a veteran credited with more than half a million observations, had taken a good look at the Tarantula Nebula at 9:30 UT but had seen nothing unusual. Robert McNaught, another amateur, photographed the explosion at 10:30 UT in Australia, confirming Shelton's timing. So the light arrived somewhere between 9:30 and 10:00.

That is how one of the greatest astronomical discoveries of the twentieth century unfolded. A key theory explaining how the universe works was confirmed thanks to amateurs in New Zealand and Australia, a former amateur trying to turn professional in Chile, and professional physicists in the United States and Japan. When a scientific paper finally announced the discovery to the world, all of them shared authorship.

Demos, a British think tank, described this in a 2004 report as a key moment in the arrival of a "Pro-Am" era, a time when professionals and amateurs work side by side: "Astronomy used to be done in 'big science' research institutes. Now it is also done in Pro-Am collaboratives. Many amateurs continued to work on their own and many professionals were still ensconced in their academic institutions. But global research networks sprang up, linking professionals and amateurs with shared interests in flare stars, comets and asteroids."

As Timothy Ferris points out in *Seeing in the Dark*, his history of modern amateur astronomy: "If one were to choose a date at which astronomy shifted from the old days of solitary professionals at their telescopes to a worldwide web linking professionals and amateurs . . . a good candidate would be the night of February 23, 1987." Demos concludes: "Astronomy is fast becoming a science driven by a vast open-source Pro-Am movement working alongside a much smaller body of professional astronomers and astrophysicists."

The enabling technologies of this Pro-Am movement in astronomy are Dobsonian optics, CCDs, and the arrival of the Internet as a mechanism for sharing information. These tools have swelled the ranks of the amateur astronomers and vastly increased their impact. Over the past two decades, astronomy has become one of the most democratized fields in science, in part because it's so clear what an important role the amateurs play.

NASA often calls on amateurs to watch for specific asteroids that might be headed for Earth, an observation task coordinated via an email message group called the Minor Planet Mailing List that's run by Richard Kowalski, a forty-two-year-old baggage handler at US Airways in Florida by day and an astronomer by night. Some of the eight hundred amateurs on the list record their observations for fun; others hope to be immortalized by having an important discovery named after them. What's notable is that none of them do it for money.

Astronomy has a natural place for volunteer manpower. Again, the problem with the sky is that you need to be looking at the right place at the right time to witness most interesting new phenomena, such as asteroids or stellar evolution. It's less a matter of how big or expensive the telescope, and more a matter of how many eyeballs are transfixed on the sky at any given moment. Amateurs multiply the manpower of astronomy many times—and not just by looking at the stars from their backyards.

SETI@home ("Search for Extraterrestrial Intelligence at home") is a project that harnesses the spare computing power of more than half a million home computers. After collecting hours and hours of white noise recorded from space, the project distributes its radio telescope data to the computers of volunteers. When they're not using their computers, a special screen-saver kicks in. While it displays cosmic imagery, it scans bits of each recording in the hopes of locating a signal that may have come from alien intelligence. By divvying up its data to these volunteer computers, the project is able to examine a far greater number of signals than it would otherwise; and all anyone has to do to participate is download some software.

Another project has open-sourced the analysis of Mars imagery.

NASA put up decades-old photos snapped by the Viking orbiters and asked Web visitors to click on all the craters they could see, classifying them as fresh, degraded, or "ghost." Usually, this is a tedious job for scientists and grad students that can take months or years, but in just three months the "Mars Clickworkers" project got volunteers to identify more than 200,000 craters. Averaged over all the clicks, this amateur collective was almost as accurate as expert planetary geologists.

In "open-source" software, where anyone can contribute to a project, the mantra is "With enough eyes, all bugs are trivial." Likewise for astronomy: With enough eyes, we'll see the asteroid with our name on it—and early enough to do something about it.

Of course, there are limits to what Pro-Ams can achieve. They're largely collecting data, not creating new theories of astrophysics. Sometimes, they are unable to analyze properly the data they collect. Nevertheless, their place in the field seems assured. As John Lankford, a historian of science, put it in *Sky & Telescope* magazine, the bible of U.S. amateur astronomers: "There will always remain a division of labor between professionals and amateurs. But it may be more difficult to tell the two groups apart in the future."

DEMOCRATIZING THE TOOLS OF PRODUCTION

What's new about this is the way it's done, not the concept itself. Indeed, Karl Marx was perhaps the original prophet of the Pro-Am economy. As Demos notes, "In *The German Ideology*, written between 1845 and 1847, Marx maintained that labor—forced, unspontaneous and waged work—would be superseded by self-activity." Eventually, he hoped, there would be a time when "material production leaves every person surplus time for other activities." Marx evoked a communist society in which ". . . nobody has one exclusive sphere of activity but each can become accomplished in any branch he wishes . . . to hunt in the morning, fish in the afternoon, rear cattle in the evening, criticize after dinner, just as I have a mind without ever becoming hunter, fisherman, shepherd or critic."

To continue with Marx's vocabulary, Pro-Ams are a creation of the first force of the Long Tail, the democratization of the tools of production.

The same effect we see in astronomy is playing out in countless other fields. Just as the electric guitar and the garage democratized pop music forty years ago, desktop creation and production tools are democratizing the studio. Apple's GarageBand, free with every Mac, greets a user with the suggestion to "Record your next big hit," and provides the tools to do just that. Likewise, digital video cameras and desktop editing suites (free with every copy of Windows and every Mac) are putting the sort of tools into the hands of the average home moviemaker that were once reserved for professionals alone.

Then there's the written word, always the leading edge of egalitarianism. Although it was the photocopier that first put lie to the aphorism that "the power of the press goes to those who own them," it's blogging that has really sparked the renaissance of the amateur publisher. Today, millions of people publish daily for an audience that is collectively larger than any single mainstream media outlet can claim. What sparked blogging was, again, democratized tools: the arrival of simple, cheap software and services that made publishing online so easy that anyone could do it.

So, too, for desktop photo editing and printing, video games that encourage players to create and share their own alternative levels, and print-on-demand book publishing. A few decades ago, there were two reasons why most of us weren't making hit movies: (1) we didn't have access to the necessary tools, and (2) we didn't have the talent. Today, there's only one excuse—and even that is not as solid as it was. Hollywood, for all its efficiencies, can't find every potentially great filmmaker on the planet. Technology, cheap and ubiquitous, can do far better. Once upon a time, talent eventually made its way to the tools of production; now it's the other way around.

The consequence of all this is that we're starting to shift from being passive consumers to active producers. And we're doing it for the love of it (the word "amateur" derives from the Latin *amator*, "lover," from *amare*, "to love"). You can see it all around you—the extent to which amateur blogs are sharing attention with mainstream media, small-time bands are releasing music online without a record label, and fellow consumers dominate online reviewing. It's as if the default setting of production has shifted from "Earn the right to do it" to "What's stopping you?"

Author Doc Searls calls this a shift from consumerism to participative "producerism":

> The "consumer economy" is a producer-controlled system in which consumers are nothing more than energy sources that metabolize "content" into cash. This is the absolutely corrupted result of the absolute power held by producers over consumers since producers won the Industrial Revolution.
>
> Apple is giving consumers tools that make them producers. This practice radically transforms both the marketplace and the economy that thrives on it.

I can see it in my own young children, who are, as I write, into machinima—short computer-animated movies made with video-game software. Using the 3D rendering engines of games such as Halo 2 or the Sims for all the visuals, machinima directors need only write a script, control the characters, and voice the lines. Everything else— sets, camera, character, and vehicle models—is done by the game software. It's like having a mini-Pixar in every Xbox or PC.

The first reaction of the kids was to watch and enjoy the machinima movies as entertainment. Their second was to express curiosity as to how they're made. And their third was to ask if they could make one themselves. (The answer, of course, is *yes*.) What machinima lacks in Hollywood polish, it more than makes up for in creative inspiration. A generation is growing up watching people just like them produce impressive works of creativity. This can't help but make an impression.

It's one thing to see a movie or listen to music and to think "genius"—that some gifted person and exalted apparatus has put together this unique work of art we appreciate. However, once you know what's behind the curtain, you begin to realize that it could be *you*. It is when the tools of production are transparent that we are inspired to create. When people understand how great work is made, they're more likely to want to do it themselves.

Today, millions of ordinary people have the tools and the role models to become amateur producers. Some of them will also have talent and vision. Because the means of production have spread so widely and to so many people, the talented and visionary ones, even if they're just a small fraction of the total, are becoming a force to be reckoned with. Don't be surprised if some of the most creative and influential work in the next few decades comes from this Pro-Am class of inspired hobbyists, not from the traditional sources in the commercial world. The effect of this shift means that the Long Tail will be populated at a pace never before seen.

THE WIKIPEDIA PHENOMENON

In January 2001, a wealthy options trader named Jimmy Wales set out to build a massive online encyclopedia in an entirely new way—by tapping the collective wisdom of millions of amateur experts, semi-experts, and just regular folks who thought they knew something. This encyclopedia would be freely available to anyone; and it would be created not by paid experts and editors, but by whoever wanted to contribute. Wales started with a few dozen prewritten articles and a software application called a Wiki (named for the Hawaiian word meaning "quick" or "fast"), which allows anybody with Web access to go to a site and edit, delete, or add to what's there. The ambition: Nothing less than to construct a repository of knowledge to rival the ancient library of Alexandria.

This was, needless to say, controversial.

For one thing, this is not how encyclopedias are supposed to be made. From the beginning, compiling authoritative knowledge has been the job of scholars. It started with a few solo polymaths who dared to try the impossible. In ancient Greece, Aristotle single-handedly set out to record all the knowledge of his time. Four hundred years later, the Roman nobleman Pliny the Elder cranked out a thirty-seven-volume set of the day's knowledge. The Chinese scholar Tu Yu wrote an encyclopedia on his own in the ninth century. And in the 1700s, Diderot and a few of his pals (including Voltaire and Rousseau) took twenty-nine years to create the *Encyclopédie, ou Dictionnaire Raisonné des Sciences, des Arts et des Métiers.*

Individual work gradually evolved into larger team efforts, especially after the arrival of the Industrial Revolution. In the late eighteenth century, several members of the Scottish Enlightenment started to apply the industrial principles of scientific management and the lessons of assembly lines to the creation of an encyclopedia such as the world had never before seen. The third edition of the *Encyclopædia Britannica,* published between 1788 and 1797, amounted to eighteen volumes plus a two-volume supplement, totaling over 16,000 pages. Groups of experts were recruited to write scholarly articles under the direction of a manager, organized by a detailed work chart.

Now Wales has introduced a third model: the open collective. Instead of one really smart guy or a number of handpicked smart guys, Wikipedia draws on tens of thousands of people of all sorts—ranging from real experts to interested bystanders—with a lot of volunteer curators adopting entries and keeping an eye on their progression. In Wales's encyclopedia calculus, 50,000 self-selected Wikipedians equal one Pliny the Elder.

As writer Daniel Pink puts it, "Instead of clearly delineated lines of authority, Wikipedia depends on radical decentralization and self-organization; open source in its purest form. Most encyclopedias start to fossilize the moment they're printed on a page. However, add Wiki software and some helping hands and you get something self-repairing and almost alive. A different production model creates a product that's fluid, fast, fixable, and free."

In 2001, that idea seemed preposterous. But by 2005, this non-profit venture had became the largest encyclopedia on the planet. Wikipedia offers more than 1 million articles in English—compared with *Britannica's* 80,000 and *Encarta's* 4,500—fashioned by more than 20,000 contributors. Tack on the editions in seventy-five other languages, including Esperanto and Kurdish, and the total Wikipedia article count tops 3.5 million.

All you need to contribute to Wikipedia is Internet access: Every entry has an "Edit This Page" button on it, available to all. Each of us is an expert in something, and the beauty of Wikipedia is that there is practically no subject so narrow that it can't have an entry. This is in stark contrast to *Britannica*. If you open that great encyclopedia and find either no entry for what you're looking for or an entry that seems deficient, there's little you can do but shake your fist or write a letter to the editor (expecting no response). With Wikipedia, however, you fix it or create it yourself. This kind of shift from passive resentment to active participation makes the big difference. To remix the old joke about the weather, everybody complains about the encyclopedia, but now you *can* do something about it.

THE PROBABILISTIC AGE

Much is made of the fact that Wikipedia's entries are "non-authoritative," which is a way of saying they're not invariably accurate. This is, of course, inevitable when anyone can write them. Unlike *Britannica*, where each entry is scrubbed, checked, and labored over by responsible professionals, each Wikipedia entry simply arrives, conjured from the vacuum by the miracle of the "Edit This Page" button.

In late 2005, John Seigenthaler Sr. wrote an op-ed in *USA Today* about his own Wikipedia entry; the entry started this way:

> John Seigenthaler Sr. was the assistant to Attorney General Robert Kennedy in the early 1960's. For a brief time, he was thought to have been directly involved in the Kennedy assassinations of both John, and his brother, Bobby. Nothing was ever proven.

Aside from the part about him being Robert Kennedy's assistant in the 1960s, virtually everything else about the entry was false and slanderous. Seigenthaler called Wales and got him to delete the entry (although he could have easily done that himself), but after he wrote about the experience it led to a national debate over whether Wikipedia could be trusted, a question that continues today.

The answer is not a simple yes or no, because it is the nature of user-created content to be as messy and uncertain at the microscale, which is the level at which we usually experience it, as it is amazingly successful at the big-picture macroscale. It just has to be understood for what it is.

Wikipedia, like Google and the collective wisdom of millions of blogs, operates on the alien logic of probabilistic statistics—a matter of likelihood rather than certainty. But our brains aren't wired to think in terms of statistics and probability. We want to know whether an encyclopedia entry is right or wrong. We want to know that there's a wise hand (ideally human) guiding Google's results. We want to trust what we read.

When professionals—editors, academics, journalists—are running the show, we at least know that it's someone's job to look out for such things as accuracy. But now we're depending more and more on systems where nobody's in charge; the intelligence is simply "emergent," which is to say that it appears to arise spontaneously from the number-crunching. These probabilistic systems aren't perfect, but they are statistically optimized to excel over time and large numbers. They're designed to "scale," or improve with size. And a little slop at the microscale is the price of such efficiency at the macroscale.

But how can that be right when it feels so wrong?

There's the rub. This tradeoff is just hard for people to wrap their heads around. There's a reason why we're still debating Darwin. And why *The Wisdom of Crowds*, James Surowiecki's book on Adam Smith's invisible hand and how the many can be smarter than the few, is still surprising (and still needs to be read) more than two hundred years after the great Scotsman's death. Both market economics and evolution are probabilistic systems, which are simply counterintuitive to our mammalian brains. The fact that a few smart humans figured this out and used that insight to build the foundations of our modern economy, from the stock market to Google, is just evidence that our mental software (our collective knowledge) has evolved faster than our hardware (our neural wiring).

Probability-based systems are, to use writer Kevin Kelly's term, "out of control." His seminal book by that name looks at example after example, from democracy to bird-flocking, where order arises from what appears to be chaos, seemingly reversing entropy's arrow. The book is more than a dozen years old, and decades from now we'll still find the insight surprising. But it's right.

Is Wikipedia "authoritative"? Well, no. But what really is? *Britannica* is reviewed by a smaller group of reviewers with higher academic degrees on average. There are, to be sure, fewer (if any) total clunkers or fabrications than in Wikipedia. But it's not infallible either; indeed a 2005 study by *Nature,* the scientific journal, reported that in forty-two entries on science topics there were an average of four errors per entry in Wikipedia and three in *Britannica.* And shortly after the report came out, the Wikipedia entries were corrected, while *Britannica* will have to wait for its next reprinting.

Britannica's biggest errors are of omission, not commission. It is shallow in some categories and out of date in many others. And then there are the millions of entries that it simply doesn't—and can't, given its editorial process—have. But Wikipedia *can* scale itself to include those and many more. And it is updated constantly.

The advantage of probabilistic systems is that they benefit from the wisdom of the crowd and as a result can scale nicely both in breadth and depth. But because they do this by sacrificing absolute certainty on the microscale, you need to take any single result with a grain of salt. Wikipedia should be the first source of information, not the last. It should be a site for information exploration, not the definitive source of facts.

The same is true for blogs, no single one of which is authoritative. Blogs are a Long Tail, and it is always a mistake to generalize about the quality or nature of content in the Long Tail—it is, by definition, variable and diverse. But collectively blogs are proving more than an equal to mainstream media. You just need to read more than one of them before making up your own mind.

Likewise for Google, which seems both omniscient and inscrutable. It makes connections that you or I might not, because they emerge naturally from math on a scale we can't comprehend. Google is arguably the first company to be born with the alien intelligence of the Web's "massive-scale" statistics hardwired into its DNA. That's why it's so successful, and so seemingly unstoppable.

Author Paul Graham puts it like this:

The Web naturally has a certain grain, and Google is aligned with it. That's why their success seems so effortless. They're sailing with the wind, instead of sitting becalmed praying for a business model, like the print media, or trying to tack upwind by suing their customers, like Microsoft and the record labels. Google doesn't try to force things to happen their way. They try to figure out what's going to happen, and arrange to be standing there when it does.

The Web is the ultimate marketplace of ideas, governed by the laws of big numbers. That grain Graham sees is the weave of statistical mechanics, the only logic that such really large systems understand. Perhaps someday we will, too.

THE POWER OF PEER PRODUCTION

As a whole, Wikipedia is arguably the best encyclopedia in the world: bigger, more up-to-date, and in many cases deeper than even *Britannica*. But at the individual entry level, the quality varies. Along with articles of breathtaking scholarship and erudition, there are plenty of "stubs" (placeholder entries) and even autogenerated spam.

In the popular entries with many eyes watching, Wikipedia shows a remarkable resistance to vandalism and ideological battles. One study by IBM found that the mean repair time for damage in high-profile Wikipedia entries such as "Islam" is less than four minutes. This is not the work of the professional encyclopedia police. It is simply the emergent behavior of a Pro-Am swarm of self-appointed curators. Against all expectations, the system works brilliantly well. And as Wikipedia grows, this rapid self-repairing property will spread to more entries.

The point is not that every Wikipedia entry is probabilistic, but that the *entire encyclopedia* behaves probabilistically. Your odds of getting a substantive, up-to-date, and accurate entry for any given subject are excellent on Wikipedia, even if every individual entry isn't excellent.

To put it another way, the quality range in *Britannica* goes from, say, 5 to 9, with an average of 7. Wikipedia goes from 0 to 10, with an average of, say, 5. But given that Wikipedia has ten times as many entries as *Britannica*, your chances of finding a reasonable entry on the topic you're looking for are actually higher on Wikipedia.

What makes Wikipedia really extraordinary is that it improves over time, organically healing itself as if its huge and growing army of tenders were an immune system, ever vigilant and quick to respond to anything that threatens the organism. And like a biological system, it evolves, selecting for traits that help it stay one step ahead of the predators and pathogens in its ecosystem.

The traditional process of creating an encyclopedia—professional editors, academic writers, and peer review—aims for perfection. It seldom gets there, but the pursuit of accuracy and clarity results in a work that is consistent and reliable, but also incredibly time-consuming and expensive to produce. Likewise for most other products of the professional publishing industry: One can expect that a book will, in fact, have printing on both sides of the pages where intended and will be more or less spelled correctly. There is a quality threshold, below which the work does not fall.

With probabilistic systems, though, there is only a statistical level of quality, which is to say: Some things will be great, some things will be mediocre, and some things will be absolutely crappy. That's just the nature of the beast. The mistake of many of the critics is to expect otherwise. Wikipedia is simply a different animal from *Britannica*. It's a living community rather than a static reference work.

The true miracle of Wikipedia is that this open system of amateur user contributions and edits doesn't simply collapse into anarchy. Instead, it has somehow self-organized the most comprehensive encyclopedia in history. Reversing entropy's arrow, Jimmy Wales's catalytic moment—putting up a few initial entries and a mechanism for others to add to them—has actually created order from chaos.

The result is a very different kind of encyclopedia, one completely unbounded by space and production constraints. It offers all the expected entries of any world-class reference work and then hundreds of thousands of unexpected ones, ranging from articles that go into textbook-like depth in fields such as quantum mechanics to biographical entries on comic book characters. Or, to put it another way, it's got all the hits plus a huge number of niches.

The classic model of the encyclopedia is a curated list of received cultural literacy. There is the basic canon, which must be recognized by authorities. Then, there are other entries of diminishing length until you get to that line at which the priests of *Britannica* decide "This is not worthy." There, the classic encyclopedia ends. Wikipedia, on the other hand, just *keeps going*.

In a sense, you can think of Wikipedia as equivalent to Rhapsody, the music site. There are the popular top 1,000, which can be found in any encyclopedia: Julius Caesar, World War II, Statistics, etc. These are like the hit songs. With these, Wikipedia is competing with professionals at their best, who produce well-written, authoritative entries that deploy facts with the easy comfort that comes with great scholarship. The main advantage of the user-created Wikipedia model for these entries is its ability to be up-to-date, have unlimited length and visual aids (such as photos and charts), include copious links to support material elsewhere, and perhaps, better represent alternate views and controversies.

In the middle of the curve, from the 1,000th entry to where *Britannica* ends at 80,000, are the narrower subjects: Caesarian Section, Okinawa, Regression Analysis, etc. Here, the Wikipedia model begins to pull ahead of its professional competition. Unlimited space means that the Wikipedia entries tend to be longer and more comprehensive. While the average length of a *Britannica* entry is 678 words, more than 200,000 Wikipedia entries (more than two entire *Britannicas*) are longer than that. Meanwhile, the external links and updated information emerge as a key advantage as Wikipedia becomes a launching place for further research.

Then there is the Tail, from 80,000 to 1 million. These are the entries that Wikipedia has that no other encyclopedia even attempts to include. Its articles on these subjects—Caesar Cipher, Canned Spam, Spearman's Rank Correlation Coefficient—range from among the best in Wikipedia (those written by passionate experts) to the worst (self-promotion, score-settling, and pranks). While many critics focus on the worst entries, the really important thing about Wikipedia's Tail is that there is nothing else like it *anywhere*. From hard-core science to up-to-the-minute politics, Wikipedia goes where no other encyclopedia—whether constrained by paper or DVD limitations—can. *Britannica* doesn't have an entry about the Long Tail phenomenon (yet), but Wikipedia's entry is not only well written and thorough, it's also 1,500 words long (and none of it was written by me!).

Wikipedia authors tend to be enthusiastically involved, liberated, and motivated by the opportunity to improve public understanding of some subject they know and love, a population that has, in five short years, grown a thousandfold with an invasion of empowered amateurs using the simple, newly democratized tools of encyclopedia production: a Web browser and an Internet connection.

This is the world of "peer production," the extraordinary Internet-enabled phenomenon of mass volunteerism and amateurism. We are at the dawn of an age where most producers in any domain are unpaid, and the main difference between them and their professional counterparts is simply the (shrinking) gap in the resources available to them to extend the ambition of their work. When the tools of production are available to everyone, everyone becomes a producer.

THE REPUTATION ECONOMY

Why do they do it? Why does anyone create something of value (from an encyclopedia entry to an astronomical observation) without a business plan or even the prospect of a paycheck? The question is a key one to understanding the Long Tail, partly because so much of what populates the curve does not start with commercial aim. More important, this question matters because it represents yet another example of where our presumptions about markets must be rethought. The motives to create are not the same in the head as they are in the tail. One economic model doesn't fit all. You can think of the Long Tail starting as a traditional monetary economy at the head and ending in a nonmonetary economy in the tail. In between the two, it's a mixture of both.

Up at the head, where products benefit from the powerful, but expensive, channels of mass-market distribution, business considerations rule. It's the domain of professionals, and as much as they might love what they do, it's a job, too. The costs of production and distribution are too high to let economics take a backseat to creativity. Money drives the process.

Down in the tail, where distribution and production costs are low (thanks to the democratizing power of digital technologies), business considerations are often secondary. Instead, people create for a variety of other reasons—expression, fun, experimentation, and so on. The reason one might call it an economy at all is that there is a coin of the realm that can be every bit as motivating as money: *reputation*. Measured by the amount of attention a product attracts, reputation can be converted into other things of value: jobs, tenure, audiences, and lucrative offers of all sorts.

Tim Wu, a Columbia University law professor, calls this the "exposure culture." Using blogs as an example, he writes,

> The exposure culture reflects the philosophy of the Web, in which getting noticed is everything. Web authors link to each other, quote liberally, and sometimes annotate entire articles. E-mailing links to favorite articles and jokes has become as much a part of American work culture as the water cooler. The big sin in exposure culture is not copying, but instead, failure to properly attribute authorship. And at the center of this exposure culture is the almighty search engine. If your site is easy to find on Google, you don't sue—you celebrate.

Once you think of the curve as being populated with creators who have different incentives, it's easy to extend that to their intellectual property interests as well. Disney and Metallica may be doing all they can to embrace and extend copyright, but there are plenty of other (maybe even more) artists and producers who see free peer-to-peer ("P2P") distribution as low-cost marketing. Musicians can turn that into an audience for their live shows, indie filmmakers treat it as a viral resume, and academics treat free downloads of their papers as a way to increase their impact and audience.

Each of these perspectives changes how the creators feel about copyright. At the top of the curve, the studios, major labels, and publishers defend their copyright fiercely. In the middle, the domain of independent labels and academic presses, it's a gray area. Farther down the tail, more firmly in the noncommercial zone, an increasing number of content creators are choosing explicitly to give up some of their copyright protections. Since 2002, a nonprofit organization called Creative Commons has been issuing licenses of the same name to allow for a flexible use of certain copyrighted works for the sake of the greater value (for the content creators) of free distribution, remixing, and other peer-to-peer propagation of their ideas, interests, and fame. (Indeed, I've done that with my own blog, for all of the reasons above.)

In short, some creators care about copyright and some don't. Yet the law doesn't distinguish between them—copyright is automatically granted and protected unless explicitly waived. As a result, the power of "free" is obscured by fears over piracy and is often viewed with suspicion, not least because it evokes unfortunate echoes of both communism and hippie sloganeering.

Regardless, it's something we're starting to reconsider as the power of the "gift economy" becomes clear—in everything from the blogosphere to open source. In one part of my professional life (the 600,000-circulation magazine I edit), I'm near the head of the curve, and in another (my 5,000-reader blog) I'm in the tail. My decisions on intellectual property are different in each. Someday soon, I hope, marketplace and regulation will more accurately reflect this reality.

SELF-PUBLISHING WITHOUT SHAME

We think of books through a commercial lens, assuming that most authors want to write a best-seller and get rich. But the reality is that the vast majority of authors not only won't become best-sellers, but also aren't even trying to write a hugely popular book. Each year, nearly 200,000 books are published in English. Fewer than 20,000 will make it into the average book superstore. Most won't sell.

In 2004, 950,000 books out of the 1.2 million tracked by Nielsen BookScan sold fewer than ninety-nine copies. Another 200,000 sold fewer than 1,000 copies. Only 25,000 sold more than 5,000 copies. The average book in America sells about 500 copies. In other words, about 98 percent of books are noncommercial, whether they were intended that way or not.

The quest for mass-market acceptance requires compromise—a willingness to pick topics of broad rather than narrow interest, and to write in conversational rather than academic style. Most writers can't do that and many others won't. Instead, the vast majority of authors choose to follow their passions and assume they won't make money. Many want no more than to be read by some group that matters to them—from their peers to like-minded souls.

Such profitless publishing can be lucrative all the same. The book becomes not the product of value but the *advertisement* for the product of value—the authors themselves. Many such noncommercial books are best seen as marketing vehicles meant to enhance the academic reputation of their authors, market their consultancy, earn them speaking fees, or just leave their mark on the world. Seen that way, self-publishing is not a way to make money; it's a way to distribute your message.

To get a glimpse of that world, consider Lulu.com, which is a new breed of DIY publisher. For less than two hundred dollars, Lulu can not only turn your book into a paperback or hardcover and give it an ISBN number, but also ensure that it gets listed with online retailers. Once it's listed, the book will be available to an audience of millions and potentially side by side with *Harry Potter*, if the winds of the recommendation engines blow that way. With Lulu, the copies are printed in batches as small as a few dozen and the inventory is replenished as needed via print-on-demand. It's an extraordinary improvement over the scorned "vanity" publishing model of just a few years ago. As a result, thousands of authors are now choosing this route.

Here are the top five self-published books on Lulu, as I write:

1. *Raw Foods for Busy People: Simple and Machine-Free Recipes for Every Day*

2. *The Havanese* ("The quintessential handbook for Havanese dog owners, breeders and fanciers.")
3. *Investigating Biology—A Laboratory Manual for BIO 100*, 12th Edition
4. *Maximum SAT*
5. *How to Start a Wedding Planning Business*

All of them have sold between 5,000 and 50,000 copies, which is not bad. Eighty percent of the profits from these sales go directly to the authors, compared to 15 percent for standard publishers. So much for the notion that self-publishing is just for losers.

Still, most authors don't use such self-publishing services to make money, nor do they expect to hit it big. The vast majority of Lulu's other few thousand customers choose to self-publish because they know that what they're writing isn't likely to sell enough to make the search for a commercial publisher worthwhile. That doesn't mean they don't have a potential audience; it's just that it's a small one.

A few years ago, most of these authors wouldn't have been published at all—and that would have been enough to discourage many of them from writing a book in the first place. But today, the economics of publishing have fallen so low that nearly everyone can do it. That means people can write books for whatever reason they want, and they don't need to depend on some publisher deciding if the book is worth taking to market.

The effect of this is being felt throughout the industry, right up to the giant booksellers. In 2005, Barnes & Noble sold 20 percent more unique titles than it had in 2004, something its CEO, Steve Riggio, attributes to three forces: (1) the efficiencies of print-on-demand, which keeps more books in print; (2) the increase in the number of smaller and independent publishers; and (3) self-publishing.

"Over the next few years, the traditional definition of what a 'published book' is will have less meaning," he says. "Individuals will increasingly use the Internet as a first stage to publish their work, whether they are books, short stories, works in progress, or articles on their area of expertise. The best of this work will turn into physical books. I tend to be sanguine about the book industry's prospects because a whole new and efficient means of first-step publishing is emerging and rapidly becoming more sophisticated."

One of the big differences between the head and the tail of producers is that the farther down you are in the tail, the more likely you are to have to keep your day job. And that's okay. The distinction between "professional" producers and "amateurs" is blurring and may, in fact, ultimately become irrelevant. We make not just what we're paid to make, but also what we *want* to make. And both can have value.

South Korea's "citizen journalism" phenomenon, created in 2000 by OhmyNews, is another example. At OhmyNews, about fifty professional reporters and editors screen, edit, and complement news articles written by more than 40,000 amateurs, from elementary school students to professors. These volunteers submit between 150 and 200 articles a day, which account for more than two-thirds of OhmyNews's content. For this, they receive a pittance: If the article goes to the front page, which only a small fraction do, the author gets around $20. Why do they do it? "They are writing articles to change the world, not to earn money," says Oh Yeon Ho, the site's founder.

From filmmakers to bloggers, producers of all sorts that start in the Tail with few expectations of commercial success can afford to take chances. They're willing to take more risks, because they have less to lose. There's no need for permission, a business plan, or even capital. The tools of creativity are now cheap, and talent is more widely distributed than we know. Seen this way, the Long Tail promises to become the crucible of creativity, a place where ideas form and grow before evolving into commercial form.

CASE STUDY: LONELY ISLAND

One size of incentive doesn't fit all. People create things for all sorts of reasons, ranging from expression to reputation. What makes this important is that there is increasingly frictionless mobility in the Long Tail. In a seamless digital marketplace, from iTunes to the Web itself, content that starts at the bottom can easily move to the top if it

strikes a chord. Understanding the diverse incentives that can moti-
vate the creators of such content becomes essential in finding and encouraging it.

Speaking at a conference in mid-2005, Barry Diller, the media
mogul chairman of IAC/InterActiveCorp, acknowledged that peer production is interesting, but he scoffed at the idea that it is a force capa-
ble of rivaling Hollywood. "People with talent won't be displaced by
18 million people producing stuff they think will have appeal," he con-
fidently predicted.

What are the odds that he's right? Well, if you define "people with
talent" only as those who have a proven ability to make mass-market
blockbusters, Diller may have a point. But there's more to creativity
than Hollywood hits, and people who can strike a chord can come
from anywhere, via any path.

Take Akiva Schaffer, Jorma Taccone, and Andy Samberg. Until recently, they fit nicely into the category of people Diller's talent-
identification machine had efficiently filtered out.

After college, the three high school buddies relocated to Hollywood together. They moved into a big house with low rent on Olympic
Boulevard and dubbed it the Lonely Island. Then they tried to figure
out how to break into the entertainment industry as a comedy troupe.

It isn't easy for an individual comic to make it in TV—even as a
writer—but it's even harder for a preassembled team. Sure enough, the
threesome quickly ran up against all the usual barriers in their hunt for
work in Hollywood. However, rather than subject themselves to endless rejection, the three took their act—now named after their home—
online. Borrowing some video gear, the Lonely Island crew started
producing short-form comedy videos and songs. Schaffer's kid brother
Micah—a tech consultant and Internet agitpropster—threw together
their Web site, thelonelyisland.com, in 2001.

The Lonely Islanders started with white-boy rap music videos, presented with signature deadpan humor. One of the first videos was
about things that are "ka-blamo!" (as in, "You kissed Shannen Do-
herty") and things that aren't ("I majored in pottery"). As is sometimes
the case for such amusing ephemera, the video circulated widely on

the Internet. At one point, a Dutch DJ "mashed" it up (mixed it with other video footage), further boosting its popularity.

Soon more videos and fan mashups followed, something the group encouraged by releasing their videos under a Creative Commons license that freely permitted creative reuse. In just a few years, the Lonely Island was "Internet famous," which is to say they were big with the demographic that has traded its TV time for online time, constantly surfing the contours of online subculture.

Capitalizing on their online celebrity, the Dudes—as they're known to fans—scored better writing and performing gigs. Still, their main show continued to be online. The first episode of their "Internet prime time" series was called "The 'Bu." "Young, sexy people that live in Malibu call it The 'Bu," reads thelonelyisland.com, "because when you say the entire word, it takes time, and then you wouldn't be young anymore."

As the group's cult following grew, word of their shorts got to *Saturday Night Live* star Tina Fey and the show's creator, Lorne Michaels. In mid-2005, the threesome flew to Manhattan for auditions with the most famous team in comedy. In short order, all of the Dudes were hired.

In December 2005, the Lonely Island crew did another one of their white-boy rap sendups on *SNL*. Riffing on the *Chronicles of Narnia* film, the sketch was, as expected, twisted, wrong, and very, very funny. Now that the crew is on network TV, the skit went out as broadcast on a Saturday night, when it was watched by the usual (dwindling) audience, most of whom no doubt laughed and forgot about it.

But some people had recorded the show to their DVRs, and a few of them recognized a flash of brilliance in the *Narnia* skit. So they uploaded the video to the Internet. After it started to take off in the usual link frenzy, NBC heard the stampede and put the video on the official *SNL* site and even iTunes. Then, once again, the viral video effect kicked in—this time bigger than ever.

Jeff Jarvis, a media commentator, described the impact like this: "I haven't heard anyone buzz about, recommend, or admit to watching *SNL* in, oh, a generation. But suddenly, I hear lots of buzz about the show. And it's not because millions happened to start watching when the show happened to actually be funny again. No, the buzz is born because folks started distributing the *Narnia* bit, which indeed is funny, on the Internet, and people are linking to it. NBC is learning the power of the network that no one owns." And sure enough, links to the *SNL* site increased more than 200-fold in the two weeks after the video started circulating.

The Lonely Island tale has come full circle. Misfits rejected by the entertainment industry go online and get popular. Entertainment industry wakes up to this phenomenon in the hard-to-reach demographic of influential twenty-somethings and hires the misfits. The kids do the same thing on broadcast TV, but since that influential demographic doesn't actually watch much TV, it isn't until the skit *goes back online* (now amplified by the net-kids-make-it-big appeal) that the skit gets really popular. Thus *SNL,* previously scorned by the online generation, suddenly gets cool again by tapping into the authentic underground spirit blossoming online. Once upon a time, the show used to handpick its talent pool from obscure regional theaters and improv troupes. Now they also find it online.

So what's the lesson in this story? Well, on one hand, the existing entertainment industry filters did recognize the appeal of the Lonely Island and found a way to tap it. In that sense, maybe the system works. Yet if three kids with a video camera doing goofy raps and putting them on their Web site isn't "18 million people producing stuff they think will have appeal"—to borrow Diller's scornful phrase—I really don't know what is.

The truth is that the next generation of talent will probably come from the 18 million people doing their own thing—and these are the people who are most likely to save Hollywood and the rest of the entertainment industry from grinding formula. Maybe Diller is right. Maybe there are only a small number of people who can write *Friends.* But just think about how many people can produce quirkier fare, like the *Narnia* sketch, content that can resonate with an audience that has grown up online—the place where niches, not networks, rule. Think about how many of those potential talents now have a chance to find a real audience, thanks to the democratized distribution of the Internet.

It may still require the full might of the Hollywood machine to make a multiseason drama with high production qualities. But over that same time hundreds of grassroots videos can collectively capture a similar size audience. That comparison would seem like apples and oranges—lasting commercial brands versus transient amateur amusements—were it not for the fact that the two compete for the time of a generation of Web-savvy viewers. If they're watching one kind of video, they're not watching the other.

What Diller neglects to consider is that today there seems to be less demand for blockbusters than there is for focused or targeted content that *isn't* for everybody. As the audience continues to move away from Top 40 music and blockbusters, the demand is spreading to vast numbers of smaller artists who speak more authentically to their audience. So what if 99 percent of blogs will never attract an audience of more than a few dozen? The fraction of a percent that *do* emerge with broader reach still number in the thousands. And collectively, that 1 percent can draw as much traffic as many mainstream media. The typical "viral video" sensation is seen by several million people, something that can only be said for the most popular TV shows.

As with authors who self-publish their books via Lulu, the products themselves aren't usually making much if any money, but that's not the point. The point is simply that the product exists and it's taking audience share. It isn't a creation of the traditional commercial industry, but it competes with it. Today, the number of people who produce content is far more than the usual talent finders of the media can process—the wave of grassroots creativity would overwhelm the script-readers and tape-listeners of any studio and label. Because the tools of production have entirely democratized, the population of producers is expanding exponentially, and now there's little stopping those with the will and skill to create from doing just that.

THE ARCHITECTURE OF PARTICIPATION

We've seen parts of this story before. In the late 1970s and early 1980s, the combination of the electric guitar, the arrival of cheap multitrack recorders, and the fine example set by the Sex Pistols gave license to a generation of kids with no musical training, obvious talent, or permission from anyone to start bands and record music. When punk rock exploded onto the scene, it was a shocking epiphany for a generation of kids in the mosh pit. Watching someone your age play three chords badly, while jumping around on stage, one couldn't but think: "I could do *that*."

For a while, the assumption was that to be a musician, the right way of learning was to copy the masters. So you should start by playing covers, reading music, and maybe going to music school. This was the notion of paying your dues: Do the circuit, and play the standards, because that's what people want (no one wants to hear your crappy original compositions). Do it *right*.

But punk rock changed the game. Punk rock said: "Okay, you have your guitar, but you *don't* have to do it right. You can do it wrong! It doesn't matter one bit if you're a skilled musician; it just matters if you have something to say."

Through punk rock, we saw a premium on fresh voices, new sounds, vigor, and an antiestablishment sentiment that could have only come from outside the system. It was inspirational to see people out there with no more talent than you, having fun, being admired, doing something novel. To put it in economic terms, punk rock lowered the barriers of entry to creation.

The traditional line between producers and consumers has blurred. Consumers are also producers. Some create from scratch; others modify the works of others, literally or figuratively remixing it. In the blog world, we talk about "the former audience"—readers who have shifted from passive consumers to active producers, commenting and blogging right back at the mainstream media. Others contribute to the process nothing more than their Internet-amplified word of mouth, doing what was once the work of radio DJs, music magazine reviewers, and marketers.

The result is starting to look like what Tim O'Reilly, a book publisher and seer of the DIY age, calls the "The New Architecture of Participation."

A team at the University of California, Berkeley, illustrated this with a new map of creation, as follows.

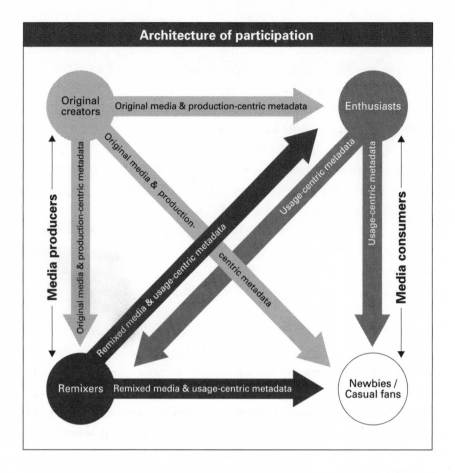

As this figure shows, a once-monolithic industry structure where professionals *produced* and amateurs *consumed* is now a two-way marketplace, where anyone can be in any camp at any time. This is just a hint of the sort of profound change that the democratized tools of production and distribution can foster.

6

THE NEW MARKETS

HOW TO CREATE AN AGGREGATOR THAT
CAN STRETCH FROM HEAD TO TAIL

In 1982, a bookseller named Richard Weatherford realized that the then-new personal computer could revolutionize the used-book business. There are thousands of used-book stores around the country, all with different inventories. Virtually any book you might want is out there somewhere, but good luck in finding it. Weatherford saw this as primarily an information problem, exactly the sort of thing computers are good at solving, and he wrote a business plan for a company that would build an online database for antiquarian booksellers. He called it Interloc, short for interlocutor, a fancy way of saying "go-between."

Weatherford was a few decades ahead of his time, and he failed to get funding. But in 1991, he was hired by Faxon, a book and magazine service firm, to salvage BookQuest, which had attempted to do the same thing. It didn't work—this was still about a decade too early—but the funding at least was starting to become available. With $50,000 from other booksellers, Weatherford launched Interloc in 1993, before the Web. It was a closed network to enable booksellers to search other merchants' inventory to find books for their own customers. It created a data standard (which is still in use today) and software that allowed sellers to transfer files of book listings over a modem. In 1996 it expanded to the Web.

In 1997, Marty Manley, a former union leader, McKinsey consultant, and assistant secretary of labor under Bill Clinton, was looking for an out-of-print book. He found Interloc, and was immediately struck by the potential of such a rich database of information in the fragmented book market. He got in touch with Weatherford and proposed merging Interloc into a new company, tailored to both consumers and booksellers alike; later that year they launched Alibris in Manley's home in Berkeley.

It's worth taking a moment here to understand the used-book market. For most of the past few decades it has actually been comprised of two very different markets. About two-thirds of it was the thriving and efficient textbook business that centered around college campuses. The other third was a relatively sleepy trade in around 12,000 small used-book stores scattered around the country.

Used textbooks are a model of an efficient market—every year millions of students buy and then resell expensive volumes they need only for a single semester. The set of books with resale value is determined by the published curriculum of core classes; the price is set by what competition there is between campus bookstores; and the supply is replenished twice a year.

Textbook publishers don't mind this very much because it means they can actually charge more for new copies, since the buyers know they have a predictable resale value. Indeed, the economic model at work here is more like a rent than a purchase. Typically, stores buy books for 50 percent of the cover price and then resell them for 75 percent. Depending on whether the student is buying new or used, that "rental fee" is between half and a quarter of the list price of the book. This arrangement works so well that the used-textbook market in the United States is now a $1.7 billion enterprise, accounting for 16 percent of all college store sales.

Publishers ensure that the used books don't circulate forever, which would depress new book sales, by releasing new editions with different page numbers (so the old ones can't be used). This purges the market of old inventory from time to time.

In the case of the non-academic used-book market, however, there were few of these efficiencies. The typical used-book store's access to secondhand books is limited to whomever happens to be local and selling volumes from his or her own collection. As a result, the selection at these stores tends to be pretty random, reflecting the taste of the proprietor and the luck of the catch rather than any comprehensive slice of the book market. For patrons of used-book stores, this randomness is part of the appeal, providing a serendipitous sense of exploration and discovery. But if you're looking for a particular book, that process of cruising around the store and browsing the shelves can be unrewarding.

In economic terms, what makes the textbook market work is ample liquidity. There are so many sellers and so many buyers of a relatively small set of traded commodities that the odds of finding what you want at the right price are excellent. By contrast, what ailed the non-academic used-book market was poor liquidity—not enough sellers and buyers of an *unbounded* set of commodities. The result of too many products and not enough players was that the odds of finding what you want were poor. Thus, most buyers simply never consider a used-book store when they're shopping for something specific.

Weatherford had realized that although the economics of each individual bookstore didn't make a lot of sense, together (with all the bookstores combined or linked up) the overall used-book market made a *huge* amount of sense. The collective inventory of some 12,000 used-book stores could rival the best library in the world. The individual store owners uploaded their inventory, and Alibris collected them all together and ensured that the used books were displayed right alongside the new ones at the online booksellers that used Alibris data.

It made that database available to the big online booksellers such as Amazon and bn.com, which integrated the used-book listings alongside new books, effectively making "out of print" obsolete and offering a low-price alternative to new books. By bringing millions of customers to the used-book market, this gave used-book stores even more incentive to computerize their inventories, which, in turn, gave Alibris (and by extension its online retailing partners) even more inventory to sell. It was a classic virtuous circle, and the effect supercharged used-book sales. After years of stagnation, the $2.2 billion market is now growing at double digits, with all that growth coming from a $600 million on-line market that's growing by more than 30 percent a year, according to the Book Industry Study Group.

ENTER THE AGGREGATORS

Alibris is a Long Tail "aggregator"—a company or service that collects a huge variety of goods and makes them available and easy to find, typically in a single place. What it did by connecting the distributed inventories of thousands of used-book stores was to use information to create a liquid market where there was an illiquid market before. With a critical mass of inventory and customers, it tapped the latent value in the used-book market. And it did it at a tiny fraction of the cost that it would have required to assemble that much inventory from scratch, by outsourcing most of the work of assembling the catalog to the individual booksellers, who type in and submit the product listings themselves.

That's the root calculus of the Long Tail: The lower the costs of selling, the more you can sell. As such, aggregators are a manifestation of the second force, democratizing distribution. They all lower the barrier to market entry, allowing more and more things to cross that bar and get out there to find their audience.

There are literally thousands of other examples, but I'll give just a few here. Google aggregates the Long Tail of advertising (small- and medium-sized advertisers and publishers that make their money from advertising). Rhapsody and iTunes aggregate the Long Tail of music. Netflix does the same for the Long Tail of movies. EBay aggregates the Long Tail of physical goods and the Long Tail of merchants who sell them, right down to the millions of regular people getting rid of unwanted birthday presents.

It goes far beyond selling, too. Software, such as Bloglines, that collects "feeds" of online content using the RSS standard are also referred to as "aggregators," and for good reason—they pull together and coherently order the Long Tail of online content, including millions of blogs. Wikipedia is an aggregator of the Long Tail of knowledge and those who have it. The list of examples goes on and on, aggregating every-thing from ideas to people.

In this chapter, I'll focus on the business aggregators. They fall mostly into five categories:

1. Physical goods (e.g., Amazon, eBay)
2. Digital goods (e.g., iTunes, iFilm)
3. Advertising/services (e.g., Google, Craigslist)
4. Information (e.g., Google, Wikipedia)
5. Communities/user-created content (e.g., MySpace, Bloglines)

Each of these categories can range from massive companies to one-person operations. A single blog that collects all the news and infor-mation that it can about a topic, let's say needlework, is an aggregator, as is Yahoo! Some aggregators attempt to straddle an entire category, such as Netflix (films) or iTunes (music), while others simply find their niche, such as services that aggregate only SEC filings or techno music.

Many aggregators occupy multiple categories. Amazon aggregates both physical goods (from electronics to cookware) and digital goods (from ebooks to downloadable software). Google aggregates informa-tion, advertising, and digital goods (Google Video). MySpace, the hugely popular networking site for bands and their fans, aggregates both content (millions of free songs) and the people who listen to it and, in turn, generates more content *about* those bands in the form of reviews, news, and other fan ephemera.

HYBRID VERSUS PURE DIGITAL

Let's start by contrasting the first category of online aggregator busi-nesses, selling physical goods online, with the second, selling digital goods online. They're both Long Tail opportunities, but the second one can extend farther down the Tail than the first.

The online retailers of physical goods, from BestBuy.com's camera selection to Netflix's DVD library, can offer inventory hundreds of times greater than their bricks-and-mortar counterparts, but eventually even they hit a limit. By contrast, the companies that sell digital goods, from albums or songs on iTunes to TV shows or amateur clips on Google Video, can theoretically go all the way down the Tail, expanding the variety they offer to encompass everything available. (The other three categories of aggregator—services, user-created content, and communities—are largely based on digital information, so they share this quality.)

We call the first type a *hybrid retailer* because it's a cross between the economics of mail order (physical) and the Internet (digital). In this instance, the goods are usually delivered through the mail or FedEx, and the efficiencies come both in lowering the supply-chain costs with centralized warehouses and being able to offer an unlimited catalog with all the search and other informational advantages of a Web site.

Take Amazon's CD business. It lists a bit less than a half million CD titles. Combined with the collective inventories of its many third-party "marketplace" sellers, the total is probably closer to 800,000. That number is growing steadily, so in a few years there will be over a million CD titles. Still, there are limits to that catalog.

Because CDs are physical items, somebody's got to store them somewhere before they're sold. As such, there's some inventory risk associated with each Amazon listing. After all, a certain CD may never sell. Plus, there are shipping costs associated with each sale, so in practice, the price never falls below $3 or so. And, more important, the songs on a CD cannot be sold individually: it's either the whole CD or nothing.

Clearly, Amazon's CD economics are a whole lot better than the average record store's, which is why it's able to offer as much as one hundred times the choice. That takes Amazon well down the Tail. But not all the way. According to SNOCAP, a digital licensing and copyright management service that tracks the usage of peer-to-peer file-trading networks, there are at least 9 million tracks circulating online. That works out to nearly a million albums' worth—and that doesn't even include most music from before the age of CDs, much of which will eventually appear in digital form. Plus, there are many thousands of garage bands and bedroom remixers who make music and distribute but have never released a CD at all. Together, all that music could easily amount to another million albums' worth. So Amazon, despite all of its economic advantages, can actually get only a quarter of the way down the Long Tail of music.

The only way to reach all the way down the Tail—from the biggest hits down to all the garage bands of past and present—is to abandon atoms entirely and base all transactions, from beginning to end, in the world of bits. That's the structure of the second class of aggregator, the pure digital retailer.

With the pure digital model, each product is simply a database entry, costing effectively nothing. The distribution costs are simply broadband megabytes, bought in bulk at fast-dropping costs incurred only when the product is ordered. What's more, pure digital retailers can choose between selling goods as stand-alone products (ninety-nine-cent downloads at iTunes) or as a service (unlimited access music subscriptions at Rhapsody).

Those commercial digital services have all the advantages of Amazon's online CD catalog, plus the additional savings of delivering their goods over broadband networks at virtually no cost. This is the way to achieve the holy grail of retail—near-zero marginal costs of manufacturing and distribution. Since an extra database entry and a few megabytes of storage on a server cost effectively nothing, these retailers have no economic reason not to carry everything available. And someday (once they get past messy issues such as rights clearance and contracts) they will.

Seen this way, there is no simple divide between traditional retailers and Long Tail ones. Instead, it's a progression from the economics of pure atoms, to a hybrid of bits and atoms, to the ideal domain of pure bits. Digital catalogs of physical goods lower the economics of distribution far enough to get partway down the potential Tail. The rest is left to the even more efficient economics of pure digital distribution. Both are Long Tails, but one is potentially longer than the other.

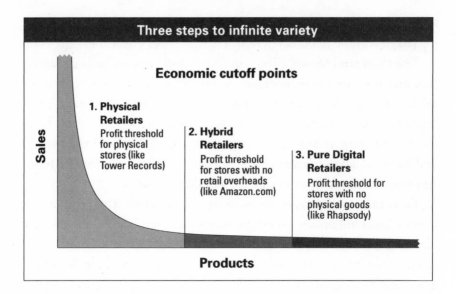

Three steps to infinite variety

Economic cutoff points

1. Physical Retailers
Profit threshold for physical stores (like Tower Records)

2. Hybrid Retailers
Profit threshold for stores with no retail overheads (like Amazon.com)

3. Pure Digital Retailers
Profit threshold for stores with no physical goods (like Rhapsody)

Sales

Products

TRIPPING DOWN THE TAIL

Let's return to the Amazon story to see how this works in practice. Amazon embodies both the hybrid and pure digital models, which have emerged as it sought new ways to lower its costs and work its way farther down the Tail.

Step one, as we've already seen, was Bezos's original insight: that online commerce could have the basic advantage of a mail-order merchant's centralized distribution, as well as the direct-buying advantage of a catalog retailer, without the corresponding costs of printing and mailing millions of catalogs. Thus, Amazon 1.0 (circa 1994–96).

The next step was to reduce the company's inventory risk even further by not paying for items that it kept even in its own warehouses. Amazon did that with a consignment program. Again, the company started with books. The Amazon Advantage program offered authors what at first blush sounded like a pretty one-sided deal: Pay a yearly $29.95 fee, ship your books to Amazon, and when it sells them, let it keep 55 percent of the proceeds. Why would an author do that? Because the consignment program was one more step away from the delays and uncertainty of special order. In a nutshell, it ensured that the author's book would be in stock—and easily accessible—without having to beg a publisher to keep it that way.

The third step toward even lower costs involved extending the virtual inventory model by bringing in other big retailers and their own existing relationships with manufacturers and distributors. Offering its sophisticated e-commerce technology to large retailers such as Toys "R" Us and Target, Amazon created storefronts for those big partners and let *them* deal with the inventory entirely. With each new partner, Amazon's effective inventory grew by millions of items.

Of course, not all big retailers were willing to put their digital future in Amazon's hands, and those that were often asked to be the exclusive supplier in their domain of housewares or toys. While this limited how far Amazon could extend the model, in principle, being an aggregator-for-hire allowed Amazon to enjoy the sweet economics of a services business, free of the fuss of fulfillment. As eBay can attest, selling your software and servers for a fee is about the highest-margin business around.

But the big growth in the virtual inventory model turned out not to be in moving up to larger and larger partners, but moving down to smaller ones. In 1999, Amazon introduced its "Marketplace" program, which extended its storefront service model farther into eBay territory by offering its services to all merchants. Retailers and distributors of any size, from specialty shops to individuals, could have their goods listed on Amazon.com just like the products in Amazon's own warehouses—and the customers could buy either just as easily. By the end of 2004, Amazon had more than 100,000 Marketplace sellers, and these third-party sales represented nearly 40 percent of the company's total sales volume.

The rise of this virtual selling model turned the traditional inventory problem on its head. Again, a chain retailer like Best Buy has to distribute its supply of, say, digital cameras across all of its stores, hoping to guess roughly at where the demand will be and how big it might get. Needless to say, the people and the products must be in the same place—supply and demand must meet right there in the store's aisles. But invariably the retailer will guess wrong, at least to some degree, running out in some stores and having surplus stock depreciating and taking up valuable space in others.

With the Amazon Marketplace form of distributed inventory, the products are still on shelves around the country, but they're collectively cataloged and offered in one central place—Amazon's Web site. Then, when people order them, the products are boxed up and shipped directly to the customer by the small merchants who have held the inventory all along. Like the chain retailers, Amazon also connects centralized supply with scattered demand, but the genius of its model is that the store and customer don't have to be in the same place. Ironically, this makes it *more* likely that the supply and demand will actually connect. Regardless, even if they don't, Amazon bears none of the cost—the surplus stock simply depreciates on the shelves of a third party.

As this program continues to grow, Amazon gets closer and closer to breaking the tyranny of the shelf entirely. It doesn't have to guess ahead of time where the demand is going to be, and it doesn't have to guess at how big that demand will be. All the risk within the Marketplace program is outsourced to a network of small merchants who make their own decisions, based on their own economics, on what to carry. (We'll get more into the tyranny of the shelf in the "Short Head" chapter.)

INVENTORY ON DEMAND

Virtual and distributed inventory is a dramatic way to move down the Tail, but getting rid of physical inventory altogether can take you even farther. Amazon's next step was to attempt to get closer to this economic nirvana by building a business that kept inventory as bits until it was shipped.

One of the problems with carrying books is that a lot of them sell only one or two copies a year. In that case, even orders of 10 copies— instead of 100 or 1,000—might not be viable. Even if it costs a retailer just a dollar to store a book until it sells (which could mean holding on to it for a whole year), the retailer is going to ask itself whether carrying that book is ultimately worth it if it is going to sell in such low numbers. What retailers need is an efficient, economically sustainable way to sell a book that sells just one copy per year. And that means near-zero inventory costs.

Amazon's solution was *print-on-demand*. In its idealized form books stay as digital files until they're purchased, at which time they're printed on laser printers and come out looking just like regular paperbacks. Since bits are turned into atoms only when an order comes in, the costs scale perfectly with the revenues. Or, to put it in the simplest terms, the production and inventory cost of a print-on-demand book that is never bought is zero. These economics are potentially so efficient that they may someday make it possible to offer any book ever made. If you're a bookseller, that means you won't have to be discriminating about what you do and do not carry in a print-on-demand edition, because the costs of making a mistake are also essentially zero.

That's the ideal form. The current reality is that most print-on-demand is used to top off inventory with small print runs of a few hundred. But the falling price of the technology is bringing that number down closer to idealized single-copy form.

Amazon started by placing industrial printers in its own warehouses. Then, in mid-2005, the company massively expanded its capacity by acquiring BookSurge, a leading print-on-demand business. A few months later, it did the same for movies, buying CustomFlix, a DVD-on-demand company. Now Amazon can retain an inventory that takes up no space and has no cost at all: These books and movies remain files in a database somewhere until they're ordered.

Of course, Amazon didn't invent the notion of print-on-demand. It has long been a dream of the book industry, but until recently, print-on-demand was hobbled by technical and economic constraints. Printing a paperback that looks good is not, surprisingly, the problem. Unless you know what to look for (mostly the reproduction of images on inside pages), you probably can't tell if that paperback that just arrived from Amazon was printed in a batch of 50,000 by the publisher or in a lot of one by a laser printer in one of Amazon's warehouses.

Despite the compelling economics, the publishing industry is still far from a widespread shift to print-on-demand. Traditional printing is considerably cheaper for large batches. It is still costly to turn a book manuscript into a file that's formatted correctly for print-on-demand. As I write, print-on-demand is also limited to a few set paper sizes, meaning that books whose pages are larger or smaller than certain dimensions absolutely must be redesigned and reformatted. Then, there is the gnarly question of rights. For older books, the author's permission is required to make a book available as a print-on-demand edition. Yet many authors are afraid that the price premium now required of on-demand printing (a few dollars to cover the slightly higher production costs compared to bulk printing) will suppress sales; so they resist.

But the potential of print-on-demand is extraordinary, and not just for the onesies and twosies. The biggest cost to publishers is the cost of returns from booksellers, which the publishers freely accept as a matter of industry practice. The reason booksellers over-order is that they want to make sure they don't run out between print runs, and since the cost of any excess is borne by the publisher, there's little risk in ordering a bit more than they might need. But if the booksellers knew that demand could be filled via small print-on-demand batches between big print runs, they might be willing to order no more than they actually need, potentially reducing returns radically.

Thus the economic efficiencies of print-on-demand wouldn't just be extending the Long Tail, but also improving the economics of the head, where there are far more dollars at stake. This is, needless to say, a powerful attraction and will only accelerate the adoption of the technology.

THE END OF INVENTORY ALTOGETHER

The ultimate cost reduction is eliminating atoms entirely and dealing only in bits. Pure digital aggregators store their inventory on hard drives and deliver it via broadband pipes. The marginal cost of manufacturing, shelving, and distribution is close to zero, and royalties are paid only when the goods are sold. It's the ultimate on-demand market: Because the goods are digital, they can be cloned and delivered as many times as needed, from zero to billions. A best-seller and a never-seller are just two entries in a database; equal in the eyes of technology and the economics of storage.

Today this is the model that iTunes, Rhapsody, and the other digital music services are so dramatically demonstrating. But the opportunity goes much farther than just music. The overwhelming trend of our age is to take products that were once delivered as physical goods, find ways to turn them into data, and stream them into your home.

For video, pure digital markets range from commercial video-on-demand services provided by cable companies to Web-based video aggregators such as Google Video. Peer-to-peer file trading technologies such as BitTorrent are the underpinnings of hundreds of noncommercial digital video markets, while iTunes is building a thriving pay-per-download video business for its video iPod. Some of this is television content, making these network-based digital video markets a sort of TiVo in the sky. Other aggregators offer movies, a market that will someday take Netflix's massive selection and make it all instantaneously available (a move that will presumably be led by Netflix itself).

Video games, once delivered on cartridges and then on DVDs, are now increasingly streamed as bits to game consoles in the living room. This creates a new market in everything from older titles and niche titles to supplemental content such as new characters and levels. Nintendo is putting this at the core of its next console, code-named Revolution, which will be backward compatible with its previous consoles, making most of its back catalog available as Long Tail content—fun or nostalgia downloadable and playable for a small fee.

And so, too, for ebooks and audio books, online newspapers and magazines, and software. All were once delivered on paper or plastic, necessitating all the complexities of physical inventory and delivery. All are now joined by digital versions, with corresponding digital economics. The experience is not always the same, which is why paper books and magazines are still the preferred version for many. But the functional gap is shrinking. And the distribution advantages of the digital versions are irresistible.

7

THE NEW TASTEMAKERS

THE ANTS HAVE MEGAPHONES.
WHAT ARE THEY SAYING?

Once upon a time, there was really only one way to launch a hit album: radio. Nothing else reached as many people, as often. Getting on
a radio playlist was tricky (especially after payola was outlawed), but
once a song was in heavy rotation it had a high probability of selling.
Then, in the 1980s, came MTV, which became the second way to create a hit. It had even more limited capacity for new music, but its influence over a generation was unparalleled. For the music labels, those
were good times. It was a brutally competitive business, but it was a
business they knew. They understood the rules, and they could earn
their keep by working them.

But now rock radio is in seemingly terminal decline and MTV
doesn't show many music videos anymore. So how to market music?
Labels know the answer lies online, tapping the word-of-mouth forces
that are replacing traditional marketing in creating demand, but they're
still trying to figure out exactly how best to do it.

We're entering an era of radical change for marketers. Faith in advertising and the institutions that pay for it is waning, while faith in individuals is on the rise. Peers trust peers. Top-down messaging is
losing traction, while bottom-up buzz is gaining power. Dell spends

hundreds of millions each year on promoting its quality and customer service, but if you Google "dell hell" you'll get 55,000 pages of results. Even the word "dell" returns customer complaints by the second page of results. The same inversion of power is now changing the marketing game for everything from individual products to people. The collective now controls the message.

For a generation of customers used to doing their buying research via search engine, a company's brand is not what the company says it is, but what Google says it is. The new tastemakers are us. Word of mouth is now a public conversation, carried in blog comments and customer reviews, exhaustively collated and measured. The ants have megaphones.

The question of how to drive demand in such a world is a key one, and in this chapter I'll describe many of the techniques that work best. But first, I'll start with the music industry, ground zero of the Long Tail explosion. Three bands tell the story of an era where the power has shifted from music executives to fans, to the consternation of suits everywhere. The results are mixed—one is a disappointment, another a success, and the third a sobering lesson in how bands may soon not need labels at all—but together they illuminate the challenges of selling in a new era of empowered consumers.

BONNIE MCKEE

In September 2004, the record label Reprise (a subsidiary of Warner) released the debut album by a then-nineteen-year-old singer named Bonnie McKee. It was a rocky start. The record had been recorded twice and delayed a year while the label tried to figure out what to do with it—and her. Although young, McKee had a mature, throaty voice, wrote her own songs, and had had a troubled adolescence that involved drugs and sexual experimentation. She had married at eighteen but openly dated other men, sometimes those twice her age. Her hero was the delightfully unhinged Fiona Apple, another artist whom record labels have had trouble categorizing.

Based on her hard-luck story and rough edges, Reprise eventually decided McKee fit into the singer-songwriter rock category that included the likes of Sheryl Crow. They titled her album *Trouble* and began a marketing plan that would pitch her to so-called adult contemporary radio stations, which appeal mostly to women in their late twenties and early thirties.

Such guesswork is risky—even the labels can't predict whether and where an artist will resonate—yet for new acts without a touring history there have been few alternatives. But today radio is no longer the only way to launch new artists. So while it was preparing its radio roll-out, Reprise prereleased several tracks to online music sites, including Yahoo!, which has a free Internet radio service called LAUNCHcast. One of the most popular features of LAUNCHcast is its customized radio station, which allows its millions of users to select bands and genres they like and then listen to those bands and others like them for free. Reprise decided to see if this audience could help them find out where McKee fit in.

LAUNCHcast is built around an "adaptive" recommendation system that decides based on your preferences what else you might like. While each song is played, a little window display encourages you to rate the song, artist, and album on a scale of one to five stars, from "Never play again" to "Can't get enough." As you listen to music and rate it, Yahoo!'s software is getting to know you and changing the playlist of upcoming songs accordingly.

But it's not just software. LAUNCHcast is also learning from other listeners and using their opinions to guide its recommendations. Because this is an online service with millions of users, Yahoo! is able to record hundreds of millions of likes and dislikes each year, measuring the taste of its listeners with remarkable precision. This tells it something not only about each of its users, and how to provide them with more music that they'll like, but also about the music itself. LAUNCHcast, along with being a free music service, is a polling machine of remarkable size and fine-grained resolution. It is, in a sense, constantly taking the pulse of the culture, learning how artists fit into it through the clicks of millions of music fans.

If enough people say they like Groove Armada as well as The Crystal Method, there may well be a stylistic connection between them, despite the fact that one's categorized as "downtempo" and the other "beats and breaks." Such strong associations tell Yahoo! to put the two on the same playlists more often, and if the positive ratings continue to come in, that connection is reinforced.

As Yahoo!'s software makes custom playlists for each listener, it occasionally sprinkles in a few new artists and tracks to see if they resonate. Radio stations do this, too, but typically only with artists who have a good track record, and even then only after much pretesting and record-label marketing. The difference is that Yahoo! has literally millions of radio stations, each one of them a stream customized for a user. It effectively has infinite broadcast capacity, and thus, just as with infinite shelf space, it can afford to be a lot less discriminating. So it can try to break more new artists and albums—thousands of new songs each year, almost all of which will get no airplay on traditional radio.

If a new song gets high ratings from the few listeners who first hear it, Yahoo! will add it to more playlists. Unlike a traditional radio station, Yahoo! knows quite a bit about those listeners who liked the song. It knows their gender, age, zip code, and a lot about their musical taste from having tracked their listening behavior and ratings. These data streams, used cleverly, can unlock a powerful new way of marketing music—word of mouth amplified by the feedback effect of adaptive recommendations.

This is what drew Reprise to the service. Unsure of where to find an audience for the talented McKee, Reprise decided to use Yahoo!'s ability to test new artists by pushing her first single, "Somebody," to adult contemporary playlists, which were similar to the listenership of the radio stations they intended to market her to. The label paid for extra placement and promotion to push McKee out to more listeners, hoping that the ratings feedback would support their instincts about her natural audience. And after a few weeks, Yahoo! did indeed have its answer. "Somebody" was very popular, but not equally with all demographic groups—and not, surprisingly, with the 25–35 female group the label had aimed it at.

The report from LAUNCHcast showed the following demographic information about McKee's listeners:

AUDIENCE COMPOSITION

Females 13–17	29.9%
Females under 13	17.2%
Females 18–24	15.9%
Males 13–17	8.0%
Males 18–24	6.4%
Males under 13	4.4%
Females 25+	11%
Males 25+	7.2%

The lesson was clear. Reprise had guessed wrong. Instead of appealing to women in their twenties and thirties, Bonnie actually appealed to a far younger audience, with nearly half of her listener base under the age of seventeen. Instead of showing an affinity to artists like Sheryl Crow, this listener constituency most commonly searched for artists like Avril Lavigne, Britney Spears, and Gwen Stefani. It turned out that many teenage girls could relate to the troubled adolescence and bruised romance story in McKee's lyrics.

By the middle of November 2004, "Somebody" had become the tenth most played song on LAUNCHcast. Finally, as a result of the promotional campaign, Bonnie McKee became a Top 50 search term on the service.

This data prompted label executives to make a major change in how they marketed Bonnie McKee. They gave her a makeover, emphasizing her edgier side, a sort of bubblegum Lolita-gone-wrong look. She was neither a Sheryl Crow nor a Britney Spears, they decided; she was the rebel anti-poptart, appealing to an angsty subset of the teen girl audience.

It was a smart move, but it didn't work. Her album sold fewer than 17,000 copies. Despite demographic and geographic data of where McKee's most receptive audience could be found, she still got virtually no airplay. "What we've learned is that if a band builds an online fan base first, they have a better chance of selling CDs when the song gets on the radio or MTV," says Robin Bechtel, who ran the marketing campaign. "Many artists who don't do that either fail at radio or get on the radio and only the hit song gets downloaded, rather than people buying the whole album. It seems the fans aren't invested in the artist, just the song."

She speculates that demand for McKee's single was pretty much satisfied by all the free online access. Her appeal was apparently not deep enough to get people to go beyond the single they'd already heard online. The problem wasn't positioning or marketing, it was a lack of authentic grassroots support. Getting online consumers to pay for music today takes more than a catchy single; it requires a real fan base, ideally one spreading the word online.

MY CHEMICAL ROMANCE

Reprise found a perfect example of just that kind of fan base with a punk-pop fivesome from New Jersey called My Chemical Romance. Although the band's album *Three Cheers for Sweet Revenge* came out around the same time as McKee's, it was their second album. The first, on an independent label, had sold 10,000 copies, which suggested a small but strong core following. So five months before the second album's launch in May 2004, Reprise started giving tracks to Web sites focused on that core, such as Shoutweb.com and AbsolutePunk.net, to get the buzz going among the faithful in hopes that it would spread.

The label also pushed the band on PureVolume.com and MySpace.com, two relatively new (at the time) music-heavy social-networking sites with an exploding user base. It gave exclusive live tracks to PureVolume for promotions and premiered an Internet-only video for the band's first single, "I'm Not Okay (I Promise)."

Once the tracks were out there, Reprise could watch how they did. Using BigChampagne file-trading data, the label could see growing interest in "Not Okay," but also heavy trading and searching on the track "Helena." On the basis of that, it made "Helena" the next single, and, helped by requests from the band's core fans, the song got airplay. By the end of the summer, "Helena" had become the band's biggest radio single by far.

As the band went on tour in September, Reprise extended the promotions to Yahoo! Music and AOL, including audio, video, and a heavily promoted live performance from Yahoo!'s studios. Meanwhile, fans flocked to the band's Web site and MySpace page. My Chemical Romance now has Warner's largest email list.

The album went on to sell 1.4 million units, making it one of the biggest hits of the year. Most of that came after radio and MTV embraced the band and brought it to a larger audience, but it all started online, where the band's core audience had cemented its credibility.

What was the difference between My Chemical Romance and Bonnie McKee? Talent differences aside, My Chemical Romance had the advantage of an existing base of fans, both of its first album and its live shows. There were thousands of people already hungry for more from the band, and when the label gave them what they wanted, in the form of early online content, they returned the favor with strong word of mouth, including radio requests. And that, in turn, got the band the airplay that took it to the next level of popularity, acquiring a new, larger, set of fans.

McKee, by contrast, was a relatively unknown artist, who had rarely played live. Although people liked what they heard on Yahoo!, it wasn't enough to trigger real fan behavior. They didn't buy the album, and they didn't clamor for more. On MySpace, My Chemical Romance has nearly 450,000 "friends"; McKee has 9,000. Word of mouth makes all the difference.

BIRDMONSTER

This last example is a much smaller one, but one I know well, since it involves a former colleague. In the course of researching this book, I decided to track the progress of Birdmonster, an up-and-coming San Francisco band fronted by Peter Arcuni, an editorial assistant at *Wired*. The experience proved all too instructive.

Birdmonster is a prime example of how the three forces of the Long Tail are overturning the status quo in the music industry. Like all new rock bands, Birdmonster started by hustling for gigs. But rather than pestering club owners for a break, the band members realized that there was now a smarter way. In club booking, the headliners are typically signed up first. Then, once the dates are set in the calendar, the club looks for opening acts to support them. Since virtually all club schedules are now online, opportunities for opening acts can be found simply by searching for the letters "TBA" and some other keywords to limit the search to local clubs. Then it's simply a matter of contacting the club and offering to fill that gap in their lineup.

But getting the club owners' attention isn't enough; they need to know that you'll be able to attract a crowd, too. For that Birdmonster used grassroots Internet marketing. It started an online mailing list and encouraged fans to register as "friends" on the band's MySpace page. It put a few songs on that page and listed its other gigs, along with pictures. Bookers could check it out, listen to songs, and see pictures from previous shows, while reading raves from the band's fans.

Birdmonster also courted Internet radio stations, which have none of the constraints of traditional broadcast. As it happened, it was "Ted," the owner of San Francisco's BagelRadio.com, who convinced the booker to give Birdmonster its first big break, an opening gig for Clap Your Hands Say Yeah. That (and a battle-of-the-bands contest) led to opening for the White Stripes, which was at that moment the pinnacle of indie rock. Birdmonster had arrived.

It was time to go beyond live gigs. The band recorded three tracks in a local independent studio and self-published them as a mini album, which they sent to a music service called CD Baby, which takes albums on consignment and sells them online. CD Baby, in turn, transferred the digital tracks to iTunes and other top music services, so they could be bought or streamed just like the biggest label hits.

The band then emailed song tracks and personal notes to various MP3 blogs, getting a positive mention on several, such as Music for Robots, which brought yet more attention. The band's MySpace page started filling up with fans, and soon managers, labels, and industry folks came calling with deals.

But then something surprising happened: Birdmonster turned the offers down. As Arcuni put it, "We're not anti-label in principle, but the numbers (risk vs. reward) didn't add up."

A music label exists primarily to fulfill four functions: (1) talent scouting; (2) financing (the advances bands get to pay for their studio time is like seed capital invested by a venture capitalist); (3) distribution; and (4) marketing.

From Birdmonster's perspective, they didn't need a label to provide that. A growing local fan base, amplified online, had already spotted their talent. Improving digital recording technology had made studio time cheaper than ever—they could record the tracks in a few days in the studio and then mix and overdub them at home using personal computers. The cost to record the entire album was less than $15,000, which they covered with credit cards and savings. CD Baby and a similar company called Cinderblock provided the distribution, which gave them a reach as broad as iTunes, Rhapsody, and the other top services. And MP3 blogs and MySpace were free marketing.

Why sign their life away now to a label, they reasoned, when they could record and distribute their music themselves and keep their creative independence? If the first self-released album did well, they'd be in a much stronger negotiating position with the label, for rereleasing the first album in stores, or for the second album, much as My Chemical Romance was after its first album. And if it didn't, there were still live shows and touring, which are really the best part of being in a band anyway. And so Arcuni quit his day job (our loss!) and set off to become a professional musician, emboldened in a DIY age where technology has shifted the balance of power from label to band.

THE POWER OF COLLECTIVE INTELLIGENCE

Yahoo! music ratings, Google PageRank, MySpace friends, Netflix user reviews—these are all manifestations of the wisdom of the crowd. Millions of regular people are the new tastemakers. Some of them act as individuals, others are parts of groups organized around shared interests, and still others are simply herds of consumers automatically tracked by software watching their every behavior.

For the first time in history, we're able to measure the consumption patterns, inclinations, and tastes of an entire market of consumers in real time, and just as quickly adjust the market to reflect them. These new tastemakers aren't a super-elite of people cooler than us; they *are* us.

The trend watchers at Frog Design, a consultancy, see this as nothing less than an epochal shift:

> We are leaving the Information Age and entering the Recommendation Age. Today information is ridiculously easy to get; you practically trip over it on the street. Information gathering is no longer the issue—making smart decisions based on the information is now the trick. . . . Recommendations serve as shortcuts through the thicket of information, just as my wine shop owner shortcuts me to obscure French wines to enjoy with pasta.

Amplified word of mouth is the manifestation of the third force of the Long Tail: tapping consumer sentiment to connect supply to demand. The first force, democratizing production, populates the Tail. The second force, democratizing distribution, makes it all available. But those two are not enough. It is not until this third force, which helps people find what they want in this new superabundance of variety, kicks in that the potential of the Long Tail marketplace is truly unleashed.

The new tastemakers are simply people whose opinions are respected. They influence the behavior of others, often encouraging them to try things they wouldn't otherwise pursue. Some of these new tastemakers are the traditional professionals: movie and music critics, editors, or product testers. As our interests expand with the exploding availability of wide variety, the demand for such informed and trusted advice is now extending to the narrowest niches. Companies such as Weblogs, Inc. have built thriving businesses around starting blogs to serve narrow interests, from scuba diving and the WiMax wireless standards, to medical informatics.

Other tastemakers are celebrities, who are another sort of trusted guide, and whose influence on consumption continues to grow. From product placement in TV shows to the remarkable success of *InStyle* magazine (its great innovation was not cropping the photos at the knees, so as to show the shoes), the power of celebrity is increasingly measured in terms of their ability to move merchandise. Whether you like it or not, Jessica Simpson is a tastemaker.

But not all celebrities are Hollywood stars. As our culture fragments into a million tiny microcultures, we are experiencing a corresponding rise of microcelebrities. In the technology world, these take the form of power bloggers, such as the team that writes DailyCandy, a fashion blog, or BoingBoing, a site focusing on technology and subculture, which is at the time of this writing the world's most popular blog. BoingBoing has the capacity to discover a cool toy, such as a $15 "20Questions" game built on a neural network trained online, and drive enough traffic to an online marketplace to sell it out in a day. Other microcelebrities are even more micro, ranging from high-ranking playlist contributors on iTunes to the taste mavens behind popular music blogs such as Pitchfork Media.

And then there is crowd behavior, which is best seen as a form of distributed intelligence. Examples of crowds are taggers on Flickr, the photo-sharing site that encourages you to invent your own categories for pictures (you may see Paris Hilton in the picture, but I see her Sidekick phone, and so I tag the photo "Sidekick"), and linkers who build online lists of Web pages they want to be able to find again.

People who are part of such a crowd may not think of themselves as offering recommendations or guidance at all. They're just doing what they do for their own reasons. But every day there is more and more software watching their actions, and drawing conclusions from them. The rise of the search engine as the economic force of Silicon Valley is simply a reflection of the value that we now recognize in the measurement and analysis of the actions of millions of individuals.

FILTERS RULE

The catch-all phrase for recommendations and all the other tools that help you find quality in the Long Tail is *filters*. These technologies and services sift through a vast array of choices to present you with the ones that are most right for you. That's what Google does when it ranks results: It filters the Web to bring back just the pages that are most relevant to your search term. It's also what the "Most Popular Tracks" in the acid jazz subgenre on Rhapsody is doing.

Filters make up what Rob Reid, one of the founders of Listen.com, calls the "navigation layer" of the Long Tail. It's not unique to the Internet and, as he points out, it's not new:

> Interestingly, the power and importance of the navigation layer is not strictly an online phenomenon. For many years American Airlines made more money from its Sabre electronic reservation system (essentially the travel industry's shared navigation layer for the bewildering world of routes and airfares in the seventies and eighties) than the entire airline industry made collectively from charging people money to ride on planes. From time to time, certain Baby Bells were bringing in more profits from their yellow pages—essentially the navigation layer of all local business before the Web came along—than from their inherited monopolies. And at its peak, *TV Guide* famously rivaled the actual networks in profitability.
>
> In a world of infinite choice, context—not content—is king.

In today's Long Tail markets, the main effect of filters is to help people move from the world they know ("hits") to the world they don't ("niches") via a route that is both comfortable and tailored to their tastes. In a sense, good filters have the effect of driving demand down the tail by revealing goods and services that appeal more than the lowest-common-denominator fare that crowds the narrow channels of traditional mass-market distribution.

Reed Hastings, the CEO of Netflix, describes the effect of filters—in this case, sophisticated recommendation engines and ranking algorithms—in driving demand down the DVD Tail on his site.

> Historically Blockbuster has reported that about 90% of the movies they rent are new theatrical releases. Online they're more niche: about 70% of what they rent from their website is new releases and about 30% is back catalog. That's not true for Netflix. About 30% of what we rent is new releases and about 70% is back catalog and it's not because we have a different subscriber. It's because we create

demand for content and we help you find great movies that you'll really like. And we do it algorithmically, with recommendations and ratings.

Hastings believes that recommendations and other filters are one of Netflix's most important advantages, especially for non-blockbusters. Recommendations have all the demand-generation power of advertising, but at virtually no cost. If Netflix suggests a film to you based on what it knows about your taste and what others thought of that film, that can be more influential than a generic billboard aimed at the broadest possible audience. But these recommendations arise naturally from Netflix's customer data, and it has an infinite number of "billboards" (Web pages customized for each customer and each visit) on which to display them.

Advertising and other marketing can represent more than half of the costs of the average Hollywood blockbuster, and smaller films can't play in that game. Netflix recommendations level the playing field, offering free marketing for films that can't otherwise afford it, and thus spreading demand more evenly between hits and niches. They're a remarkable democratizing force in a remarkably undemocratic industry.

ONE SIZE FILTER DOESN'T FIT ALL

As we get deeper into filters and how they work, it helps to get an overview of their many types. Let's start with music. Here are some of the many different filter types a typical user on Rhapsody might encounter in a single session as he or she looks for new music. From the front page, a user might start with categories, which is a form of a *multi-level taxonomy*.

Let's say you begin in Alternative/Punk and then choose the subgenre Punk Funk. In that category, there's a *best-seller list,* which is led by Bloc Party as I write. If you click on Bloc Party, you'll find that *pattern matching* has created a list of related artists, which includes the Gang of Four. A click on that produces a list of "followers" (the Gang of Four created the category of Punk Funk in their first incarnation, in the early eighties), which is a form of *editor recommendation* (you may also be persuaded by the *editorial review*).

Among those Gang of Four followers is the Rapture. Click on that, and if you like it, try a custom radio station tailored around that artist, which is a stream of songs by the Rapture and bands that other people who like the Rapture also like, which is a form of *collaborative filtering*. As you listen to that custom stream, you may find that among the bands that play, the one you like best is LCD Soundsystem. Click on that, listen for a while, and when you hunger for something new, try a *playlist* that features the band. That, in turn, will introduce you to Zero 7, where you may want to stay awhile.

A half dozen recommendation techniques have taken you from punk to soul, from the middle of the Head to the bottom of the Tail, and every step along the way made sense.

As great as music recommendations are getting these days, they aren't perfect. One of the problems is that they tend to run out of suggestions pretty quickly as you dig deeper into a niche, where there may be few other people whose taste and preferences can be measured. Another problem is that even where a service can provide good suggestions and encourage you to explore a genre new to you, the advice often stays the same over time. Come back a month later, after you've heard all the recommendations, and they're probably pretty much as they were.

Yet another limitation is that many kinds of recommendations tend to be better for one genre than for another—rock recommendations aren't useful for classical and vice versa. In the old hit-driven model, one size fit all. In this new model, where niches and sub-niches are abundant, there's a need for specialization. An example of this is iTunes, which, for all of its accomplishments, shows a pop-music bias that undermines its usefulness for other kinds of music.

In iTunes and services like it different genres—such as rock, jazz, or classical—are all displayed in a similar way, with the main classification scheme being "artist." But who is the "artist" for classical—the composer, the orchestra, or the conductor? Is a thirty-second sample of a concerto meaningful? In the case of jazz, you may be more interested in following the careers of the individual performers, rather than the band, which may have come together only for a single album. Or perhaps you're more interested in the year, and would like to find other music that came out at the same time. In all these cases, you're out of luck. The iTunes software won't let you sort by any of those.

These are the failures of one-size-fits-all aggregation and filtering. ITunes may be working its way down the Tail, but its emphasis on simplicity—and lowest-common-denominator metadata—forces it into a standard presentational model that can't cater effectively to every genre—and therefore, every consumer. And this is not to pick just on iTunes—the same is true for every music service out there.

Because no one kind of filter does it all, listeners tend to use many of them. You may start your exploration of new music by following a recommendation, then once it's taken you to a genre you like, you may want to switch to a genre-level top ten list or browse popular tracks. Then, when you've found a band you particularly like, you might explore bands that are like it, guided by the collaborative filters. And when you come back a week later and find that nothing's changed, you'll need another kind of filter to take you to your next stop on your exploration. That could be a playlist—catching a magic carpet ride on someone else's taste—which can take you to another genre, where you can settle in and start the process again.

NOT ALL TOP TEN LISTS ARE CREATED EQUAL

Not long ago, there were far fewer ways to find new music. Aside from personal recommendations, there were editorial reviews in magazines, perhaps the advice of a well-informed record store clerk, and the biggest of them all, radio airplay. Radio playlists, especially today, are the prime example of the best-known filter of all, the popularity list. The Top 10, 40, and 100 are the staples of the hit-driven universe, from Nielsen ratings to the *New York Times* book best-seller list. But in a Long Tail world, with so many other filters available, the weaknesses of Top 10 lists are becoming more and more clear.

There's nothing wrong with ranking by popularity—after all, that's just another example of a "wisdom of crowds" filter—but all too often these lists lump together all sorts of niches, genres, subgenres, and categories into one unholy mess.

A case in point: blogs. As I write, Technorati lists the top ten blogs as:

1. BoingBoing: A Directory of Wonderful Things
2. Daily Kos: State of the Nation
3. Drew Curtis' FARK.com
4. Gizmodo: The Gadgets Weblog
5. Instapundit.com
6. Engadget
7. PostSecret
8. Talking Points Memo: by Joshua Micah Marshall
9. Davenetics Politics Media Musings
10. dooce

What have we learned? Well, not much. There are a couple of gadget blogs in the list, two or three political blogs, some uncategorizable sub-culture ones (BoingBoing, FARK, PostSecret), and a personal blog (dooce).

These lists are, in other words, a semi-random collection of totally disparate things.

To use an analogy, top-blog lists are akin to saying that the best-sellers in the supermarket today were:

1. DairyFresh 2% vitamin D milk
2. Hayseed Farms mixed grain bread
3. Bananas, assorted bunches
4. Crunchios cereal, large size
5. DietWhoopsy, 12-pack, cans
6. and so on . . .

Which is pointless. Nobody cares if bananas outsell soft drinks. What they care about is which soft drink outsells which *other* soft drink. Lists make sense only in context, comparing like with like within a category.

My take: This is another reminder that you have to treat niches as niches. When you look at a widely diverse three-dimensional marketplace through a one-dimensional lens, you get nonsense. It's a list, but it's a list without meaning. What matters is the rankings *within* a genre (or subgenre), not *across* genres.

Let's take this back to music. As I write, the top ten artists on Rhapsody overall are:

1. Jack Johnson
2. Eminem
3. Coldplay
4. Fall Out Boy
5. Johnny Cash
6. Nickelback
7. James Blunt
8. Green Day
9. Death Cab for Cutie
10. Kelly Clarkson

Which is, as I count it, two "adult alternative," one "crossover/hiphop," one "Brit-rock," one "emo," one "outlaw country," one "post-grunge," one "punk-pop," one "indie-rock," and one "teen beat." Does anybody care if outlaw country outsells teen beat this week or vice versa? Does this list help anyone who is drawn to any of these categories find more music they'll like? Yet the Top 10 (or Top 40, or Top 100) list is the lens through which we've looked at music culture for nearly half a century. It's mostly meaningless, but it was all we had.

Let's contrast that with a different kind of top ten list, that for the music subgenre Afro-Cuban jazz:

1. Tito Puente
2. Buena Vista Social Club
3. Cal Tjader
4. Arturo Sandoval
5. Poncho Sanchez
6. Dizzy Gillespie

7. Perez Prado
8. Ibrahim Ferrer
9. Eddie Palmieri
10. Michel Camilo

Now *that's* a top ten list. It's apples-to-apples and thus useful from top to bottom. Such lists are possible because we have abundant information about consumer preference and enough space for an infinite number of top ten lists—there doesn't have to be just one. In this case Tito Puente is number one in a very niche category—a big fish in a small pond. For people into this genre, this is a big deal indeed. For those who aren't, he's simply another obscure artist and safely ignored. Tito Puente's albums don't rise to the top of the overall music charts—they're not blockbusters. But they do dominate their category, creating what writer Erick Schonfeld calls "nichebusters." Filters and recommendations work best at this scale, bringing the mainstream discovery and marketing techniques to micromarkets.

IS THE LONG TAIL FULL OF CRAP?

Why are filters so important to a functioning Long Tail? Because without them, the Long Tail risks just being noise.

The field of "information theory" was built around the problem of pulling coherent signals from random electrical noise, first in radio broadcasts and then in any sort of electronic transmission. The notion of a signal-to-noise ratio is now used more broadly to refer to any instance where clearing away distraction is a challenge. In a traditional "Short Head" market this isn't much of a problem, because everything on the shelf has been prefiltered to remove outliers and other products far from the lowest common denominator. But in a Long Tail market, which includes nearly everything, noise can be a huge problem. Indeed, if left unchecked, noise—random content or products of poor quality—can kill a market. Too much noise and people don't buy.

The job of filters is to screen out that noise. Call it pulling wheat from chaff or diamonds from the rough, the role of a filter is to elevate the few products that are right for whoever is looking and suppress the many that aren't. I'll explain this by considering one commonly held misperception.

One of the most frequent mistakes people make about the Long Tail is to assume that things that don't sell well are "not as good" as things that do sell well. Or, to put it another way, they assume that the Long Tail is full of crap. After all, if that album/book/film/whatever were excellent, it would be a hit, right? Well, in a word, no.

Niches operate by different economics than the mainstream. And the reason for that helps explain why so much about Long Tail content is counterintuitive, especially when we're used to scarcity thinking.

First, let's get one thing straight: *The Long Tail is indeed full of crap.*

Yet it's also full of works of refined brilliance and depth—and an awful lot in between. Exactly the same can be said of the Web itself. Ten years ago, people complained that there was a lot of junk on the Internet, and sure enough, any casual surf quickly confirmed that. Then along came search engines to help pull some signal from the noise, and finally Google, which taps the wisdom of the crowd itself and turns a mass of incoherence into the closest thing to an oracle the world has ever seen.

This is not unique to the Web—it's true everywhere. Sturgeon's Law (named after the science fiction writer Theodore Sturgeon) states that "ninety percent of everything is crud." Just think about art, not from the perspective of a gallery but from a garage sale. Ninety percent (at least) is crud. And the same is true for music, books, and everything else. The reason we don't think of it that way is that most of it is filtered away by the scarcity sieve of commercial retail distribution.

On a store shelf or in any other limited means of distribution, the ratio of good to bad matters because it's a *zero sum game*: Space for one eliminates space for the other. Prominence for one obscures the other. If there are ten crappy toys for each good one in the aisle, you'll think poorly of the toy store and be discouraged from browsing. Likewise it's no fun to flip through bin after bin of CDs if you haven't heard of any of them.

But where you have unlimited shelf space, it's a *non-zero sum game*.

The billions of crappy Web pages about whatever are not a problem in the way that billions of crappy CDs on the Tower Records shelves would be. Inventory is "non-rivalrous" on the Web and the ratio of good to bad is simply a signal-to-noise problem, solvable with information tools. Which is to say it's not much of a problem at all. You just need better filters. In other words, the noise is still out there, but Google allows you to effectively ignore it. Filters rule!

This leads to the key to what's different about Long Tails. They are *not* prefiltered by the requirements of distribution bottlenecks and all those entail (editors, studio execs, talent scouts, and Wal-Mart purchasing managers). As a result their components vary wildly in quality, just like everything else in the world.

One way to describe this (using the language of information theory again) would be to say that Long Tails have a *wide dynamic range* of quality: awful to great. By contrast, the average store shelf has a relatively *narrow dynamic range* of quality: mostly average to good. (There's some really great stuff, but much of that is too expensive for the average retail shelf; niches exist at both ends of the quality spectrum.)

So tails have a wide dynamic range and heads have a narrow dynamic range. Graphically, that looks like this:

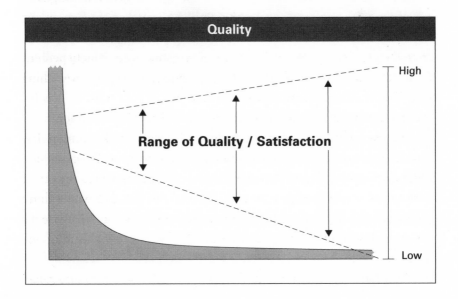

It's crucial to note that there are high-quality goods in every part of the curve, from top to bottom. Yes, there are more low-quality goods in the tail and the average level of quality declines as you go down the curve. But with good filters, averages don't matter. Diamonds can be found anywhere.

To clarify, here are some examples of criteria people might use to evaluate content.

"High Quality"	"Low Quality"
Addresses my interests	Not for me
Well made	Badly made
Fresh	Stale
Substantive	Superficial
Compelling	Boring

Obviously, the terms "high quality" and "low quality" are entirely subjective, so all of these criteria are in the eye of the beholder. Thus, there are no absolute measures of content quality. One person's "good" could easily be another's "bad"; indeed, it almost always is.

This is why niches are different. One person's *noise* is another's *signal*. If a producer intends something to be absolutely right for one audience, it will, by definition, be wrong for another. The compromises necessary to make something appeal to everyone mean that it will almost certainly not appeal perfectly to anyone—that's why they call it the *lowest common denominator*.

The remarkable consequence of the above graphic is that for many people, the best stuff is in the Tail. If you're interested in audiophile stereo equipment, the finest gear is not going to be among the top-sellers at Best Buy. It will be too expensive, too complicated, and too hard to sell to the average customer. Instead, it's going to be available at a specialist, and in overall sales ranking will be far down the Tail. Because this gear is so right for the audiophiles, it's probably *not* right for people with less focused interests. Niche products are, by definition, not for everyone.

Down there in the low-selling side of the curve, there are also products that just aren't very good. The challenge of filtering is to be able to tell one from the other. If you've got help—smart search engines, recommendations, or other filters—your odds of finding something just right for you are actually *greater* in the Tail. Best-sellers tend to appeal, at least superficially, to a broad range of taste. Niche products are meant to appeal strongly to a narrow set of tastes. That's why the filter technologies are so important. They not only drive demand down the Tail, but they can also increase satisfaction by connecting people with products that are *more* right for them than the broad-appeal products at the Head.

THE TAIL THAT WAGS EVERYTHING ELSE

Another way to look at the situation is the graph below. As the Tail gets longer, the signal-to-noise ratio gets worse. Thus, the only way a consumer can maintain a consistently good enough signal to find what he or she wants is if the filters get increasingly powerful:

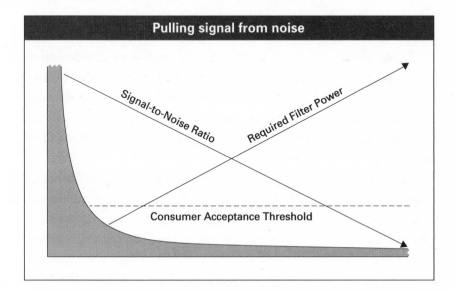

Why does the signal-to-noise ratio fall as you go down the Tail? Because there's so much stuff there that what you're looking for is overshadowed by all the things you aren't looking for. The reason for this is simple: The vast majority of everything in the world is in the Tail.

One of the consequences of living in a hit-driven culture is that we tend to assume that hits are a far bigger share of the market than they really are. Instead, they are the rare exception. This is what Nassim Taleb calls the "Black Swan Problem."

The phrase comes from David Hume, the eighteenth-century Scottish philosopher, who gave it as an example of the complications that lie in deriving general rules from observed facts. In what has now become known as Hume's Problem of Induction, he asked how many white swans one need observe before inferring that all swans are white and that there are no black swans. Hundreds? Thousands? We don't know. (The Black Swan is not just a hypothetical metaphor: Until the discovery of Australia, common belief held that all swans were white. That belief was shattered with the sighting of the first *Cygnus atratus*.)

The problem is that we have a hard time putting rare events in context. In any given population there will be a few people who are tremendously rich. Some are smart and some are lucky and we really can't tell which is which. In *Fooled by Randomness,* Taleb pokes fun at a bestseller called *The Millionaire Next Door,* which catalogs the investing tricks and work habits of multimillionaires, so that you can follow them and get rich, too. But as Taleb notes, random factors are just as likely to be responsible for that neighborly millionaire as investing strategies.

He defines a Black Swan as:

> A random event satisfying the following three properties: large impact, incomputable probabilities, and surprise effect. First, it carries upon its occurrence a disproportionately large impact. Second, its incidence has a small but incomputable probability based on information available prior to its incidence. Third, a vicious property of a Black Swan is its surprise effect: at a given time of observation there is no convincing element pointing to an increased likelihood of the event.

He could just as easily be describing a blockbuster hit.

The reality is that the vast majority of content (from music to movies) is not hits. Indeed, the vast majority of content is about as far from a hit as it's possible to be, counting its audience in hundreds rather than millions. Sometimes that's because it's not very good. Sometimes it's because it wasn't marketed well or made by people with the right connections. And sometimes it's because of some random factor that got in the way, which is just as likely as the random factors that sometimes make a blockbuster out of the flimsiest novelty fare ("Who Let the Dogs Out" comes to mind).

This is simply the natural consequence of what's called a "power-law" distribution, a term for a curve where a small number of things occur with high amplitude (read: sales) and a large number of things occur with low amplitude. A few things sell a lot and a lot of things sell a little. (The phrase comes from the fact that the curve has a $1/x$ shape, which is the same as x raised to the -1 power.)

Since most stuff doesn't sell very well, the volume of the material available—and by extension the volume of stuff you *don't want*—rises as the Long Tail falls. Here's some actual data from the book industry, showing the number of titles in each sales category for 2004:

Book Sales, 2004		
Sales Range	**Titles**	**Units**
1,000,000 or more	10	17,396,510
500,000 to 999,999	22	13,798,299
250,000 to 499,999	64	22,252,491
100,000 to 249,999	324	46,932,031
50,000 to 99,999	767	51,858,835
5,000 to 49,999	23,047	280,000,591
1,000 to 4,999	67,008	149,093,614
100 to 999	202,938	69,548,499
sold 99 or less	948,005	14,346,417
Total	**1.2 Million**	**665 Million+**

Source: Book Industry Study Group

The consequence of this is that whatever you *are* looking for, there's more stuff you *aren't* looking for the farther you go down the Tail. That's why the signal-to-noise ratio gets worse, despite the fact that you're often more likely (i.e., if you have access to good search and filters) to find what you want as you go down the Tail. It sounds like a paradox, but it isn't. It's just a problem for filters to solve.

PRE-FILTERS AND POST-FILTERS

When you think about it, the world is already full of a different kind of filter. In the scarcity-driven markets of limited shelves, screens, and channels that we've lived with for most of the past century, entire industries have been created around finding and promoting the good stuff. This is what the A&R talent scouts at the record labels do, along with the Hollywood studio executives and store purchasing managers ("buyers"). In boardrooms around the world, market research teams pore over data that predicts what's likely to sell and thus deserves to win a valuable spot on the shelf, screen, or page . . . and what's unlikely to sell and therefore *doesn't* deserve a spot.

The key word in the preceding paragraph is "predicts." What's different about those kinds of filters and the ones I've been focusing on is that they filter *before* things get to market. Indeed, their job is to decide what will make it to market and what won't. I call them "pre-filters."

By contrast, the recommendations and search technologies that I'm writing about are "post-filters." The post-filters find the best of what's already out there in their area of interest, elevating the good (i.e., what is relevant, interesting, original, etc.) and downplaying, even ignoring, the bad. When I talk about throwing everything out there and letting the marketplace sort it out, these post-filters are the voice of the marketplace. They channel consumer behavior and amplify it, rather than trying to predict it.

Here, in table form, are some examples of each:

Pre-Filters	Post-Filters
Editors	Blogs
Record label scouts	Playlists
Studio executives	Reviews
Department store buyers	Customers
Marketers	Recommendations
Advertisers	Consumers

The fact that post-filters amplify, rather than predict, behavior is an important distinction. In the existing Short Head markets, where distribution is expensive and shelf space is at a premium, the supply side of the market has to be exceedingly discriminating in what it lets through. These producers, retailers, and marketers have made a science of trying to guess what people will want, to improve their odds of picking winners. Obviously they don't always guess right. There are surely as many things that deserved to make it to market but were overlooked as there are things that made it to market and then flopped. Nevertheless, the survivors obtain a credible reputation for having some sort of mystical insight into the consumer psyche.

However, in Long Tail markets—where distribution is cheap and shelf space is plentiful—the safe bet is to assume that *everything* is eventually going to be available.

As such, in Long Tail markets, the role of filter then shifts from gatekeeper to advisor. Rather than *predicting* taste, post-filters such as Google *measure* it. Rather than lumping consumers into predetermined demographic and psychographic categories, post-filters such as Netflix's customer recommendations treat them like individuals who reveal their likes and dislikes through their behavior. Rather than keeping things off the market, post-filters such as MP3 blogs *create* a market for things that are already available by stimulating demand for them. Jeff Jarvis calls this the difference between "first-person and third-person markets."

In general, blogs are shaping up to be a powerful source of influential recommendations. There are independent enthusiast sites such as PVRblog and Horticultural (an organic gardening blog), commercial blogs such as Gizmodo and Joystiq, and then the random recommendations of whichever blogger you happen to read for any reason. (There does seem to be a natural connection between mavens, who know a lot and like to share their knowledge, and blogging.) What they may lack in polish and scope, they more than make up in *credibility*: Their readers know that there is a real person there that they can trust.

Of course, just as pre-filters aren't perfect—e.g., the talent scouts don't always pick artists that sell records—the same is true of post-filters. Because post-filters tend to be amateurs, oftentimes that means less critical independence and more random malice. Moreover, the problem with post-filtering is that feedback comes *after* publication, not before. As a result, errors that would have been caught by editors and other wise eyes can sneak through, and even though the collective post-filter feedback can eventually correct them, they may never disappear entirely.

Interestingly, when I consider my own role, I find that I do both. As the editor of a magazine with a finite number of pages, I'm a classic pre-filter. I indulge in all sorts of brutal discrimination and guesswork to decide which articles to run. But *Wired* also does lots of product reviews, and in that respect, we're a post-filter. We look at the universe of what's already out there and bring the best stuff to our readers' attention.

As long as there's a market for a pre-filtered package in the deliciously finite medium of bound glossy paper, I suspect there will continue to be demand for my old-fashioned discriminatory side. But the day when people like me decide what makes it to market and what doesn't is fading. Soon everything will make it to market and the real opportunity will be in sorting it all out.

8

LONG TAIL ECONOMICS

SCARCITY, ABUNDANCE, AND THE DEATH
OF THE 80/20 RULE

In the summer of 1897 an Italian polymath named Vilfredo Pareto busied himself in his university office in Switzerland, studying patterns of wealth and income in nineteenth-century England. It was the age of Marx, and the question of wealth distribution was in the air. Pareto found that the spread of wealth was indeed unequal in England—most of it went to a minority of the people. When he calculated the exact ratios, he found that about 20 percent of the population owned 80 percent of the wealth. More important, when he compared that with other countries and regions, he found that the ratio remained the same.

What Pareto had discovered is that there is a predictable mathematical relationship in the patterns of wealth and populations, something he called the Law of the Vital Few. It seemed constant over time, and across countries. Pareto was a brilliant economist, but he was a poor explainer, so not many understood the importance of his insight. He went on to write obscure sociological tracts about elites, which unfortunately were taken up at the end of his life by Mussolini's fascists. But the theory of unequal distribution took on a life of its own, and Pareto's observation is now known as the 80/20 Rule.

In 1949, George Zipf, a Harvard linguist, found a similar principle at work in words. He observed that while a few words are used very often, many or most are used rarely. Although that's not surprising, what Zipf also observed was that that relationship was entirely predictable, and indeed was the same as Pareto's wealth curve. The frequency with which a word was used was proportional to 1 divided by the word's frequency rank among all words. This means that the second item occurs approximately ½ as often as the first, and the third item ⅓ as often as the first, and so on. This is now called Zipf's Law.

The same is true, Zipf found, for a host of other phenomena, from population statistics to industrial processes. He analyzed Philadelphia marriage licenses within one twenty-block area and showed that 70 percent of the marriages were between people who lived no more than 30 percent of that distance apart.

Since then, other researchers have extended the rule to everything from atoms in a plasma to the size of cities. At the heart of these observations is the ubiquity of powerlaw distributions, the $1/x$ shape that Pareto first saw in his wealth curves.

Powerlaws are a family of curves that you can find practically anywhere you look, from biology to book sales. The Long Tail is a powerlaw that isn't cruelly cut off by bottlenecks in distribution such as limited shelf space and available channels. Because the amplitude of a powerlaw approaches but never reaches zero as the curve stretches out to infinity, it's known as a "long-tailed" curve, which is where I derived the name of this book.

As far as consumer markets go, powerlaws come about when you have three conditions:

1. Variety (there are many different sorts of things)
2. Inequality (some have more of some quality than others)
3. Network effects such as word of mouth and reputation, which tend to amplify differences in quality

In others words, powerlaw distributions occur where things are different, some are better than others, and effects such as reputation can work to promote the good and suppress the bad. This results in what

Pareto called the "predictable imbalance" of markets, culture, and society: Success breeds success. Needless to say, these forces describe a good fraction of the world around us.

HOW DISTRIBUTION BOTTLENECKS DISTORT MARKETS

To see what happens to powerlaws in the real world, let's look at the example of Hollywood box office. If you plot the data the usual way, it's the familiar shape: A few blockbusters dominate the high part of the curve at the left and a vast population of others (non-hits, to use the least pejorative term) account for the low part at the right.

Because all powerlaws tend to look alike when plotted like this, it's often useful to put them on a scale that shows their differences more clearly. One way to do that is to graph them on a logarithmic scale, where each division is a factor of 10 larger than the one that came before it: 10, 100, 1,000, and so on. (Common examples of logarithmic scales are the Richter scale of earthquakes and the decibel scale of sound volume.)

When you plot a proper powerlaw on a log scale on both axes (called a "log-log graph"), you should get a straight line sloping down. The exact angle of that slope varies from market to market, but whether it's the sales of soup or the distribution of publicly listed companies by stock-market capitalization, the natural shape of a market is a straight line.

But all too often in the real world, it doesn't look like that at all. Instead, the curve starts off as a straight line and then simply dies. In our box office case, that looks like the curve on page 128.

Notice what happens around rank 100. Box-office revenues fall sickeningly until they approach zero at around 500. (In fact, the lowest recorded box office of the year was $423 for *The Dark Hours*, a Canadian horror film made on a shoestring budget with a cast of unknowns. According to those who have seen it, it's actually not bad at all.)

What happened? Did the movies suddenly get worse at rank 100? Did they stop making movies after the first 500? Or is that heart-stopping fall just a measurement error?

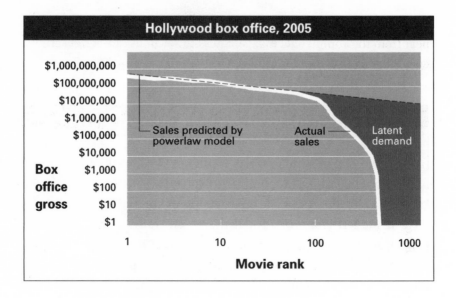

Sadly, here's your answer: *None of the above.* It's not a measurement error. The movies don't get worse at rank 100 (some would argue they actually get better). And they didn't stop making movies at 500. Indeed, an estimated 13,000 feature films are shown in festivals each year in the United States alone, and that doesn't include the tens of thousands of foreign films not shown in the United States.

What happened is that the films past the first 100 or so simply failed to get much theatrical distribution. Or, to put it another way, the "carrying capacity" of the U.S. theatrical industry is only about 100 films a year. The economics of local movie theaters are cruel and unforgiving. It's not enough that a film be good or big in Bombay. It's got to be big enough in Stamford, Connecticut, or wherever else a theater happens to be, to pull more than a couple thousand people through the door over a two-week run. Typically, that necessitates a big marketing budget, a distribution deal, and probably a star or two—if you can afford them.

Movies that don't have all that don't make it to the big theater chains. In effect, these chains lop off the consumer supply of films at the point where the economics stop making sense. They simply truncate the curve. Filmmakers don't stop making movies there, of course; a phantom line keeps going along the curve past the cutoff point, marking the box office sales that these other films would have earned if they had only gotten distribution. In the "real world," however, those films disappear from the commercial mainstream. Simply put, they don't make the cut. What should be a Long Tail instead looks roughly like this:

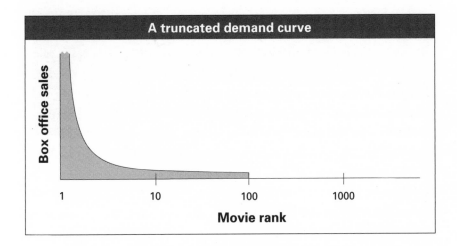

Granted, it's not quite as bad as I'm making it out to seem. If they're lucky, a few of the really good films that knocked out audiences at Sundance do get picked up by a few repertory houses in college towns. That, mostly likely, is the group that accounts for the 100–500 line on page 128, the members of which have low—but not quite zero—revenues. And the rest—the 500 to at least 13,000? Well, sadly most of them garnered no theatrical distribution at all. And if they're not seen in a theater, they have no box-office gross. This means that from the perspective of the earlier chart they just don't exist.

Of course, they do exist. It's just that they don't show up in the charts of an industry that judges merit through a box-office lens. Where do these other movies go? Most of them are never seen outside of film festivals and private showings. Some of them make it to TV or DVD if their makers can clear the rights to the music and get other necessary permissions. Others might be distributed for free online.

That sounds pretty bleak, but some of those derided nontheatrical distribution channels, such as direct-to-DVD and the Internet, are starting to become major markets in their own right. TV shows on DVD are by far the fastest growing part of the DVD business. And the market for video delivery over the Internet, while still just taking shape, may become bigger yet. With box office shrinking and DVD sales and retail growing, theatrical release is no longer the only worthwhile path to market.

The lesson is that what we thought was a naturally sharp drop-off in demand for movies after a certain point was actually just an artifact of the traditional costs of offering them. In other words, give people unlimited choice and make it easy for them to find what they want, and you discover that demand keeps on going into niches that were never even considered before—instructional videos, karaoke, Turkish TV, you name it. Netflix changed the economics of offering niches and, in doing so, reshaped our understanding about what people actually *want* to watch.

The same is true for virtually every other market you can imagine. In books, Barnes & Noble found that the bottom 1.2 million titles represent just 1.7 percent of its in-store sales, but a full 10 percent of its online (bn.com) sales. PRX, which licenses a huge library of public radio programming online, reports that the bottom 80 percent of its content now accounts for half of its sales. And in India, rediff.com, one of the largest Web portals and ringtone providers, saw what happened as ringtone demand shifted from being driven by Top 20 lists published in newspapers to an online business driven by search. The top 20 ringtones, which had accounted for 80 percent of sales in the newspaper era, fell to just 40 percent when users could search online from a catalog that now has nearly 20,000 songs.

Music shows some of the most dramatic effects. In traditional retail, new album releases accounted for 63 percent of sales in 2005; the rest were older "catalog" albums, according to Nielsen SoundScan. Online, that percentage is reversed: New music accounts for about a third of sales and older music accounts for two-thirds.

THE 80/20 RULE

The best known manifestation of Pareto/Zipf distributions is the 80/20 Rule, which is often used to explain that 20 percent of products account for 80 percent of revenues, or 20 percent of our time accounts for 80 percent of our productivity, or any number of other comparisons that all share this characteristic of a minority having disproportionate impact.

The 80/20 Rule is chronically misunderstood, for three reasons. First, it's almost never exactly 80/20. Most of the large-inventory markets I've studied are 80/10 or even less (no more than 10 percent of products account for 80 percent of sales).

If you're troubled by the fact that 80/10 doesn't add up to 100, you've discovered the second confusing thing about the Rule. The 80 and the 20 are percentages of *different things,* and thus don't need to equal 100. One is a percentage of products, the other a percentage of sales. Worse, there's no standard convention on how to express the relationship between the two, or which variable to hold constant. Saying a market has an 80/10 shape (10 percent of products account for 80 percent of sales) can be the same as saying it's 95/20 (20 percent of products account for 95 percent of sales).

Finally, the Rule is misunderstood because people use it to describe different phenomena. The classic definition is about products and revenues, but the Rule can just as equally be applied to products and *profits*.

One of the most pernicious misinterpretations is to assume that the 80/20 Rule is an invitation to carry *only* the 20 percent of goods that account for the most sales. This derives from the observation that the 80/20 Rule is fundamentally an encouragement to be discriminating in what you carry, because if you guess right, the product can have a disproportionate effect on your business.

This is why I've described the Long Tail as the death of the 80/20 Rule, even though it's actually nothing of the sort. The real 80/20 Rule is just the acknowledgment that a Pareto distribution is at work, and some things will sell a lot better than others, which is as true in Long Tail markets as it is in traditional markets.

What the Long Tail offers, however, is the encouragement to not be dominated by the Rule. Even if 20 percent of the products account for 80 percent of the revenue, that's no reason not to carry the other

80 percent of the products. In Long Tail markets, where the carrying costs of inventory are low, the incentive is there to carry everything, regardless of the volume of its sales. Who knows—with good search and recommendations, a bottom 80 percent product could turn into a top 20 percent product.

Because a traditional bricks-and-mortar retailer has significant inventory costs, products that don't sell well tend to be unprofitable. Thus, virtually all the profit comes from the 20 percent that do sell well. I've shown that in the top part of the graphic below, which gives an idealized case for a hypothetical bricks-and-mortar retailer:

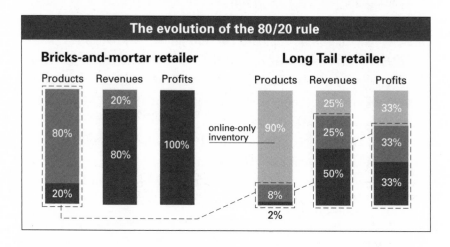

For a Long Tail retailer, however, the picture is very different. First, let's assume it has ten times as much inventory, so in this hypothetical example the 20 percent of products that make up most of the revenues of the first retailer become just 2 percent of the Long Tail retailer's inventory, as per the bottom left bar in the graphic above.

The revenue picture, in the second bar, reflects the natural consequences of a powerlaw distribution. The top 2 percent of products still account for a disproportionate share of the sales, in this case 50 percent. The next 8 percent of products account for the next 25 percent of sales. And the bottom 90 percent of products account for the remaining 25 percent of sales. (Although this is just a hypothetical example, those numbers are quite close to the actual statistics from both Rhapsody and Netflix.)

Where Long Tail economics really shines, however, is in the third bar, profits: Because of the low cost of inventory, the margins for non-hits can be far higher in Long Tail markets than in traditional bricks-and-mortar.

Let's use DVDs as an example. The chart below gives a rough sense of DVD economics for a retailer such as Wal-Mart:

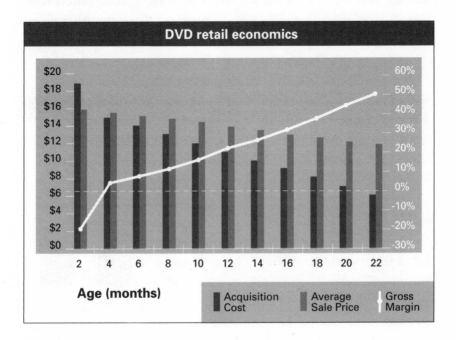

What you see here is that the economics of new releases these days is simply awful. The studios charge $17–$19 for the DVDs and the "big box" retailers (Wal-Mart, BestBuy) sell them for $15–$17 for the first week or two, for an average loss of $2 per DVD. (This is before overheads; the actual loss is larger.)

After the first month or so, the wholesale price (what the distributors charge the stores) of the DVDs goes down faster than the retail price (what the stores charge us), and they gradually become profitable to sell. Yet nearly 80 percent of the sales for DVD retailers are of titles within their first two months of release, before they've moved significantly into profitability. Why do stores sell new releases so cheaply? Because for the big-box retailers, at least, they're a loss leader, designed to draw people to other titles in the DVD section or items else-where in the store, where the margins are better. DVD distributors en-courage this by allowing unsold new releases to be returned, lowering the risk for retailers.

The problem is that while this makes sense for the big-box retailers who have other things to sell, it has the effect of also setting the price for everyone else, including the specialty DVD retailers like Block-buster. The big-box retailers have thus driven down the margins for new releases across the industry, making the economics of the Head even tougher. No wonder Blockbuster is struggling.

But if you could shift demand farther into the Tail, creating a market that wasn't so dependent on new releases, you could improve the profit picture immensely. As you can see in the graphic on the previous page, the older the title the more profitable it is. That's why Long Tail retailers have such an advantage—they have the shelf space to carry the older titles. This is also why recommendations and other filters are so important to Long Tail markets. By encouraging people to venture from the hits world (high acquisition costs) to the niche world (low acquisition costs), smart retailers have the poten-tial to improve the economics of retail dramatically. (This is, by the way, exactly what Netflix does: It underbuys new releases—despite the fact that such unavailability and delay annoys some customers and increases churn—because that allows Netflix to maintain its margins.)

The above explains why the Long Tail profit bar in the graph on page 132 shows a more even distribution of profit than of revenues. Long Tail products may not account for most of the sales, but because they're often cheaper to acquire, they can be very profitable, as long as inventory costs are kept close to zero. So the 80/20 Rule changes in three ways in Long Tail markets:

1. You can offer *many* more products.
2. Because it is so much easier to find these products (thanks to recommendations and other filters), sales are spread more evenly between hits and niches.

3. Because the economics of niches is roughly the same as hits, there are profits to be found at *all* levels of popularity.

While the 80/20 Rule is still alive and well, in a Long Tail market it has lost its bite.

DOES A LONGER TAIL MEAN A SHORTER HEAD?

One of the main questions that came up as I got deeper into quantifying Long Tail markets was about the effect of increased variety on the overall shape of the demand curve. As aggregators are able to carry more and more products, lengthening their Tail, will the relatively few hits at the Head sell less? More? The same?

There are three aspects of the Long Tail that have the effect of shifting demand down the tail, from hits to niches. The first is the availability of greater variety. If you offer people a choice of ten things, they will choose one of the ten. If you offer them a thousand things, demand will be less concentrated in the top ten.

The second is the lower "search costs" of finding what you want, which range from actual search to recommendations and other filters. Finally, there is sampling, from the ability to hear thirty seconds of a song for free to the ability to read a portion of a book online. This tends to lower the risk of purchasing, encouraging consumers to venture farther into the unknown.

There are several ways to try to quantify this with hard data. One is to compare a market that offers relatively limited variety with one that offers much more variety of the same sort of products. Another is to track a Long Tail aggregator/retailer over time, watching what happens as its inventory grows. Yet another would be to just look at the effect of lowered search costs online, making an apples-to-apples comparison with a similar offline inventory.

A 2005 study by a team at MIT lead by Erik Brynjolfsson, who did some of the early work on Amazon's Long Tail inventory, looked at this effect at a women's clothing retailer. The company has a catalog business and an online business, both of which offer the exact same inventory and prices. The difference is that online, it has search, easy browsing of both products and variations of those products, and ways to organize the offerings using "rank by" filters.

The result was that consumers—even those that shopped in both the catalog and online—tended to buy farther down the Tail online. The bottom 80 percent of products accounted for 15.7 percent of catalog sales, but 28.8 percent of online sales. Or to switch it around and see it from the top 20 percent perspective, the catalog exhibited an 84/20 rule, while the online site was closer to 71/20.

That's the effect of lowered search costs for the same inventory. To measure the effect of different inventories—one much larger than the other—we worked to construct an apples-to-apples comparison between a retailer with limited shelf space and one with unlimited shelf space. In practice, that means comparing a bricks-and-mortar store with an online one selling or renting the same things. We decided to use entertainment examples because the online markets were mature enough to measure with confidence and the data was available. We looked at both music and DVDs.

Rather than pick a single bricks-and-mortar retailer, we used industry-wide data compiled by Nielsen divisions—SoundScan for music and DVDScan for movies. We compared that with online data from Rhapsody and Netflix, respectively.

(There are several corrections required to do these comparisons properly. In music we had to find a way to compare album sales offline with track sales online, and then from individual sales to streams under a subscription plan. In DVDs it was a matter of comparing sales and single-copy rental data offline with subscription rental online. Although the methodologies are beyond the scope of this book, they broadly revolve around using other data sets, such as pay-per-track online sales, to calibrate the curves and eliminate as many systematic biases as we could.)

After the corrections, the results were striking: The online demand curve is much flatter. The average niche music album title—those beyond the top 1,000—sold about twice as well online than offline. And the average niche DVD—again those beyond the top 1,000—was *three* times as popular online as it was offline.

Another way to look at this is to see how much less dominated the online market is by the top hits. Here's the data for music. Offline, in bricks-and-mortar retailers, the top 1,000 albums make up nearly 80 percent of the total market. (Indeed, in a typical big-box retailer, which carries just a fraction of available CDs, the top 100 albums can account for more than 90 percent of the sales.) By contrast, online that same top 1,000 accounts for less than a third of the market. Seen another way, a full half of the online market is made up of albums *beyond* the top 5,000.

DOES THE LONG TAIL INCREASE DEMAND OR JUST SHIFT IT?

Does the Long Tail grow the pie or simply slice it differently? In other words, as the number of available products grows many-fold with the infinite shelf space of virtual retailers, does it encourage people to buy more stuff or just less popular stuff? In general, the answer depends on the sector: Some do seem to have huge opportunities for growth as their niches become widely available, and some do not.

Although human attention and spending power are finite, you can get *more* for your time and money. Some forms of entertainment, such as music, are "non-rivalrous" for attention, which is to say you can consume them while you're doing something else. For instance, some explanations for the rise of average hours of TV watching in the seventies and eighties involved the idea that a generation had grown up used to television on in the background of their lives; as the novelty wore off, it went from a rivalrous to a non-rivalrous medium, and thus we consumed more of it.

Other media, such as text, may not be consumed faster, but they can be consumed more efficiently and with greater satisfaction through better preselection. Indeed, it's quite extraordinary how much we've been able to increase our consumption bandwidth of information, scanning pages of Google search results and custom blog feeds. I may not read any more words than I once did, but they're more likely to be meaning-ful to me, thanks to much better filters (better at suiting my own inter-ests than, say, the editors of any newspaper) preselecting what I do read. So because the words are more relevant, my meaningful bandwidth has increased; I have, in a sense, compressed my reading attention.

But once you combine the scarcity of disposable income with the scarcity of time, some non-rivalrous media may become rivalrous. The reason people have the television on in the background is that it doesn't cost them anything to do so. But if that were pay-per-view video, you can bet it would suddenly become the center of their atten-tion. From a consumer perspective, this highlights the advantages of all-you-can eat subscription services, which offer risk-free exploration down the Tail. You're likely to consume more if it doesn't cost you more to do so.

So bottom line: Human attention is more expandable than money. The primary effect of the Long Tail is to shift our taste toward niches, but to the extent we're more satisfied by what we're finding, we may well consume more of it. We just won't necessarily pay a lot more for the privilege.

SHOULD PRICES RISE OR FALL DOWN THE TAIL?

I'm often asked about the effect of the Long Tail on pricing. Should prices go down with demand as you travel down the Tail? Or should they rise, as more specific and narrowly focused goods appeal more strongly to their niche audiences?

The answer is that it depends on the product. One way to look at it is to distinguish between "want" markets and "need" markets, each of which has different implications for pricing.

Need markets are those in which customers know what they're look-ing for and just can't find it anywhere but, say, online. Take, for instance, a relatively hard-to-find nonfiction book on a topic of keen interest to you. When you find it, you're probably going to be relatively price in-sensitive. You can see this effect writ large in the discounting policy at Amazon. The online bookseller discounts best-sellers by 30 to 40 percent, gradually reducing the discount until it's around zero for the books with sales ranks in the hundred thousands.

By comparison, music and other forms of entertainment are typically "want" markets. For the right price, you can be encouraged to try something new, venturing down the Tail with diminished risk of wasting your money. Thus, many music labels have experimented with discount pricing for their older titles and more obscure new acts.

The ultimate manifestations of this would be dynamic variable pricing, where prices for music would automatically fall with popularity. That is, in fact, what Google does with its automatic auctions for keyword ads, and what eBay's similar auctions do for everything else. The more demand there is, the higher the price goes.

A really efficient variable pricing market would presumably lead to a more gradual sales decay, and a flatter demand curve overall. But for music, at least, the adoption of such a model runs up against the advantages of single-price simplicity (as in iTunes' fixed-price $0.99 model) and the perils of dreaded "channel conflict" with CD retailers who cannot so easily change their prices. As the music industry gets more desperate it will probably grow more bold in its search for new business models. And then we'll have better data with which to answer this question.

"MICROSTRUCTURE" IN THE LONG TAIL

One of the features of powerlaws is that they are "fractal," which is to say that no matter how far you zoom in they still look like powerlaws. Mathematicians describe this as "self-similarity at multiple scales," but what it means is that the Long Tail is made of many mini-tails, each of which is its own little world.

When you look closely at the data, you can see that the big powerlaw curve of, say, "music" is really just the superposition of all the little powerlaw curves formed by each musical genre. Music is made up of thousands of niche micromarkets, miniature ecosystems that, when smooshed together into an overall ranking, look like one Long Tail. But look closer and each has its own head and tail.

As an example, I've broken out the Long Tail of music on Rhapsody by genre (just the A's), plotting the average track rank in terms of downloads for each genre on the plot below. I then broke out one—Afro-Cuban Jazz—even further, showing the curve of track popularity *within* that genre.

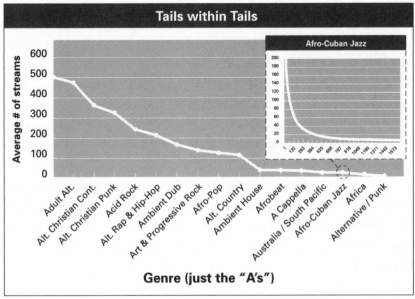

Source: Rhapsody

What you can see is that the genre averages themselves make up a Long Tail, and within each genre there is another Long Tail of individual tracks. And so it goes for the entire music universe, which appears to be one big popularity curve but is actually curves within curves within curves.

The same is true for other markets, from books to blogs. Peter Hirshberg, an executive at the blog search company Technorati, describes the emergence of "topical Long Tails" that the company has been tracking, showing the popularity powerlaw for such categories as cooking blogs and parenting blogs. "As when you apply a prism to white light, there is a spectrum of individual long tail communities in the blogosphere," he says. Rankings are most meaningful *within* such communities, not across them.

Why does this matter? First, because it suggests that the filtering is often most effective at the genre level rather than across the entire market. And second, because it explains an apparent paradox of the Long Tail. The characteristic steep falloff shape of a popularity power-law comes from the effect of powerful word-of-mouth feedback loops that amplify consumer preference, making the reputation-rich even richer and the reputation-poor relatively poorer. Success breeds success. In network theory such positive feedback loops tend to create winner-take-all phenomena, which is another way of saying that they're awesome hit-making machines.

Compounding matters, today's filters make word-of-mouth even more powerful by measuring so much more of it from so many more people and for so many more products. Shouldn't that then have the effect of making the powerlaw even steeper, *increasing* the gap between hits and niches rather than having a leveling effect?

In other words, why don't network-effect recommendation systems, which are essential in driving demand down the Tail, actually do the opposite: drive content *up* the Tail, further amplifying hit/niche inequality? That's what you'd expect with more powerful network effects, yet what we actually see in Long Tail markets is a flattened powerlaw, with *less* of a difference between hits and niches.

The explanation, it turns out, is that these filters and other recommendation systems actually work most strongly at the niche level, within a genre and subgenre. But *between* genres their effect is more muted. There are breakout hits that rise to the top of a genre and then go on to become mainstream hits, topping the overall charts. Yet they're the exception. More common are titles that use their genre popularity to break into the middle of the overall charts, at which point they have to compete with many other hits from other genres and thus tend to not rise much farther.

Thus the most popular "ambient dub" artist at the very head of the ambient dub popularity curve can hugely outsell the others in that category, but that doesn't mean that artist will snowball and tear up the charts to knock 50 Cent out of the top ten. The lesson from this microstructure analysis is that popularity exists at multiple scales, and ruling a clique doesn't necessarily make you the homecoming queen.

THE LONG TAIL OF TIME

Why are some things less popular than others? So far we've been fo-cusing mostly on the depth and breadth of certain items' appeal—how mainstream or niche they are, or how high or low their quality. But there is another factor that influences popularity: age. Just as things of broad appeal tend to sell better than things of narrow appeal, new things tend to sell better than old things.

When you look at a basic demand curve, the reasons why some things sell less well than others are lost in the merged rankings. But popularity is actually multidimensional: Factors that determine an al-bum's rankings, for instance, can include not just the quality of the music but also its genre, its release date, the fame and/or nationality of the band, similarity to other artists, and so on. Yet it's all blended into the single dimension of a best-seller list, which obscures all those fac-tors in a mushed-together mélange.

If you think about it, today's hit is tomorrow's niche. Almost all products, even hits, see their sales decay over time. *Twister* was the number two movie of 1996, but its DVD version is now outsold two-to-one on Amazon by a 2005 History Channel documentary on the French Revolution.

Einstein described time as the fourth dimension of space; you can think of it equally as the fourth dimension of the Long Tail. Both hits and niches see their sales slow over time; hits may start higher, but they all end up down the Tail eventually. The research to quan-tify this conclusion is continuing, but conceptually the picture looks like the graph on the next page.

What's particularly interesting about time and the Long Tail is that Google appears to be changing the rules of the game. For online media, like media anywhere, there is a tyranny of the new. Yesterday's news is fishwrap, and once content falls off the front page of a Web site, its popularity plummets. But as sites find more and more of their traffic coming from Google, they're seeing this rule break.

Google is not quite time-agnostic, but it does measure relevance mostly in terms of incoming links, not newness. So when you search for a term, you're more likely to get the *best* page than the *newest* one.

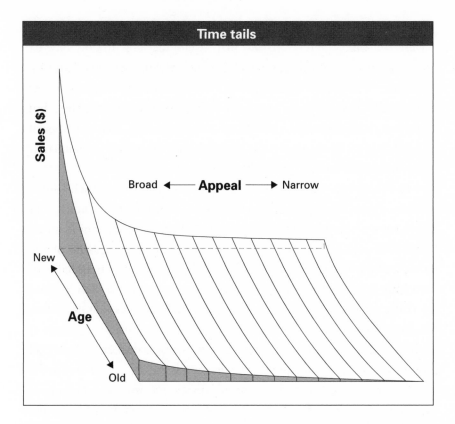

And because older pages have more time to attract incoming links, they sometimes have an advantage over the newer ones. The result is that the usual decay of popularity for blog posts and online news pages is now much more gradual than it was, thanks to the amount of traffic that comes via search. Google is in a sense serving as a time machine, and we're just now being able to measure the effect this has on publishing, advertising, and attention.

THE TRAGICALLY NEGLECTED ECONOMICS OF ABUNDANCE

Broadly, the Long Tail is about abundance. Abundant shelf space, abundant distribution, abundant choice. How awkward, then, that one of the definitions of economics given by Wikipedia is:

eco-nom-ics: *n* The social science of choice under scarcity.

There are other definitions ("the allocation of scarce resources to satisfy unlimited wants," and so on), but many share the same troublesome element: a focus on scarcity, especially on how to allocate scarce resources. In an age of abundance in the form of everything from Moore's law (the observation that computer price/performance doubles every eighteen months) to its equivalents in storage and bandwidth, this is a problem.

It's hard to overstate how fundamental to economics the notion is that you can't have it all for free—the entire discipline is oriented around studying trade-offs and how they're made. Adam Smith, for instance, created modern economics by considering the trade-off between time, or convenience, and money. He discussed how a person could live near town, and pay more for rent of his home, or live farther away and pay less, "paying the difference out of his convenience." And since then, economics has been all about how to divide finite pies.

That's just the way it is. Neoclassical economics explicitly does not deal with abundant inputs. It doesn't deny that oxygen is free when you're trying to light a fire; it just doesn't include that in its equations. It leaves that to other disciplines, such as chemistry.

But we are entering the era of effectively infinite shelf space. Two of the main scarcity functions of traditional economics—the marginal costs of manufacturing and distribution—are trending to zero in Long Tail markets of digital goods, where bits can be copied and transmitted at almost no cost at all. Surely economics has something to say about that?

Clearly abundance (also known as "plentitude") is all around us, especially in technology. Moore's Law is a classic example. What Carver Mead, the semiconductor pioneer and Caltech professor, recognized in 1970 when he encouraged his students to "waste transistors" was that transistors were becoming abundant, which is to say effectively free. The shift in thinking from making the most of scarce computing resources to "wasting" cycles by, say, drawing windows and icons on the screen led to the Mac and the personal computing revolution. To say nothing of the scandalous profligacy—a supercomputer used for fun!—of an Xbox 360.

We also have similar abundance laws working in storage and bandwidth and virtually everything else digital. Outside of technology, the green revolution brought abundance to much of agriculture (so now, to prop up prices, we pay farmers *not* to plant their crops). And what is the motive force behind China and India's rise if not abundant labor, allowing them to, in a sense, waste people?

Even ideas can on some level be considered abundant, because they can propagate without limit due to their "non-rivalrous" nature. As Thomas Jefferson, the father of the U.S. patent system, put it, "He who receives an idea from me, receives instruction himself without lessening mine; as he who lights his taper at mine, receives light without darkening me."

More than a decade ago George Gilder, the apostle of abundance, offered a good way to think about all this:

> For most of human history, most people have believed that economics is essentially a zero-sum game—that scarcity will ultimately prevail over abundance. Pastor Malthus was the famous exponent of the view that populations increase geometrically while agricultural output rises arithmetically. In the Malthusian view, food scarcity eventually chokes off growth. Karl Marx saw all economics ultimately reducing to a class struggle over scarce "means of production."
>
> The economists' focus on scarcity stems from the fact that shortages are measurable and end in zero. They constrain an economic model to produce a clearly calculable result, an identifiable choke point in the industrial circuitry. Abundances are incalculable and have no obvious cap. When they are ubiquitous, like air or water, they are invisible—"externalities." Yet abundance is the driving force in all economic growth and change.

So how to reconcile this with neoclassical economics? Gilder recommends embracing waste.

> In every industrial revolution, some key factor of production is drastically reduced in cost. Relative to the previous cost to achieve that function, the new factor is virtually free. Physical force in the industrial revolution became virtually free compared to its expense when it derived from animal muscle power and human muscle power. Suddenly you could do things you could not afford to do before. You

could make a factory work 24 hours a day churning out products in a way that was just incomprehensible before the industrial era. It really did mean that physical force became virtually free in a sense. The whole economy had to reorganize itself to exploit this physical force. You had to "waste" the power of the steam engine and its derivatives in order to prevail, whether in war or in peace.

That suggests a way to put this in an economic context. If the abundant resources are just one factor in a system otherwise constrained by scarcity, they may not challenge the economic orthodoxy. They are then like learning curves and minimized transaction costs—drivers of production efficiency that serve to lower prices and increase productivity but do not invalidate the laws of economics.

And, indeed, the abundance of the Long Tail, for all its power, is surrounded by such constraints. Although there may be near infinite selection of all media, there is still a scarcity of human attention and hours in the day. Our disposable income is limited. On some level, it's still a fixed-pie game. Offer a couch potato a million TV shows and he or she may end up watching no more television than before, just different television, better suited to that individual.

Finally, it's worth noting that economics, for all its charms, doesn't have the answer to everything. Many phenomena are simply left to other disciplines, from psychology to physics, or left without an academic theory at all. Abundance, like growth itself, is a force that is changing our world in ways that we experience every day, whether we have an equation to describe it or not.

9

THE SHORT HEAD

THE WORLD THE SHELF CREATED,
FOR BETTER OR WORSE

Hits, like it or not, are here to stay. So are retail stores with limited shelf space and broadcast networks, lowest-common-denominator fare and all. For all the growth in e-commerce, online shopping is still less than 10 percent of American retail, having just passed catalog shopping. Even the biggest boosters of online shopping don't expect that they'll pass a quarter of consumer spending for decades.

It's not just the instant-gratification convenience and tactile advantages of bricks and mortar. We're also a gregarious species, and sometimes we *like* to do things together with other people. There's comfort in numbers, and shared experiences bring us closer.

That's why the unequal shape of powerlaws is unavoidable. Long Tail markets tend to be a bit flatter than traditional markets, but they still have their share of blockbusters. For each way that we differ from one another, there are more ways that we're alike. This is not only inevitable, but it's actually essential in helping kickstart recommendations and other filters that make the rest of the online market work.

In this chapter we'll return to the left side of the powerlaw, the land of the A list. We'll look at both the virtues of shelves and their costs, and likewise for broadcast technologies and Hollywood's hit-making machine. Let's start with their advantages.

Hits may not dominate society and commerce as much as they did over the past century, but they still have unmatched impact. And part of that is their ability to serve as a source of common culture around which more narrowly targeted markets can form.

Successful Long Tail aggregators need to have both hits *and* niches. They need to span the full range of variety, from the broadest appeal to the narrowest, to be able to make the connections that can illuminate a path down the Long Tail that makes sense for everyone.

Consumers want one-stop shopping. They want to have some confidence that what they're looking for is in one specific place. Stores that give consumers the most confidence that everything they want is there are going to be the ones that succeed. This notion of ultimate selection, of knowing that the filters are selecting the best from a choice of *everything* (or at least everything in that domain) is why good Long Tail aggregators are so compelling.

If you just have the products at the Head, you find that very quickly your customers want more and you can't offer it. If you just have the products at the Tail, you find that customers have no idea where to start. They're unable to get traction in the marketplace because everything you're offering is unfamiliar to them. The importance of offering the stuff at both the Head and the Tail is that you can start in the world that customers already know: familiar products that tap into and define a space.

A good example of why this is so necessary is the story of MP3.com, one of the early online music services. In 1997, an entrepreneur named Michael Robertson started what looked like a classic Long Tail business. It let anyone upload music files that would be available to all. The idea was that the service would bypass the record labels, allowing artists to connect directly to listeners. MP3.com would make its money in fees paid by bands to have their music promoted on the site. The tyranny of the labels would be broken, and a thousand flowers would bloom.

But although MP3.com grew quickly and soon had hundreds of thousands of tracks, struggling bands did not, as a rule, find big new audiences, and independent music was not transformed. Indeed, MP3.com got a reputation for being exactly what it was: an undifferentiated mass of mostly bad music that deserved its obscurity.

The problem with MP3.com was that it was *only* Long Tail. For most of its life it didn't have license agreements with the labels to offer mainstream fare or much popular commercial music at all. Therefore, there was no familiar point of entry for consumers, no known quantity from which further exploring could begin. (In the search for a viable business model, it later offered a service that allowed users to upload commercial CDs they owned, which brought on massive record industry lawsuits that eventually shut down the company.)

The reason MP3.com's model didn't succeed and the iTunes model—which is less oriented toward independent musicians—did is that iTunes began by making deals with major record labels, which gave it a critical mass of mainstream music. Then it added more and more niche content, as "rights aggregators" shipped it hard drives full of hundreds of thousands of independent musicians. Thus, iTunes customers were able to dive into an already working market where the categories were defined by known commercial acts, which served as a natural leaping-off point for the discovery of niche music.

(As an aside, it's worth asking why MySpace, which has a free independent music model that is very reminiscent of MP3.com, is such a success. The answer at this point appears to be that it is a very effective combination of community and content. The strong social ties between the tens of millions of fans there help guide them to obscure music that they otherwise wouldn't find, while the content gives them a reason to keep visiting. This helps the site avoid the burnout phenomenon that has sunk previous social networking services that were mostly about connection for connection's sake.)

THE URBAN TAIL

Another sort of "hit" is major cities. If you chart population clusters around the globe, you'll get a powerlaw. A small number of places, from Shanghai to Paris, have huge populations, while many more places have smaller populations. As Richard Florida, in his book *The Rise of the Creative Class,* puts it, "the world is spiky":

> People cluster not simply because they like to be around one another or they prefer cosmopolitan centers with lots of amenities, though both those things count. They and their companies also cluster because of the powerful productivity advantages, economies of scale, and knowledge spillovers such density brings. Ideas flow more freely, are honed more sharply, and can be put into practice more quickly when large numbers of innovators, implementers, and financial backers are in constant contact with one another, both in and out of the office.

These population spikes—the great cities of the world—exist because the cultural and economic advantages of being around lots of other people more than compensate for the costs of urban living. One of those advantages, ironically enough, is massive variety in every possible niche.

Places like New York City, London, Paris, and Tokyo offer practically everything. Want international food? It's all there—from Eritrean and Bengali to Mongolian hot pots. There is entertainment of every possible variety, services to cater to every need, and if you know which side street or hole in the wall to explore, a bounty of products to rival even Amazon.

Why? Because cities have such a dense population that the usually widely distributed demand becomes concentrated. In a sense, you can think of cities as the Long Tail of urban space in the same way the Internet is the Long Tail of idea space or cultural space.

As the writer Steven Johnson puts it:

> A store selling nothing but buttons most likely won't be able to find a market in a town of 50,000 people, but in New York City, there's an entire button-store district. Subcultures thrive in big cities for this reason as well: if you have idiosyncratic tastes, you're much more likely to find someone who shares those tastes in a city of 9 million people.

The urban theorist Jane Jacobs observed many years ago that huge cites create environments where small niches can flourish. She wrote:

> Towns and suburbs . . . are natural homes for huge supermarkets and for little else in the way of groceries, for standard movie houses or drive-ins and for little else in the way of theater. There are simply not enough people to support further variety, although there may be people (too few of them) who would draw upon it were it there.
>
> Cities, however, are the natural home of supermarkets and standard movie houses plus delicatessens, Viennese bakeries, foreign groceries, art movies, and so on, all of which can be found co-existing, the standard with the strange, the large with the small. Wherever lively and popular parts of cities are found, the small much outnumber the large.

IN DEFENSE OF SHELVES

Before we bury the shelf, let us first praise it. Today's retail display rack is the human interface to a highly evolved supply chain designed to make the most of time and space. Standing as much as seven feet high and four feet wide and extending up to two feet deep, the average supermarket shelf module has the cubic capacity of a minivan.

Stacked with hundreds of packaged goods designed to fit perfectly in industry-standard racks, that shelf has become the modern-day symbol of abundance. Today the average supermarket carries more than 30,000 different items, all ideally arranged and displayed in rows of shelves for maximum sales at minimum cost. It is both a miracle of efficient storage and a fine-tuned selling machine.

The shelf reflects the absolute state of the art in retail science. The products on today's supermarket shelves are packaged and arranged according to stocking algorithms and the peaks of elastic demand curves. The optimal inventory distribution is recalculated each day in retail chain headquarters and tuned in real time on the basis of check-out data.

These shelf-stocking models are designed to press every button we've got: satisfying existing demand, stimulating new demand, and extracting the highest possible sales from the smallest space. Every dimension of the supermarket shelf has been studied, focus-grouped, and observed by retail anthropologists via hidden cameras and radio-frequency ID tags. The retail shelf is the frontline of an enterprise that accounts for nearly 60 percent of the American economy, and the research industry devoted to understanding it befits its importance.

We know the precise value gradient of the vertical dimension in a rack of shelves, from top to bottom. We also know the exact dollar value of the golden shelf just below eye level in each product category and type of retail (for instance, in supermarkets that magic place in the middle has more than five times the selling power of the bottom shelf). As a result, stores determine exactly how high a "slotting fee" they can charge manufacturers to place their products in this purchasing sweet spot, increasing both sales for the maker and margins for the seller.

Meanwhile, the horizontal dimension is a study in optimizing brand exposure. We now know exactly how wide to stack a company's products to capture a shopper's scanning eye without going too wide and wasting scarce shelf frontage. Thanks to bar codes and point-of-sale integration with stock replenishment software, we also know how to keep shelves filled with the right stuff all the time.

In short, thanks to decades of research by the best minds in super-marketology, we have learned how to make the most of each square inch of retail space. When one considers how far we've come, with the explosion of abundance and variety and the price-lowering effect of global supply chains, it is hard to quibble with the shelf. It is the very embodiment of capitalism evolved.

RENT BY THE HALF INCH

Yet the shelf is so wasteful in so many ways. Let's start with the obvious. The monthly rent on that two-by-four-foot slab is outrageous. True, you can stack six square feet of shelf space on top of one square foot of floor space, but retail rules of thumb dictate that for every square foot of floor space used for shelves, you need another two to three square feet of aisle, checkout, and common space. Depending on the type of store, backroom storage and administrative space can add another 25 percent to the floor space required. In early 2005, mall retail space in major U.S. markets was renting for an average of nearly $40 per square foot; this can put the net space cost of each square foot of shelving at between $26 and $33 a month.

Then there are the other overheads of bricks-and-mortar retail: sales staff, inventory depreciation, power and other utilities, shoplifting and other "leakage" issues, returns, insurance, and marketing costs. Combined, these types of overhead can nearly equal the space costs, bringing the total rent on that twelve-inch-by-twelve-inch square of shelving to at least $50 a month. With an average retail markup of 40 percent, this means that the average square foot of mall shelf space must account for between $100 and $150 in sales a month—and that's to simply pay its way.

Since every slot on that shelf is precious, only the most promising products—those with a certain expected popularity or profit margin—can be allowed in. It's a brutal test, and the vast majority of products don't make it. Supermarkets consider 15,000 new products a year. Out of the few that actually make it to the shelf, an estimated 70 to 80 percent don't survive for long there, according to Consumers Union. Today, the average cost of carrying a single DVD in a movie rental store is $22 a year. Only the most popular titles rent often enough to make that back (there's a reason why they call it "Blockbuster").

If that weren't bad enough, the hidden costs of selling products on shelves can actually be even higher than the direct costs. These are largely the opportunity costs of products not found and latent demand not realized because of the physical constraints of shelves. The Google era has opened our eyes to the lucrative virtues of findability. We type in what we want (misspelled or not) and, more often than not, it pops right up. We are now spoiled with useful recommendations (lessons learned by those who came before us) that introduce us to things we never would have thought of or found on our own.

Yet none of this carries over to the local Safeway, where products are shoehorned into crude taxonomies ("canned goods"), the patterns of other shoppers are known only to management, and the only search engine available is a stock clerk who works for minimum wage. This is not really Safeway's fault, or the fault of any other bricks-and-mortar retailer. Those retailers are simply fated to live in the inflexible world of racks and aisles, where products must obey the uncompromising physics of atoms, not bits.

One of those unfortunate rules of corporeal matter is that it cannot transcend time and space. Obviously, a physical item can be in only one place at any given time. For instance, a can of tuna cannot exist simultaneously in multiple categories, even though the interests and browsing paths of each shopper might suggest many: "fish," "canned food," "sandwich makings," "low-fat," "on sale," "best-selling," "back-to-school," "under $2," and so on.

A physical store cannot be reconfigured on the fly to cater to each customer based on his or her particular interests. Bottles of wine cannot be magically rearranged to suit the results of a search. They cannot be popped onto the next shelf to optimize the probability that people like you who bought aged Gouda and black olives might also like this Pinot. Atoms are stubborn this way.

When you place an item in your wire shopping basket, the store knows nothing about it until you arrive at the checkout, at which time it's too late to do anything but feebly give you a coupon for discounts on future purchases. Somewhere, retail scientists dream of smart shopping carts that detect their contents by radio frequency ID tags and then spit out recommendations on the fly. Yet even those scientists still can't transport matter into reach and make acting on those recommendations easy. In the physical world, shoppers move; products don't.

THE WAL-MART EFFECT

When I was a twenty-something slacker, I, like many of my twenty-something kin, worked in a record store. It was a pretty big record store in the business district of downtown Washington, D.C., part of a chain that no longer exists.

Catering mostly to the lawyers, admins, and paralegals who worked around the area, the store was relatively mainstream. Nevertheless I can still remember the aisle of import records, mostly British new wave (after all, this was the mid-eighties) that stretched the length of the store near the stool where I sat watching the door and answering questions. The entire back wall was twelve-inch singles (Depeche Mode and Billy Idol were big), and classical had its own room, with excellent acoustics for more refined listening.

This all came back to me recently as I wandered through the two aisles of the music department at a Wal-Mart in Oakland, California. (And really, is *wandered* even the right word for fifteen paces down one aisle and back the other?) Wal-Mart, which accounts for about one-fifth of all music sales in America, is by far the nation's largest music retailer. Some 138 million Americans shop at Wal-Mart each week, making it perhaps the single most unifying cultural force in the country.

Over the past decade, these types of big-box retailers, including stores like Best Buy, have changed the face of the music industry with their unmatchable economies of scale. Today, the number of large independent music stores like the one I once worked at has dropped dramatically; the classical listening room is now an endangered species. There are, needless to say, few import aisles left.

In the place of specialist stores' often eclectic collections, the superstores offer just a relatively small selection of hits. It's ironic that such big stores carry so little in each category, but that's what the economics of big-boxery dictates. Still, their prices are excellent and they are packed with eager shoppers. A triumph of supply-chain efficiencies and bulk pricing, these big retailers are the state of the art in bricks-and-mortar retail today.

Welcome to the Short Head.

How short is short? The average Wal-Mart now carries around 4,500 unique CD titles (as a point of comparison, Amazon lists about 800,000). More specifically, consider the music department at that Wal-Mart I strolled through in Oakland. Here's the number of records I found for each of the store's categories:

"Rock/Pop/R&B"	1,800
"Latina"	1,500
"Christian/Gospel"	360
"Country"	225
"Classical/Easy Listening"	225

Again, there were just two main aisles. One was "Rock/Pop/R&B"; the other was "Latina." All other categories were lumped into single four-by-five-foot racks. "Jazz," "Classical," "World Music," "Easy Listening," and "New Age" were all together along *one rack*.

Of the estimated 30,000 new albums released each year, Wal-Mart carries just 750, according to David Gottlieb, a former label executive. That works out to only 2.5 percent of the new music released each year; and those 4,500 titles in the total inventory are less than half a percent of all the music available. Entire categories, from Dance to Spoken-Word, are either missing or buried deep in catch-all categories such as "Rock/Pop/R&B." There are no copies of the Rolling Stones' *Exile on Main Street* or Nirvana's *Nevermind*.

There you have it. Scarcity, bottlenecks, the distortion of distribution, and the tyranny of shelf space all wrapped up in one *big* store. Again, it's ironic, this paradox of plenty: Walk into a Wal-Mart and you're overwhelmed by the abundance and choice. Yet look closer and the utter thinness of this cornucopia is revealed. Wal-Mart's shelves are a display case a mile wide and twenty-four inches deep. At first glance that may look like everything, but in a world that's actually a mile wide and a mile deep, a veneer of variety just isn't enough.

IN THE LIBRARY OF MISSHELVED BOOKS

One of the most vexing problems with physical goods is that they force us into crude categorization and static taxonomies, as we saw with Wal-Mart. That means that a windbreaker can be in the "Jackets" section or the "Sports" section, but not in a "Blue" or "Nylon" section. Generally, this isn't seen as a big problem, since most of those categories would be silly for most people (the one-size-fits-all economics of retail must ignore the few shoppers those categories would be perfect for).

As a store manager, you have to guess as to where most people would expect to find a windbreaker. So after constructing your store around a preconceived taxonomy, you can do nothing but hope that your setup corresponds to the way most people think. And those customers that don't, in fact, think this way? One hopes they'll ask for assistance.

With the evolution of online retail, however, has come the revelation that being able to recategorize and rearrange products on the fly unlocks their real value. For one, online stores are free to list products in whichever, and however many, sections they choose. This captures the attention of potential buyers who wouldn't have found the product in the default category, and it also stimulates demand in people who weren't even looking for the product in the first place but were spurred to buy because of clever positioning.

The efficiency and success of online retail have illuminated the cost of traditional retail's inflexibility and taxonomical oversimplifications. It's one thing to have high prices or limited selection; it's quite another to simply be unable to help people find what they want.

In the world of information science, the tricky question of where to put things is known as the "ontology problem." Ontology is a word that means different things in different disciplines, but for librarians and computer scientists (and for store managers, whether they know it or not), it's about ways to organize things. The Dewey Decimal System is one way to organize books; the *Encyclopædia Britannica* is one way to organize information; the Periodic Table of the Elements is one way to organize matter.

All of these are successes, as far as they go. However, as the Google era has shown, we're suddenly realizing how limited those fixed ways of making sense of the world really are.

Let's start with the Dewey Decimal System, which divides the world of knowledge into ten top-level categories:

- 000 Computers, information, and general reference
- 100 Philosophy and psychology

- 200 Religion
- 300 Social sciences
- 400 Language
- 500 Science and mathematics
- 600 Technology
- 700 Arts and recreation
- 800 Literature
- 900 History and geography

Seems reasonable so far, right? Okay, let's look at the next level of organization, the second digit. Here it is for Category 200, Religion:

- 200 Religion
- 210 Philosophy and theory of religion
- 220 Bible
- 230 Christianity
- 240 Christian moral and devotional theology
- 250 Christian orders and local churches
- 260 Social and ecclesiastical theology
- 270 History of Christianity and Christian sects
- 280 Christian denominations
- 290 Comparative religion and other religions

See the problem? Islam, Judaism, Hinduism, Taoism, and all the world's other religions, which account for most of the global population, are lumped into a subset of the "other" category. This taxonomy says more about the culture of nineteenth-century America in which the system was developed (and probably something about Melvil Dewey himself) than it does about the world of faith.

Truth be told, the Dewey Decimal taxonomy really isn't about the world of knowledge at all; it's about the world of *books*. Clay Shirky, a prominent thinker on the social and economic effects of Internet technologies, explains:

What's being optimized is the number of books on the shelf. The musculature of this scheme looks like it's about concepts. It's organized into non-overlapping categories that get more detailed at lower and lower levels—any concept is supposed to fit in one category and in no other categories. But every now and then the skeleton pokes through, and that skeleton, the supporting structure around which the system is really built, is designed to minimize seek times on shelves.

We've come a long way since the nineteenth century, of course. Libraries built card catalogs that cross-indexed books by multiple categories: authors, titles, keywords, alternative subjects. Eventually came digital catalogs and keyword search, which at least made things findable. Regardless, the physical books were still stacked on the shelves according to the Dewey Decimal System. This meant that although you could now locate the book you wanted (even if you didn't subscribe to Melvil Dewey's Victorian worldview), you might not find much relevance in the books stacked around it.

Even with the card catalog, books are still vulnerable to the physics of materiality. Consider what happens when one is stacked in the wrong place, orphaned in the wrong category. It's as if it were vaporized. Unless someone stumbles upon it and reshelves it, that book will effectively be lost to the world (even though it's still sitting *somewhere*). No wonder the semantics of shelves are often so negative. "Shelf life" refers to the mortality of expiring goods—whether literal (think: bananas just starting to brown) or figurative (think: Halloween-themed paper plates in March). In the realm of film and television, "shelved" means canceled or delayed. Shelves are places where things go to die.

On the other hand, think about a world of ad-hoc organization, determined by whatever makes sense at the time. That's more like a big pile of stuff on a desk instead of rows of items stringently arranged on shelves. Sure it may seem messy, but that's just because it's a different kind of organization: spontaneous, contextual order, easily reordered into a different context as need be. That image is a little bit like the Web itself, seen through Google's lens: a world of infinite variety and little predetermined order; a world of dynamic structure, shaped differently for each observer.

Recently, I toured the new Seattle Public Library, which was designed by famed architect Rem Koolhaas to be a model library for the twenty-first century. He faced the challenge of making stacks of books fit into a search-engine culture. Realizing that the relative balance between computers and books was changing and would probably continue to change, Koolhaas didn't make too many assumptions about how books should be shelved. He arranged the stacks on rails in a spiral, which could expand or contract as demand dictated.

Yet even within this commendably flexible system, he obviously needed to arrange the books in some order. Since it takes more than the turn of a century or two to change library culture, that order was our friend the Dewey Decimal System. However, in the Seattle Public Library the Dewey numbers are marked on the floor on rubber mats that slide into grooves in the concrete. As the stacks accordion and shift with the world's changing information priorities, the rubber mats will change as well. And if, someday, the Dewey system has reached its own expiry date, those rubber mats can be turned over to provide nothing more than a good place to wipe your shoes. A future-proof library makes no assumptions about the information landscape of tomorrow.

SHOPPING IN THE MISCELLANEOUS AISLE

What's true for libraries is doubly true for retail stores. In libraries, at least there is a standard categorization scheme—the card catalog is there to be searched, and librarians tend to know their stuff. However, good luck finding what you want quickly in an unfamiliar supermarket. The consequences of ad-hoc taxonomies and capricious shelving are frustrated customers, unsold products, and a flight to the best-known brands and products, simply because those are the ones that are easy to find. Likewise, for most other kinds of stores, from hardware to clothes.

As an example, I recently went looking in my local Blockbuster for *Akira*, a Japanese anime classic. What section to look in? Science fiction? Animation? Foreign? Action? As it turned out, it didn't matter—

they didn't have the film. Physical stores' advantages of immediate gratification are of little meaning if you can't find what you want.

On Amazon, however, it was simply a matter of typing "akira" into the search bar (and just note how there's no need to capitalize or even necessarily to spell it quite right). The film immediately came up, as did two other versions (as well as both new and used copies of all three). If I had wanted to browse by category, any of those above would have worked; the film was listed in all of them. A tempting package deal with *Ghost in the Shell* was offered, another virtue of dynamic marketing and positioning. Likewise, Amazon also recommended two other films it thought I might like: *Princess Mononoke* and *Ghost in the Shell 2*. And, of course, both of those were also in stock and cheaper than Block-buster. The experiences I had with these two stores couldn't have been more different.

In a sense, an online retailer is to a bricks-and-mortar store what Google is to a library. Because of the constraints of physical shelves, the real-world outlets are forced to create taxonomies and assign every-thing to them. I tremble to think where the Dewey Decimal System will place the book you're reading right now. Technology? Economics? Business? Culture? None of them are quite right by themselves. Sadly, there is no category for "all of the above."

Google, by contrast, will put it in no category at all. The book's nat-ural place(s) in the world will emerge spontaneously after the fact, measured in terms of incoming links. My publisher might call this a "business book," but if the world decides it's really more "popular eco-nomics" and links to it in that context, then that is what it is and what it will be, along with virtually any other description that someone may find relevant. In a Google world, meaning and ontology are entirely in the eyes and minds of the beholder. One thing can be many different things to many different people. As such, Google's algorithms simply measure the wisdom of the crowd by calculating the most appropriate results for the keywords a searcher types in.

Meanwhile, Amazon will start by giving this book five or six cate-gory designations. Customers will then have their say by "tagging" it, which means typing in any words they choose to make their own cate-gories ("Internet," "blogger," "to read later," "Pareto," "good geek gift," etc.). Others will be able to see what tags have been assigned, which is another useful piece of context that will help this book find its place in the world. This process of tagging creates what are known as "folks-onomies"—after-the-fact categorizations based entirely on whatever people choose to say is meaningful about something. Interestingly, Amazon gives these tags so much weight that they appear *before* its own list of preset categories.

Still, that is only the start of the multidimensional process of teasing out what something is in the infinite bookstore. Amazon's software will digest every word of this book's text and determine a list of "statistically improbable phrases," which are word combinations that do not appear in many, if any, other books. In a sense, these will comprise a unique fingerprint of my book, but they're also an indication of any unique ideas or subject areas, which is useful in itself. The software will also list unique capitalized words, which will help define the factual foundation of my book. Then, Amazon will deploy all its usual collaborative filtering recommendation tools to find books that other customers looked at or bought along with mine, which will help define the book through its peer set.

THE TYRANNY OF GEOGRAPHY

Shelves have another disadvantage: They are bound by geography. Their contents are available only to people who happen to be in the same place as they are. That is, of course, also their virtue: The stores near you are convenient and offer the immediate gratification of sending your purchase home with you. For all the time we may spend on-line, we do, after all, live in the physical world.

The main constraint of bricks-and-mortar retail is the need to find *local* audiences. Whether we're talking about movies, CDs, or any number of products, bricks-and-mortar retailers will carry only the content that earns its keep, products that attract the greatest amount of interest (and dollars) from the limited local population.

In America, 20 percent of the population live more than eight miles from the closest bookstore; 8 percent live more than twenty miles away. The numbers for music stores, movie theaters, and video rental shops aren't much different. Even if everyone wanted to buy that way, many can't.

Remember, in the tyranny of physical space, an audience too thinly spread is the same as no audience at all. Thus, local demand must be at a high enough concentration to compensate for the high costs of physical distribution. In other, more obvious words, not enough local demand equals no store.

This is true for goods of any sort. There is a reason why ski stores are not often found in hot climates and diving stores are not often found inland (despite the fact that lots of people fly from both sorts of places to ski and dive). There may be a local demand for the goods, but again, the question for any store owner is whether there's *enough* local demand. The calculation goes a little like this:

Sales =

The percentage of the population who might buy

Minus

The percentage not within ten miles of the store

Minus

The percentage that never comes in

Minus

The percentage that won't see the item on the shelf

And so on . . .

It doesn't have to be that way. In a sense, you can think of there being a Long Tail of customers, just like that of products. Imagine that the horizontal axis of the curve is towns, and the vertical is the number of potential customers for a product in each of those towns. A traditional retailer would have to focus on the head of the curve, where the customers are most concentrated. Yet as we've already learned, most of the customers are in the tail, distributed over many towns. That's the dirty secret of traditional retail. Stores leave business on the table simply because their economics doesn't allow them to pursue it.

In a nutshell, that is the business case for online retailers. Because they *can* reach all of those many low-density towns as efficiently as the high-density ones, they can tap the Long Tail of distributed demand. That's exactly what the Sears, Roebuck catalog did a century ago: tap the distributed demand for variety in the American heartland. Today, we just do it faster, cheaper, and with even greater variety.

SCARCE AIR

The introduction of radio—and then television—was meant to have exactly that kind of egalitarian effect. For mass-market fare, the economics of broadcast are hard to beat: They allow you to reach a million people as cheaply as one. Yet while the costs of the transmitter and license are fixed, the advertising revenues are variable. The more people you reach, the more money you make. In the Short Tail of hits, it's as simple as that.

After the arrival of broadcast in the middle of the twentieth century, there was suddenly a way to bring a show to every home and a newsreel to everyone every night. Compared to going to live theater or the movies, radio and television were an incredibly democratizing force, extending the audience for audio and video news and entertainment farther down the tail of demand than anything before or since.

Still, don't forget that broadcast technologies have limitations of their own. It's the physics: Airwaves can carry only so many stations, and coaxial cables only so many TV channels. And, most obviously, there are only twenty-four hours in a day that can be programmed.

If you're a television or radio executive, these constraints have a very real effect. Each slot on the dial, each channel on a cable lineup has a cost. Sometimes it's the cost of broadcasting licenses and cable carriage fees; other times it's the expectations of an advertiser. In either case, there's only one way to turn a profit (or at least break even): get a big enough audience to make the most of that valuable broadcast slot.

The traditional solution is to focus on hits. Aside from using scarce distribution resources efficiently by aggregating and concentrating audiences, hits also benefit from network effects in marketing, otherwise known as buzz. Once advertising gets them to a certain level of popularity, word of mouth can kick in and organically break them through to the next levels, all the way up to blockbuster status if they've really struck a chord.

But how do you make a hit? Well, there are two basic options: (1) search far and wide for rare, unpredictable genius, or (2) use lowest-common-denominator formulas to manufacture something optimized to sell. You can guess which one is most common.

The result is the hit-driven media and entertainment culture that has come to define the second half of the twentieth century. It's defined by:

- A desperate search for one-size-fits-all products
- Trying to predict demand
- Pulling "misses" off the market
- Limited choice

Umair Haque, who writes about digital media economics, phrases it in terms of "consumer attention." A formulaic TV show designed for broad, if shallow, appeal may get watched (along with commercials that go along with it). But it will get watched more if there's little else on, which was pretty much the case for most of television's history. So, too, for movies and radio:

> The general principle of the last hundred years of entertainment economics was that content and distribution were scarce and consumer attention was abundant. Not everyone could make a movie, broadcast on the airwaves or owned a press. Those who could and did had control of the means of production. It was a sellers' market, and they could afford to waste attention.

One statistic—ad clutter on television—is telling. Following deregulation in the mid-1980s, network TV ad time per hour increased from six minutes and forty-eight seconds in 1982 to twelve minutes and four seconds in 2001 (that's an increase of nearly 50 percent!). Why? Because Americans continued to watch more and more television, even as the ad load went up. Since they continued to give their attention despite getting less and less content, why not exploit that? As

Haque puts it, from a network perspective, "increased ad time was a cost borne by the players on the other side of a two-sided market." No wonder the ads were taking over.

THE DANGERS OF "HITISM"

It takes a long time to unlearn the last century's lessons in distribution scarcity. But we're starting to do so, starting with the first generation to grow up online.

In 2001, the first wave of "digital natives" came of age. Kids who started using the Internet as twelve-year-olds in 1995 turned eighteen (the beginning of Nielsen's 18–34 demographic that is highly coveted by advertisers). The males of the species, in particular, were watching less television. Given a choice between the infinite variety and easy ad-dodging online versus network TV, they were choosing the former—the 18–34 viewership figures started to drop for the first time in a half century.

Although the shift is still small, it's real: The audience is migrating away from broadcast to the Internet, where niche economics rule. Given greater choice, they are also shifting their attention to what they value most—and that turns out *not* to be formulaic fare with lots of commercials. They are, to use Haque's term, starting to take back their attention, or at least value it more highly.

The lesson for the entertainment industry should be clear: Give people what they want. If that's niche content, then give them niche content. Just as we're starting to rethink the premium we pay for hits and stars, we're also starting to realize that the nature of the goods and participants, and their incentives, in this new market are also different.

It's human nature to see things in absolutes and extremes, black or white, all one thing or all another—hits or misses. But of course the world is messy, gradated, and statistical. We forget that most products aren't big sellers, because most of the ones we see on the shelves do indeed sell in huge numbers, at least compared to those that didn't make it to the store in the first place. Yet the vast majority of virtually everything, from music to clothing, is at best only modestly popular. Most things fail the hit test, yet somehow they continue to exist. Why? Because the economics of blockbusters is not the only economics that works. Blockbusters are the exception, not the rule, and yet we see an entire industry through their rarefied air.

For instance, Hollywood economics is not the same as Web video economics, and Madonna's financial expectations are not the same as Clap Your Hands Say Yeah's. But when Congress extends copyright terms for another decade at the request of the Disney lobby, they're playing just to the top of the curve. What's good for Disney is not necessarily what's good for America. Likewise for legislation restricting technologies that allow digital file copying or video transmission. The problem is that the Long Tail doesn't have a lobby, so all too often only the Short Head is heard.

These are some of the other mental traps we fall into because of scarcity thinking:

- Everyone wants to be a star
- Everyone's in it for the money
- If it isn't a hit, it's a miss
- The only success is mass success
- "Direct to video" = bad
- "Self-published" = bad
- "Independent" = "they couldn't get a deal"
- Amateur = amateurish
- Low-selling = low-quality
- If it were good, it would be popular

And finally, there's the notion that "too much choice" is overwhelming, a belief so common and ill-founded that it deserves its own chapter.

10

THE PARADISE OF CHOICE

WE ARE ENTERING AN ERA OF UNPRECEDENTED CHOICE. AND THAT'S A GOOD THING.

In 1978, *Saturday Night Live* featured a skit about the "Scotch Boutique," a store in a trendy mall that sells nothing but Scotch tape in many varieties. Its proprietors puzzle over the absence of customers— they offer so many kinds of tape that surely one should appeal to nearly everyone. And yet no traffic. The skit reveled in the cluelessness of the tape-obsessed store owners. Could anything be more absurd than a Scotch Tape store?

Yet in 2004, a store called "Rice to Riches" actually opened in Manhattan. It sells rice pudding in more than twenty flavors and nothing else. It is reportedly doing well and expanding into a mail-order business. Meanwhile, the White Store in London just sells home furnishing in white. In America, a similar store chain, called the White House, has proven so successful that it's been joined by the Black House. Yesterday's joke is today's reality.

We are in the midst of the biggest explosion of variety in history. You can see it all around you, but sometimes a few numbers make the point even better. There are precisely 19,000 variations of Starbucks coffee, according to the advertising firm OMD. In 2003 alone, 26,893 new food and household products were introduced, including 115 deodorants, 187 breakfast cereals, and 303 women's fragrances, according to Mintil International's Global New Products database.

Back in the 1960s, Chevrolet's Impala sedan accounted for more than 1 million of the 8 million cars sold each year, close to 13 percent of a market that had no more than forty different kinds of cars. Today, in a car market nearly ten times that size, there are more than two hundred and fifty models available (more than one thousand if you count all the variants). Fewer than ten of those sell more than 400,000 units, or one-half percent of the market.

Why has there been such an explosion of variety? Part of the answer is globalization and the hyperefficient supply chains it brings. Merchants in one country can now pull from a truly global range of products. Indeed, the National Bureau of Economic Research estimates that the variety of goods imported to the United States grew more than threefold between 1972 and 2001.

Another part of the answer is demographics. As *Business Week* recently put it:

> In the 1950s and 1960s the country was far more uniform in terms not only of ethnicity—the great Hispanic influx had not yet begun—but also of aspiration. The governing ideal was not merely to keep up with the Joneses, but to be the Joneses—to own the same model of car or dishwasher or lawn mower. As levels of affluence rose markedly in the 1970s and 1980s, status was redefined. We've had a change from "I want to be normal" to "I want to be special." As companies competed to indulge this yearning, they began to elaborate mass production into mass customization.

Finally, there is the Long Tail itself. ITunes offers nearly forty times as much selection as Wal-Mart. Netflix has eighteen times as many DVDs as Blockbuster and would have even more if there were more DVDs to be had. Amazon has almost forty times as many books as a Borders superstore. For the likes of eBay and the average department store, the multiples are impossible to calculate, but no doubt go into the thousands.

TOO MUCH CHOICE?

The overwhelming reality of our online age is that *everything* can be available. Online retailers offer variety on a scale unimaginable even a decade ago—millions of products in every possible variant and combination. But does anyone need this much choice? Can we handle it?

This is the question that is being raised more and more these days as the online cornucopia expands. The conventional view is that more choice is better, because it acknowledges that people are different and allows them to find what's right for them. But in *The Paradox of Choice,* an influential book published in 2004, Barry Schwartz argued that too much choice is not just confusing but is downright oppressive.

He cited a now-famous study of consumer behavior in a supermarket. The details from the paper, "Why Choice Is Demotivating," are as follows.

Researchers from Columbia and Stanford universities set up a table at a specialty food store and offered customers a taste of a range of jams and a $1.00 coupon to use against the purchase of any single jar of jam. Half the time the table held six flavors; half the time it offered twenty-four. The researchers were careful not to include the most common flavors, such as strawberry (so that consumers didn't just pick the usual), and they also avoided weird jams such as lemon curd.

The results were clear: 30 percent of the customers who tasted from the small selection went on to buy a jar, while just 3 percent of those who sampled from the larger selection did. Interestingly, the larger selection attracted more tasters—60 percent compared to 40 percent for the smaller selection. They just didn't buy. The more choice the researchers offered, the less customers bought, and the less satisfied they were with any purchase they did make.

The customers appear to have been confused, even oppressed, by the abundance—why should they have to become an expert on jam varieties to make a selection with confidence? The extra options put them outside their jam-selection comfort zone—strawberry, blueberry, raspberry—and into the more exotic territory of boysenberry and rhubarb. Indecision and buyer's remorse began to cloud the picture. It suddenly felt like too much trouble.

Schwartz describes the conclusion this way:

> As the number of choices keeps growing, negative aspects of having a multitude of options begin to appear. As the number of choices grows further, the negatives escalate until we become overloaded. At this point, choice no longer liberates, but debilitates. It might even be said to tyrannize.

As an antidote to this poison of our modern age, Schwartz recommended that consumers "satisfice," in the jargon of social science, not "maximize." In other words, they'd be happier if they just settled for what was in front of them rather than obsessing over whether something else might be even better. (One wag commented in an Amazon review of *The Paradox of Choice* that he came across twenty books on the same topic and couldn't make up his mind, so he didn't buy any of them.)

I'm skeptical. The alternative to letting people choose is choosing for them. The lessons of a century of retail science (along with the history of Soviet department stores) are that this is not what most consumers want.

Vast choice is not always an unalloyed good, of course. It too often forces us to ask, "Well, what *do* I want?" and introspection doesn't come naturally to all. But the solution is not to limit choice, but to order it so it isn't oppressive. As Schwartz himself notes, "A small-town resident who visits Manhattan is overwhelmed by all that is going on. A New Yorker, thoroughly adapted to the city's hyperstimulation, is oblivious to it."

My suspicions about the jam research that Schwartz cites were first raised when I happened to be in the jam section of my local supermarket. The selection covered more than twenty feet. It started with the usual strawberry and raspberry and then kept going. Here's just a sample: Lemon Curd, Golden Mint, Tomato Cinnamon Clove, Cinnamon Pear, Pear Fig, Pepper Jelly, Huckleberry Raspberry, Peach Apricot, Plum Cherry, Strawberry Rhubarb, Sour Cherry, Fig, Mixed Berry, Black Cherry, Passion Fruit, Pineapple, Pineapple Papaya, Guam Strawberry, Black Currant, Jalapeno Pepper (both Red and Green varieties),

Rhubarb, Rosehip, Mint-Flavored Apple . . . and so on, including Light variants of many of the above.

There were not six varieties or twenty-four; there were more than three hundred. All in all, the store carried forty-two brands, with an average of eight kinds of jam each. I spoke to the manager. In the five years since the original jam study came out, the supermarket had roughly doubled the variety of jams it offers. "There are a lot more available and people seem to like to try the more exotic ones," he told me.

VARIETY IS NOT ENOUGH

This was confusing. Either there was something wrong with the original study or the nation's supermarket owners were remarkably oblivious to what consumers really want. I emailed the authors of the original study to ask them if they had an insight into why the people who should actually know the most about consumer choice in a supermarket were ignoring their conclusions.

As it happens, they did have an answer, which they were about to publish in a new study. In "Knowing What You Like versus Discovering What You Want: The Influence of Choice Making Goals on Decision Satisfaction," Columbia professor Sheena Iyengar and her colleagues conclude:

> Despite the detriments associated with choice overload, consumers want choice and they want a lot of it. The benefits that stem from choice, however, come not from the options themselves, but rather from the process of choosing. By allowing choosers to perceive themselves as volitional agents having successfully constructed their preference and ultimate selection outcomes during the choosing task, the importance of choice is reinstated. Consider the request in *Forbes'* recent "I'm Pro-Choice" article: "Offer customers abundant choices, but also help them search." We now know how.

The solution, they found, is to order the choice in ways that actually help the consumers. Let's turn to an online retailer to see how that might work.

As it happens, Amazon, too, sells jam. Not six kinds, or twenty-four kinds, but more than twelve hundred kinds, thanks to its Marketplace partnerships with a host of small specialty food merchants. Yet there is a huge difference between the presentation of variety in the physical world and online.

In a bricks-and-mortar store, products sit on the shelf where they have been placed. If a consumer doesn't know what he or she wants, the only guide is whatever marketing material may be printed on the package, and the rough assumption that the product offered in the greatest volume is probably the most popular.

Online, however, the consumer has a lot more help. There are a nearly infinite number of techniques to tap the latent information in a marketplace and make that selection process easier. You can sort by price, by ratings, by date, and by genre. You can read customer reviews. You can compare prices across products and, if you want, head off to Google to find out as much about the product as you can imagine. Recommendations suggest products that "people like you" have been buying, and surprisingly enough, they're often on-target. Even if you know nothing about the category, ranking best-sellers will reveal the most popular choice, which both makes selection easier and also tends to minimize post-sale regret. After all, if everyone else picked a given product, it can't be that bad.

The problem with the jam experiment is that it was disordered; all the jams were shown simultaneously and to guide them the customers had only their existing knowledge of jam or whatever was written on the labels. That's the problem on the supermarket shelf, too. All you have to go on is your domain expertise, whatever brand information has been lodged in your brain by experience or advertising, and the marketing messages of the packaging and shelf placement.

Most of the information that online retailers use to order their massive variety and make choice easy—popularity, comparative prices, reviews—is available to supermarket owners, too. But they typically don't share it with you, the customer. That's because there's no good way to do it, short of a mini-screen on each shelf. The paradox of choice is simply an artifact of the limitations of the physical world, where the information necessary to make an informed choice is lost.

The conventional wisdom was right: More choice really is better. But now we know that variety alone is not enough; we also need information *about* that variety and what other consumers before us have done with the same choices. Google, with its seemingly omniscient ability to order the infinite chaos of the Web so that what we want comes out on top, shows the way. The paradox of choice turned out to be more about the poverty of help in making that choice than a rejection of plenty. Order it wrong and choice is oppressive; order it right and it's liberating.

Virginia Postrel, a writer on the economics of variety, explains why so much academic research in choice seems to contradict the lessons from decades of real-world business experience:

> For good scientific reasons, psychology experiments systematically screen out the habits and business practices that make real-life choices, especially shopping decisions, manageable. This is because the experiments are designed to understand the mind, not the market . . . In reality people don't dislike choice, even overwhelming choice. They have mixed feelings about it. And in the real world, especially the real marketplace, they often have help making decisions.

Writing in her *New York Times* column, Postrel points out that real estate agents, financial planners, search engines, and the recommendations services at Amazon all do the same thing. "Each knows something about us and something about what's valuable. They don't just reduce the number of options. They do so intelligently, with an eye to what we're most likely to want. They help us be ourselves."

Hence the rise of wedding planners, a profession that barely existed twenty years ago. "As the constraints of tradition have loosened and the bridal market has produced more alternatives for everything from invitations to limousines, weddings have gotten more complex and personalized," Postrel explains. Membership in the Association of Bridal Consultants had grown to 4,000 in 2004, from 27 in 1981.

Adds John Hagel, a management consultant: "The more choice we have the more we have to decide what it is we really want. The more we reflect on what we really want, the more involved we get in the creation of the goods we buy and use [via customization]. The more we participate in the creation of products and services, the more choices we end up creating for ourselves."

THE ECONOMICS OF VARIETY

Does more choice encourage consumers to buy more? Anecdotally, we all know of instances where increased variety and better ways to find things encouraged people to consume more. I know, for instance, that Napster reawakened my interest in exploring new music, a passion that continues more easily (and legally) with Rhapsody, which has probably doubled my music spending. And my family certainly watches more DVDs thanks to Netflix.

The multitude of white-earbud-wearing New Yorkers are surely listening to more music than they were before the iPod, extending the effect created by the Walkman a generation before. But are they *buying* more music, too? The hard numbers are, unfortunately, inconclusive. As of early 2006, Apple had sold 42 million iPods and 1 billion tracks on iTunes, for an average of twenty-four tracks per iPod (an average of less than two CDs' worth) over the nearly four years the iTunes music store had been in business. That is not impressive.

CD sales are down nearly 20 percent since the launch of the iPod. So how are consumers filling their capacious portable hard drives and flash memory chips? Exactly as you'd expect: ripping CDs from friends, downloading them for free from peer-to-peer services (whose traffic continues to rise, despite occasional legal crackdowns), and trading them across dorm LANs on college campuses.

Indeed, although there is a general presumption that more availability leads to more sales, there is precious little statistical work that proves this is the case, especially for large numbers of products. The small-number consumer psychology work, however, does suggest that when the choice is meaningful, more is better—it simply improves the odds you'll find what you want, or at least something that strikes your fancy.

There are a few studies that look at examples such as the effect of increasing the number of yogurt flavors on offer by one or two, which does help sales. One of the better-known bits of "more is better" research is a paper entitled "The Lure of Choice," which analyzes bank, nightclub, and casino experiments to show that consumers picked options more often when they were accompanied by many other choices. Consumers preferred movie theaters with more screens, and casinos with more tables; the more options they were given, the lower their perceived risk of being stuck with something they didn't want.

Likewise, Malcolm Gladwell has highlighted the case study of would-be spaghetti sauce competitors who learned not to out-Ragú Ragú in making the platonic ideal sauce, but to instead celebrate diversity—chunky, homemade, spicy—and expand the market through multiple niche sauces and market segmentation. Partly because of this introduction of more variety, which pushed buttons consumers didn't even know they had, spaghetti sauce is now one of the top six growth categories in the dressing and sauce market.

Francis Hamit, a writer on publishing topics, explains that the link between variety and the volume of consumption is best seen as a trade-off, as found in basic economics:

> One of the classic examples was the chart in my old Economics textbook that demonstrated the trade-off between long-range bombers and new school buildings. There the constraint was money. Here, the constraint is time. It takes time to find the items you want, and most people will buy what they are looking for the first place they find it rather than look for a lesser price.
>
> This is why retail stores place all those little items next to the cash register. Availability and convenience equals more sales. For that matter, so-called "convenience stores" like 7/11 make most of their money from milk, bread, beer, and soft drinks, which they sell for far more than the price at the local supermarket. What is sold is not so much the product as the fact that it is available, right now.

Digital distribution has two effects on this model. It widens the field of possible customers and shortens the search time. Over time, this should increase sales and grow the overall market. As we saw in Chapter 8, longer tails can be thicker, too.

11

NICHE CULTURE

WHAT'S IT LIKE TO LIVE IN A LONG TAIL WORLD?

In the early 1980s, in the dark days at the very end of disco, a proto–Long Tail music culture emerged in a former industrial strip in Chicago. A half decade after the release of *Saturday Night Fever,* the craven commoditization of clap tracks and R&B had reached the end of its run and consumers were rebelling. They'd had enough of the bland and formulaic output of a music industry trying to clone its previous hits. People attending a baseball game in Chicago's Comiskey Park were invited to bring all their unwanted disco records, and after the game they tossed the vinyl refuse into a massive bonfire to the chant of "Disco Sucks."

But in a nightclub called the Warehouse, the resident DJ, Frankie Knuckles, was doing something new. He was wildly remixing, mashing up different genres of music into something brand-new. Knuckles took old disco classics, new Eurobeat pop and synthesized beats, including those produced with then-new drum machines, and turned them into a frantic, high-energy amalgamation of recycled soul. Taking its name from the club, this new sound became known as house music.

In *The History of House Sound of Chicago,* Stuart Cosgrove describes the scene:

Frankie is more than a DJ. He's an architect of sound who has taken the art of mixing to new heights. Regulars at the Warehouse remember it as the most atmospheric place in Chicago, the pioneering nerve-center of a thriving dance music scene where old Philly classics by Harold Melvin, Billy Paul and The O'Jays were mixed with upfront disco hits like Martin Circus' "Disco Circus" and imported European pop music by synthesizer groups like Kraftwerk and Telex.

The sound spread to another Chicago club called the MusicBox, where DJ Ron Hardy took it up several notches with massive volume and a frenetic pace, something, it was said, that was inspired by his heroin use. Then, eventually, the sound traveled to the north of England, where house became the foundation of what would later emerge as the Rave scene.

What was notable about the rise of house was that it was both a reaction to the bankruptcy of blockbuster culture and a vibrant culture of its own. DJs and clubs created a music industry that was radically different from pop music. Clubbing is really about surfing the Long Tail of dance music, and this ecosystem has seen the evolution of new models of innovation around it.

In order to understand why, let's chart the rise of house music. Its origins are now attributed to legendary DJs like Larry Levan, who rose to prominence as the resident DJ of New York's Paradise Garage. In the late seventies, DJs such as Levan and David Mancuso began stringing records together in the now-familiar DJ sets that clubbers dance to until the sun comes up.

What gave rise to these superstar DJs? Many of the same sort of forces that are at work today. It started with the spread of affordable technology, from mixing decks to multitrack recorders. That's the first force of the Long Tail, the democratization of the tools of production. Cheap production technology reduced the cost of studio time; and cheap mastering technology made it possible for hundreds of small indie record labels to economically press and market records. Some of the best known of these house labels, such as West End Records, pressed hundreds of records in a few short years.

The economic effect of this was an explosion of records, which created a vacuum of information about those records—and an opportunity for someone to act as a filter to help people find these records. But such a filter couldn't be effective without access to these underground records in the first place, which required distribution channels with a low barrier to entry. Which is exactly what clubs and warehouse parties offered, thus providing the necessary second force—democratized distribution.

Where mass-media radio stations are dominated by one-way information flows in the form of record-label marketing—labels push the albums they think will be hits and only later find out if they're right—clubs close the feedback loop instantly and immediately. If a DJ plays tracks that clubgoers don't value, their dissatisfaction is apparent—they don't dance. Clubgoers vote instantly with their feet, relaying their decentralized expectation and preference info to the DJ in aggregate. DJs surf the Long Tail of music and recommend the content their audience is most likely to gain satisfaction from—and dance to.

As production and mastering costs continued to drop, house music exploded and fragmented into hyperspecialized genres such as deep house, funky house, and dub house. And as it did, a new mechanism was necessary for DJs to be able to navigate a consumption landscape of bewildering complexity.

This mechanism is paradoxical when viewed from the outside. For many years, house producers have released records under a variety of aliases. Why use aliases if their goal is to sell records? After all, varieties of aliases are a kind of anti-branding, creating information clutter that can confuse the market.

But for DJs, the important information is in the label, not the track. Indie record labels are like tags, providing a clue about what hyperspecialized microgenre a track is likely to be. Labels are a way to allow DJs to cheaply and efficiently find tracks that are likely to satisfy their audience's expectations. In this sense, labels lay the infrastructure for the later aggregation of decentralized information that takes place on the dance floor.

In fact, at a certain point DJ names ceased to matter, since labels provided most of the valuable information. For example, the seminal Berlin duo of Moritz Von Oswald and Mark Ernestus, better known as Basic Channel, release records with their collaborators under a variety of labels. The Burial Mix label is for deep, dark dub with vocals; the M label is for minimal, instrumental, dub house; Rhythm & Sound is for abstract dub with strong reggae influences; and the Chain Reaction label is for instrumental abstract electronica with a strong house influence.

Each of these labels features records by a number of different artists. Multiply this by a factor of a thousand, and you begin to understand just how complex the consumption landscape of house music has become—and why the need for labels as tags arose. Since DJs can use the information embedded in the label itself, they don't have to spend time listening to each and every project Oswald and Ernestus are involved with—they can simply focus on the labels that are most relevant to their audiences. They can cheaply and efficiently surf the Long Tail of house music.

House music producers also rely on open-access product strategies. In contrast to record labels that spend more and more time on litigation to enforce copyright infringement, house music producers (and underground producers in general) have long realized that opening up their goods to being remixed and tweaked has beneficial economic consequences.

A house record that does well often attracts remixes from other producers; it becomes a kind of platform. Because these remixes are usually hyperspecialized for different microgenres, they're complements to the original track. As the number of complements increases, the value of the platform track snowballs. This snowball effect is another mechanism by which DJs-as-aggregators can efficiently navigate the Long Tail of music, quickly and easily discovering which tracks are snowballs within their respective niches.

FROM "OR" CULTURE TO "AND" CULTURE

The Long Tail is nothing more than infinite choice. Abundant, cheap distribution means abundant, cheap, and unlimited variety—and that means the audience tends to distribute as widely as the choice. From the mainstream media and entertainment industry perspective, this looks like a battle between traditional media and the Internet. But the problem is that once people shift their attention online, they don't just go from one media outlet to another—they simply scatter. Infinite choice equals ultimate fragmentation.

Writing in *Corante,* Vin Crosbie, a media analyst, explains why:

> Each individual listener, viewer, or reader is, and has always been, a unique mix of *generic* interests and *specific* interests. Although many of these individuals might share some generic interests, such as the weather, most, if not all of them, have very different specific interests. And each individual is a truly unique mix of generic and specific interests. Until about 30 years ago, the average American hadn't access to any medium that could satisfy each of their specific interests. All they had was the mass medium, which could *somewhat successfully* satisfy many of their generic (i.e., *"mass"*) interests.
>
> Then media technologies evolved in ways that started to satisfy their specific interests. During the 1970s, improvements in offset lithography led to a bloom of specialty magazines; no longer were there a dozen or two magazines on newsstands, but hundreds, most about only *specific* topics. Proliferations of, first, analog cable television systems during the 1980s, then digital ones during the late 1990s, increased the average American's number of accessible TV stations from four to hundreds, mostly *specialty* channels (Home & Garden TV, the Golf Channel, the Military Channel, etc.). Then the Internet became publicly accessible during the 1990s and the average individual quickly had access to *millions* of websites, most of those sites about *very specific* topics.
>
> The result is that more and more individuals, who had been using only the (*generic*) mass medium because that's all they had, have gravitated to these specialty publications, channels, or websites rather than continue to use only mass medium publications, channels, or websites. More and more use the mass medium less and less. And more and more will soon be most. The individuals haven't changed; they've always been fragmented. What's changing is their media habits. They're now simply satisfying the fragmented interests that they've always had. There are as many fragments as there are individuals. Always have been and always will be.

This shift from the generic to the specific doesn't mean the end of the existing power structure or a wholesale shift to an all-amateur, laptop culture. Instead, it's simply a rebalancing of the equation, an evolution from an "Or" era of hits *or* niches (mainstream culture vs. subcultures) to an "And" era. Today, our culture is increasingly a mix of head *and* tail, hits *and* niches, institutions *and* individuals, professionals *and* amateurs. Mass culture will not fall, it will simply get less mass. And niche culture will get less obscure.

We're already seeing the effects in music. In the CD world, classical music makes up about 6 percent of sales, which is too little to get more than a single rack at Wal-Mart. But on iTunes, where there's room for far more variety, it makes up 12 percent of all sales. Documentaries rarely make it into theaters, but they're one of the most popular categories on Netflix, which accounted for nearly half the U.S. business for such documentaries as *Capturing the Friedmans* and *Murderball*.

THE RISE OF MASSIVELY PARALLEL CULTURE

In July 2005, Anil Dash, an executive at the blog technology company SixApart, "hacked" the *New York Times* by wearing a T-shirt that read "GOATSE" in a photo shoot for an otherwise innocuous article about how hard it is to change what Google says about you. Marveling over his mad skilz, I was amazed to find that almost none of my staff (and obviously no *New York Times* editors) knew what GOATSE refers to. (I am compelled to disclose that it's a retina-scarring shock picture that online pranksters try to get noobs to click on by claiming it's a link to something irresistible, like a picture of Natalie Portman. It's not so much pornographic as exceedingly gross.) Yet many of my geek friends drop a reference to it into their writing as a sort of shared-context joke.

I thought everyone knew about GOATSE, but I was wrong. Indeed, it turned out that only some of the people I knew online did. I hadn't realized that I was part of a subcultural tribe, but apparently I was. And knowing about GOATSE appears to be one of its secret membership codes, which is what Anil was demonstrating when he cheekily wore the word on his T-shirt in the *Times* shoot.

I decided to test other cultural touchstones to see if they were as widely held as I had thought. I started by running a few other clichés from my little online world past real-world friends: "All Your Base Are Belong To Us"; "More Cowbell!"; "I for one welcome our new [fill in the blank] overlords," and so on. Turns out that these snippets of culture that I thought were ubiquitous are actually pretty obscure, even in my own office. When I took an informal poll at a public relations conference at which I was speaking, I found that only about 10 percent of the audience had heard of any of them—and for each phrase it was a *different* 10 percent.

If you check out the Wikipedia entry for Internet phenomena you'll find hundreds of those kinds of viral memes. Here are ten of the most famous ones (although some are a bit dated now). How many have you heard of?

- Ellen Feiss
- The Star Wars Kid
- Dancing baby
- Bert is Evil
- Bonzai Kitten
- Tourist Guy
- MC Hawking
- 1337
- Subservient Chicken
- First post

What does this show? It shows that my tribe is not always your tribe, even if we work together, play together, and otherwise live in the same world. Same bed, different dreams.

The same Long Tail forces and technologies that are leading to an explosion of variety and abundant choice in the content we consume are also tending to lead us into tribal eddies. When mass culture breaks apart, it doesn't re-form into a different mass. Instead, it turns into millions of microcultures, which coexist and interact in a baffling array of ways.

As a result, we can now treat culture not as one big blanket, but as the superposition of many interwoven threads, each of which is individually addressable and connects different groups of people simultaneously.

In short, we're seeing a shift from mass culture to *massively parallel culture*. Whether we think of it this way or not, each of us belongs to many different tribes simultaneously, often overlapping (geek culture and LEGO), often not (tennis and punk-funk). We share some interests with our colleagues and some with our families, but not all of our interests. Increasingly, we have other people to share them with, people we have never met or even think of as individuals (e.g., blog authors or playlist creators).

Every one of us—no matter how mainstream we might think we are—actually goes super-niche in some part of our lives. For instance, I'm pretty mainstream in my movies, less mainstream in my music, and incredibly niche in my reading, which seems to consist mostly of network economics these days (blame this book). Moreover, where we do go niche, we often follow it much farther than we might otherwise go, letting our enthusiasm take us deep into wine culture or vintage jewelry—because, thanks to abundant choice, we now can.

Virginia Postrel observed that the variety boom is nothing more than a reflection of the diversity inherent in any population distribution:

> Every aspect of human identity, from size, shape, and color to sexual proclivities and intellectual gifts, comes in a wide range. Most of us cluster somewhere in the middle of most statistical distributions. But there are lots of bell curves, and pretty much everyone is on a tail of at least one of them. We may collect strange memorabilia or read esoteric books, hold unusual religious beliefs or wear odd-sized shoes, suffer rare diseases or enjoy obscure movies.

This has always been true, but it's only now something we can act on. The resulting rise of niche culture will reshape the social landscape. People are re-forming into thousands of cultural *tribes of interest,* connected less by geographic proximity and workplace chatter than by shared interests. In other words, we're leaving the watercooler era, when most of us listened, watched, and read from the same, relatively small pool of mostly hit content. And we're entering the micro-culture era, when we're all into different things.

In 1958, Raymond Williams, the Marxist sociologist, wrote in *Culture and Society*: "There are no masses; there are only ways of seeing people as masses." He was more right than he knew.

IF THE NEWS FITS . . .

What will this niche culture look like? We can observe the changing media for clues. News was the first industry to really feel the impact of the Internet, and we've now had an entire generation grow up with the expectation of being able to have on-demand news on any subject at any time for free. This may be good for news junkies, but it's been hell on the news business. The decline of newspapers, which are down more than a third in circulation from their mid-eighties peak, is the most concrete evidence of the disruptive effect the Long Tail can have on entrenched industries.

Once, the power of newspapers came from their command over their tools of production. As the saying went, "Never pick a fight with someone who buys ink by the barrel." But starting in the early 1990s, news started coming on screens, not just smudgy pages. And suddenly anyone with a laptop and an Internet connection had the power of the press.

Initially, the first to take advantage of this were newspapers and other traditional media companies themselves. But as more and more people built first home pages and then blogs, it became less and less clear what the distinction was between professional journalism and amateur reportage. In their own area of interest, the bloggers often know as much as if not more than the journalists, they can write as well, and they are much faster. Sometimes, because they are partici-pants, not just observers, they even have better access to information than the journalists.

Richard Posner, the eminent judge and legal scholar, thinks this is a once-in-a-lifetime game-changer. Writing in a *New York Times* book review (perhaps for irony's sake), he observed that with virtually no costs, a blogger can target a segment of the reading public much narrower than a newspaper or a television news channel could possibly aim for. In effect, blogs pick off the mainstream media's customers one by one by being niche where their old-media precursors are mass:

> Bloggers can specialize in particular topics to an extent that few journalists employed by media companies can, since the more that journalists specialized, the more of them the company would have to hire in order to be able to cover all bases. A newspaper will not hire a journalist for his knowledge of old typewriters, but plenty of people in the blogosphere have that esoteric knowledge, and it was they who brought down Dan Rather.
>
> What really sticks in the craw of conventional journalists is that although individual blogs have no warrant of accuracy, the blogosphere as a whole has a better error-correction machinery than the conventional media do. The rapidity with which vast masses of information are pooled and sifted leaves the conventional media in the dust. Not only are there millions of blogs, and thousands of bloggers who specialize, but, what is more, readers post comments that augment the blogs, and the information in those comments, as in the blogs themselves, zips around blogland at the speed of electronic transmission.
>
> The blogosphere has more checks and balances than the conventional media; only they are different. The model is Friedrich Hayek's classic analysis of how the economic market pools enormous quantities of information efficiently despite its decentralized character, its lack of a master coordinator or regulator, and the very limited knowledge possessed by each of its participants. In effect, the blogosphere is a collective enterprise—not 12 million separate enterprises, but one enterprise with 12 million reporters, feature writers and editorialists, yet with almost no costs. It's as if The Associated Press or Reuters had millions of reporters, many of them experts, all working with no salary for free newspapers that carried no advertising.

To see this at work, consider this Technorati chart of popularity (measured by incoming links) of Web sites, including both blogs and mainstream media, or "MSM" in blog parlance:

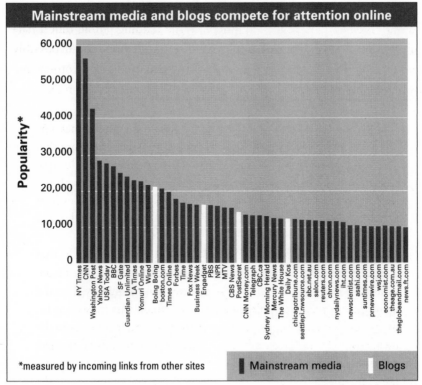

Mainstream media and blogs compete for attention online

*measured by incoming links from other sites   ▌Mainstream media   ▌Blogs

Source: Technorati

Consider just one of those white lines, Daily Kos (it's the fourth in). This is a liberal politics site run essentially solo by Markos Moulitsas Zúniga, an activist in Berkeley. It gets more incoming links than the *Chicago Tribune* and nearly a million page views a day. Or go a bit farther down the curve (to rank 65, which is slightly off the page here) to find Instapundit. This is the personal blog of Glenn Reynolds, a forty-five-year-old University of Tennessee law professor who posts on various topics of interest, from libertarian politics to nanotechnology, during his breaks at work. Because he is smart, opinionated, and fast, he is popular. And because he is popular, he has huge influence. A link from him tends to generate an "Insta-lanche" of traffic to the favored site, often exceeding that from all but the largest mainstream media sites. He gets more incoming links than *Sports Illustrated*.

Each of these two bloggers has a higher "link authority" than most of America's newspapers. This is, of course, an unfair comparison, since the newspapers still do most of their business via their print editions. But if you're in the newspaper business, the chart above raises some troubling questions about the future of the news business in a Long Tail world.

In *Letters to a Young Contrarian,* Christopher Hitchens writes that he wakes up every morning and checks his vital signs by grabbing the front page of the *New York Times*: "'All the News That's Fit to Print,' it says. It's been saying that for decades, day in and day out. I imagine that most readers of the canonical sheet have long ceased to notice the bannered and flaunted symbol of its mental furniture. I myself check every day to make sure that it still irritates me. If I can still exclaim, under my breath, *why* do they insult me and *what* do they take me for and what *the hell* is it supposed to mean unless it's as obviously complacent and conceited and censorious as it seems to be, then at least I know that I still have a pulse."

The *Times* slogan dates to the late nineteenth century. In 1897 Adolph Ochs, the paper's new owner, coined the phrase as a jab at competing papers in New York City that were at the time known for yellow journalism. Its original meaning now lost, today the tagline just sounds arrogant and superior.

Was there ever a time when that slogan was true? Probably not, and it certainly isn't today. As Jerry Seinfeld quips, "It's amazing that the amount of news that happens in the world every day always just exactly fits the newspaper."

The reality, slogan aside, is that the *New York Times* now competes not only with other New York City newspapers and newspapers elsewhere, but also with the collective wisdom and information of everyone online. Authority is in the eye of the beholder; it is not innate to the institution itself. It is a credit to the *Times* journalists and editors that they do so well, continuing to break news and set the agenda, despite this. But news and information is clearly no longer the exclusive domain of professionals.

With an estimated 15 million bloggers out there, the odds that a few will have something important and insightful to say are good and getting better. And as our filters improve, the odds that we'll see them are getting better, too. From a mainstream media perspective, this is simply more competition, whatever the source. And some audiences will prefer it. Like it or not, fragmentation is inevitable.

A MILLION LITTLE PIECES

Is a fragmented culture a better or worse culture? Many believe that mass culture serves as a sort of social glue, keeping society together. But if we're now all off doing our own thing, is there still a common culture? Are our interests still aligned with those of our neighbors?

In his book *Republic.com*, University of Chicago law professor Cass Sunstein argues that the risks are real—online culture is indeed encouraging group polarization: "As the customization of our communications universe increases, society is in danger of fragmenting, shared communities in danger of dissolving." He evokes the famous *Daily Me*, the ultimate personalized newspaper hypothesized by Nicholas Negroponte of MIT's Media Lab. To Sunstein, a world where we are all reading our own *Daily Me* is one where "you need not come across topics and views that you have not sought out. Without any difficulty, you are able to see exactly what you want to see, no more and no less."

Christine Rosen, a senior fellow at the Ethics and Public Policy Center, shares Sunstein's concerns. In an essay in *The New Atlantis*, she writes:

> If these technologies facilitate polarization in politics, what influence are they exerting over art, literature, and music? In our haste to find the quickest, most convenient, and most easily individualized way of getting what we want, are we creating eclectic personal theaters or sophisticated echo chambers? Are we promoting a creative individualism or a narrow individualism? An expansion of choices or a deadening of taste?

The effect of these technologies, Rosen argues, is the rise of "egocasting," the thoroughly individual and extremely narrow pursuit of one's personal taste. TiVos, iPods, and narrowcast content of all sorts allow us to construct our own cultural narrative. And that, she says, is a bad thing:

> By giving us the illusion of perfect control, these technologies risk making us incapable of ever being surprised. They encourage not the cultivation of taste, but the numbing repetition of fetish. In thrall to our own little technologically constructed worlds, we are, ironically, finding it increasingly difficult to appreciate genuine individuality.

Is Rosen right? I suspect not; in fact, it appears to me to be just the opposite. A world of niches is indeed a world of abundant choice, but powerful guides in the form of recommendations and other filters have emerged to encourage more exploration, not less. We load our iPods with music we get from our friends, and our TiVos ceaselessly suggest new shows we might like based on the watching patterns of others. The evidence from Netflix suggests that when given the ability to pick any movie from a selection of tens of thousands, customers don't just dive into the World War II documentary niche and never come out. Instead, they become wildly catholic in their taste, rediscovering the classics one month and going on a sci-fi bender the next.

Meanwhile, the blogosphere is the greatest vector for new voices ever created. The convention of linking to ideas and information of merit, wherever they come from, be it professional or amateur, is a powerful force of diversity. The main risk with blogs is the distraction of too many leads to pursue, not too few. Anyone who is reading online and not enlarging their cultural perspective has either found some remarkably barren corner of the blog world or needs a refresher course in the meaning of hyperlinks.

Since nothing on the Web is authoritative, it's up to you to consult enough sources so that you can make up your own mind. This is the end of spoon-fed orthodoxy and infallible institutions, and the rise of messy mosaics of information that require—and reward—investigation. The sixties told us to question authority, but they didn't provide us with the tools to do so. Now we have those tools. The question today is how best to use them without becoming overwhelmed by uncertainty.

Fundamentally, a society that asks questions and has the power to answer them is a healthier society than one that simply accepts what it's told from a narrow range of experts and institutions. If professional affiliation is no longer a proxy for authority, we need to develop our own gauges of quality. This encourages us to think for ourselves. Wikipedia is a starting point for exploring a topic, not the last word.

It's the end of the couch potato era. When you think about it, in the peak of the network TV age, we may all have been watching the same things, but we were all too often watching them by ourselves— "bowling alone" in prime time. Online today we're doing different things, but we are more likely to encounter other individuals, either by reading their writings, chatting live, or just following their example. What we've lost in common culture we've made up in our increased exposure to other people.

Today we're not so much fragmenting as we are re-forming along different dimensions. These days our watercoolers are increasingly virtual; there are many different ones; and the people who gather around them are self-selected. Rather than being loosely connected with people thanks to superficial mass-cultural overlaps, we have the ability to be more strongly tied to just as many if not more people with a shared affinity for niche culture.

Although the decline of mainstream cultural institutions may result in some people turning to echo chambers of like-minded views, I suspect that over time the power of human curiosity combined with near-infinite access to information will tend to make most people more open-minded, not less.

As much as the blockbuster era seems like the natural state of things, it is, as we've seen, mostly an artifact of late-twentieth-century broadcast technologies. Before then most culture was local; in the future it will be affinity-based and massively parallel. Mass culture may fade, but common culture will not. We will still share our culture with others, but not with everyone.

12

THE INFINITE SCREEN

VIDEO AFTER TELEVISION

"TV is not vulgar and prurient and dumb because the people who compose the audience are vulgar and dumb. Television is the way it is simply because people tend to be extremely similar in their vulgar and prurient and dumb interests and wildly different in their refined and aesthetic and noble interests."

—*David Foster Wallace*

Nobody thought the future of television would look like this. On January 19, 2006, Google unveiled Google Video, the ultimate Long Tail marketplace of the moving image. Apple's iTunes' polished video store may have had far more network TV content, but Google let anyone upload their videos for free and set their own price, right down to nothing.

The result was predictably messy, a near-random collection of everything from banned commercials to baby videos. But it was also a glimpse into a world of infinite variety, where commercial and amateur video content compete head to head . . . and the amateurs often win.

On the top half of the Google Video page were thumbnails of commercial content: *CSI, Star Trek,* basketball games, television classics such as *The Twilight Zone,* and *Charlie Rose* at $0.99 an episode. Beneath those were the most popular free videos: short clips of dumb dogs, funny commercials, and an octopus eating a shark (which was amazing, by the way). And below that was "Random": snowboarding wipeouts, Jon Stewart recorded on someone's TiVo, and people playing video games.

Broadcast networks can make Google Video a storefront for their archives, or just a place to host teasers of upcoming shows. It's already becoming a resource for the Indian diaspora, which can now find Hindi shows that are only broadcast on the subcontinent (legality: suspect). And indie filmmakers can now find out if anyone wants to pay $12 (or $3 for a day pass) to watch their masterpieces. Not having distribution is no longer an excuse for obscurity.

Meanwhile Microsoft, Yahoo!, AOL, and a host of others have started their own video marketplaces. The biggest of these sites now rival mainstream TV. Yahoo!'s music video viewership would put it between MTV and VH1 in audience share. More people watch the most popular Jon Stewart segments online than see them live. Popular online video shows, such as Tiki Bar TV, are routinely watched by several hundred thousand people a day, which puts their viewership on a par with good-sized cable TV shows.

MSNBC's *The Abrams Report*, with a multimillion-dollar budget and a crew of dozens, was at the time of this writing watched by an average of 215,000 homes per day. Rocketboom, a Jon Stewart–like comedy news program created online by exactly two people for the cost of some videotapes, two lights, and a cardboard map, was watched by 200,000 homes per day over the same period. Now it's selling advertising and got $40,000 for the five thirty-second spots in its first week. Not quite as high as broadcast TV revenues, perhaps, but the networks would kill for those margins.

This day has been predicted for a decade, but it took the mainstreaming of broadband for it to finally arrive. A generation that grew up online and developed its media consumption habits in the bandwidth paradise of American university dorm rooms is now totally comfortable watching video on a computer screen. Increasingly, though, they don't have to. The home networking boom is connecting broadband to the living room, and network TiVos, other digital video recorders, and broadband-connect video-game consoles such as the Xbox 360 are bringing online content to ordinary TVs.

It's easy to dismiss the random junk on Google Video as little threat to *The Sopranos*. After all, distribution is not the only barrier to entering TV: production costs are a hurdle, too. It takes more than a digital video camera to produce *CSI,* and only the economics of mainstream media can support elaborate dramas such as *Lost*. But there is an audience for less-produced fare that can be made at a fraction of the cost of traditional TV programming. Don't just think *America's Funniest Home Videos*, writ large. Think local sports and narrow interests; cool commercials you choose to watch and presentations from conferences you wish you could have attended.

Blogger Thomas Hawk explains:

> If today I watch *CSI Miami*, but on my weekends go out hang gliding and am a huge hang gliding fan, when the California hang gliding championships end up being broadcast through a microcontent platform I will end up watching that instead of *CSI*.
>
> If today I watch some network television but even more than my network television I love reading author Hunter S. Thompson, and my microcontent platform brings me a talk by Hunter S. Thompson from the University of Wyoming I will end up watching that instead of *CSI*.
>
> If I am 16 and my favorite band is not what hits the charts but rather the latest skate punk music thing, then the custom skate punk music shows that can easily be created and delivered to my microcontent platform will be much more interesting to me than *American Idol*.

Today, TV viewership of eighteen- to thirty-four-year-old males, the most coveted demographic for advertisers, has peaked and is beginning to decline, as the more interactive charms of Internet and video games win the competition for eyeballs. Overall TV viewership is at all-time highs, so it's not panic time in broadcast land yet. But the day when the Internet becomes a real rival to TV appears near. The question is what to do about it.

A TAIL FOR THE TAKING

As your thumb clicks through your several hundred digital cable channels, TV may appear anything but shackled. Yet it is. What seems like everything imaginable is instead a very thin slice of the video world. The existing channel structure mostly rewards focused programming with enough depth to fill a 24/7 window every day of the year. So the DIY channel and History Channel en Español now pass muster, but the Halo 2 Physics Hacks channel or the Cool Robots channel does not. An acceptable loss, you say? How about last year's great season of *Project Runway* on Bravo, long ago overwritten by your DVR to save space, or never recorded in the first place?

Today both the channel-centric reality and the ephemeral nature of TV are artifacts of the distribution bottleneck of cable broadcast. TV is still in the era of limited shelf space, while the lesson of the Long Tail is that more is almost always better. The growth of cable capacity over the past decade pales next to the growth in video creation over the same period and in the size of the potential microaudiences for anything and everything. TiVo may have helped by at least taking the tyranny of time out of the equation, but we are nowhere near the iTunes model of being able to download everything ever made, anytime.

Of all the traditional media industries, television is now the industry with the greatest potential to be transformed by Long Tail forces. Here's why:

- TV produces more content than any other media and entertainment industry. There are an estimated 31 million hours of original television content produced each year. Although that isn't as much as radio, most radio is either chat or recorded music that is available elsewhere, so it's not in the same league. In addition, 115 million digital videotapes are sold each year for personal camcorders. The amount of video produced each year is staggering, but . . .

- Only a tiny fraction of it is available to you. First, the average American household now gets one hundred channels of TV. While that sounds like a lot—it's 876,000 hours of video broadcast to the average home each year—that's still less than 10 percent of the video that's broadcast in the United States (when you include the 400-plus national channels available on high-capacity satellite and digital networks, and all the local programming across the country). Making matters much worse, unless that home has a DVR (and only about 15 percent of U.S. households do) and someone is spending a good chunk of their free time scouring listings to program it, they're going to miss virtually all of that TV. Once TV is missed, it's usually gone. Only a tiny fraction of shows are syndicated, and an even smaller fraction make it to DVD.

- Thus the ratio of produced content to available content is higher than in any other industry. Other industries may produce more content—print, for instance—but it's far more available (see Google). Only television treats its premium content as disposable. True, a lot of it actually is. But not all, and not as much as is effectively thrown away after a brief moment in the sun.

There is no shortage of smart people thinking about how TV can find its way out of its corner. But it's not easy. For starters, most of the networks are content *renters,* not content owners. This means that the archives are often not theirs to capitalize on.

Even for those who do own the content, releasing video in ways not anticipated at the original time of broadcast still can be remarkably difficult. Rights are a total hairball, made even more complicated by exclusive regional distribution deals (which conflict with the Internet's global nature) and syndication options. And then there's the music in the video, which is even worse. Want to know why you can't watch old *WKRP in Cincinnati* episodes on DVD? Because the sitcom was based in a radio station, which had loads of classic rock playing in the background. It's too expensive and difficult to license the music that was used in the show. (Indeed, that show is considered one of the hardest popular TV shows of all to clear; it's the lead standard against which all other clearance challenges are considered.) Other classic shows, such as *Married . . . with Children,* are released to DVD with different music than in their broadcast incarnations, annoying fans.

TV OUTSIDE THE BOX

But there is another class of video, one designed from the start to be distributed on the Internet. This sort of video—the product of the spread of digital camcorders and desktop animation tools—has few such legal encumbrances. Created from scratch to be streamed for free online, it's already proving to be the richest, most entrepreneurial source of programming for a post-broadcast age.

Consider Barrio305, a Web-only television service for "reggaeton" music videos, interviews, and urban Latin culture. "Think MTV . . . but in Spanglish," says its cofounder, Noah Otalvaro. Each day it streams about 50,000 minutes of video to 5,000 unique users. That's tiny by television standards (reggaeton isn't for everyone), but what's interesting is how it could grow.

The site is built on a video distribution "platform" created by Brightcove. What that means is that Otalvaro and his brothers don't have to figure out a way to stream the video to their users; they just publish the video like a blog post and Brightcove takes care of the distribution. Even better, if other sites want to use Barrio305's content, they can simply copy some HTML code onto their pages and they, too, will have streaming video. Notably, Barrio305 gets the ad revenues from the greater viewership.

Jeremy Allaire, Brightcove's founder, describes the effect:

> Just as consumers flocked to the Internet despite the hiccups of dial-up modems and clunky Web pages, they will flock to this new medium that empowers them in ways that no single company or industry can replicate. They will come to forget that their relationship to video programming used to be mediated by a black box connected to their TV set, and instead will enjoy the same degree of freedom that they have in consuming and using the text Web from any personal computer.
>
> Most importantly, the massive economies of scale and reach that the Internet already provides will extend to the realm of video production, where producing and self-distributing a video program is nearly as effortless as producing a Web site, and where millions of new producers and programmers are born.

Or as Gregg Spiradellis, the cofounder of the hugely popular Web animation site JibJab, puts it: "The Audience is the Network."

SHORTER, FASTER, SMALLER

The first thing you notice about the content of Google Video or Barrio305, aside from the near-total absence of production polish, is that most of it is three minutes long or shorter. Which is not a length often found on broadcast TV, the land of the half-hour increment (or twenty-two minutes once you take out commercials). Instead, it's something new—a medium that lies somewhere between passive television watching and interactive Web surfing.

When you think about it, there's nothing magical about half hours; they're simply an easy way to divide a broadcast programming schedule into segments that start and finish on the hour. Outside of the broadcast schedule, entertainment and news comes in all sorts of lengths, from thirty-second clips to three-hour concerts; there's no inherent premium on thirty minutes.

Like so many other conventions that we today accept as cultural choice, the rigid programming convention of producing video in multiples of thirty minutes is actually an artifact of inefficient distribution. Someday, that convention may fade away, replaced by a range of more natural lengths of video content that reflect the diversity of human attention spans and content types, not network programming convenience and advertiser priorities.

This is yet another example of the sometimes surprising implications of the shift from scarcity to abundance in distribution; it's also an example of how ingrained scarcity thinking is in our culture. The shift to broadband video and the severing of the link with fixed schedules will have the effect of making the average programming length shorter. Suddenly, it's about what *we* want; not what the distribution channel wants.

By the same token, the rise of mobile video, starting with the video iPod and video-enabled mobile phones, will be accompanied by short-form content meant to be watched in moments snatched between other things—on the bus, waiting for a friend, during a break from work. Sports, in particular, could be sliced into dozens of new lengths: full games, highlights, key quarters/innings, last two minutes, and so on.

I suspect that the thirty-minute show is the newspaper of television—a format born of distribution scarcity that is now past its prime. Demand will shift to shorter content for convenience and entertainment, and longer content for substance and satisfaction. But the arbitrary middle will not hold.

HOLLYWOOD @ HOME

The other form of video that will be transformed in a Long Tail world is movies. There, too, we've seen disruptive change before. One of the greatest shifts from mass to niche culture happened in the early 1980s with the introduction of the VCR and, more important, the video rental store. Before then, the selection of films available to a middle-class American on any given night was the three to four movies playing on broadcast TV, plus whatever local theaters happened to be featuring.

The advent of video rentals essentially placed thousands of movies on offer in every living room on every night. The result was a transition from *pushed* media (whether pushed onto the airwaves or into the local theaters) to *pulled* media. Consumers were suddenly empowered to summon movies with a degree of whim and freedom that, just a few decades before, Walt Disney himself couldn't possibly have imagined.

This huge expansion in selection was accompanied by a major shift in movie access pricing. Where before the standard was one person, one ticket, now there was one small price for as many people as you could cram into your house. This transition was loathed and resisted long before it was grudgingly accepted and finally embraced by Hollywood interests. (Recall the early attempts to sell movies at retail for $70 to $80—a price that was calculated based on the amount of money a typical family would pay at the box office to see their favorite movie two to three times.)

Rob Reid, who founded the early digital music service Listen.com, describes the economic implications of this shift:

In the early 80's, technology enabled the basic unit of consumption for a viewer-selected movie to shift from a night out to a night in—a situation that positively screamed for the "release" of a vast array of movie choices to saturate this new domain of demand. The Night In is a lower-budget affair, but boy are there a lot of them.

Initially, Hollywood was convinced that it was practically un-American for a family of five to pay less than $20 to see a movie of its choosing (as opposed to a movie of CBS's choosing, which was of course free—if you assume that 30–40 minutes of commercials can be endured at no cost to the psyche). As a result, the studios believed (wrongly, as it happened) that pricing and margin at the micro-level should be analyzed by matching a given consumer to the price paid to access a given piece of media—rather than the raw amount of time and money the consumer devotes to your products in the aggregate.

In other words, the studios were horrified when they realized that a family of five (no, not four—remember, this was the eighties) that paid $20 to see *ET: The Extraterrestrial* in the theater would never drop $20 on *ET* rentals. What they missed was twofold: Most obviously, the aggregate amount of time and money that a given family would direct toward movies was primed to explode when the family could access any movie they wanted, rather than whatever was being marketed that month; less obviously, they neglected to consider that the total amount of money *ET* could draw might similarly explode as the film started reaching the unknown millions who would not pay $20 to see *ET* but might pay, say, $2.95.

What the VCR and the video rental store hinted at was the rise of the age of infinite choice. Those stores increased the available selection of movies on any given Saturday night a hundredfold. Cable TV also increased television choice a hundredfold. Today, Netflix increases it a thousandfold. The Internet will increase it a gazillionfold.

Every time a new technology enables more choice, whether it's the VCR or the Internet, consumers clamor for it. Choice is simply what we want and, apparently, what we've always wanted.

13

BEYOND ENTERTAINMENT

HOW FAR CAN THE NICHE REVOLUTION REACH?

In this chapter I'll look at five examples of the Long Tail at work outside of media and entertainment. They range from manufacturing to services, and extend the principles of the Long Tail to industries that make up most of the world's economies.

EBAY

For a company that started less than ten years ago as little more than an experiment in whether the Internet could do a better job of selling old stuff than a garage sale, eBay is nothing less than a phenomenon. On any given day some of its 60 million active users are selling or buying more than 30 million items, making eBay one of the largest retailers in the world—brokering more than $100 million in transactions each day. But there's a big difference between eBay and Wal-Mart, which sells a roughly equal volume of stuff. Most of the goods eBay is selling can't be found on the shelves of big traditional retailers, and most of the people selling them aren't traditional retailers.

Instead, eBay is both the Long Tail of products and the Long Tail of merchants. It's a classic user-created marketplace, with eBay itself simply the facilitator. It has brought nearly every Long Tail tactic to bear, extending variety to levels unimaginable before the Internet. Like Amazon's Marketplace program, eBay is built around the notion of distributed inventory: All it provides is a Web site on which buyers and sellers meet and agree on a price (about half of the time via eBay's original auction process, and the other half with a Buy It Now fixed price). So its inventory costs are zero. It's not quite as easy as turning the computers on and watching the money roll in, but it's not far off.

EBay is also a self-service model—sellers create their own product listings and handle their own packaging and mailing. So eBay has managed to build its huge business with remarkably few people on salary. It has about $5 million in revenue per employee, nearly thirty times that of Wal-Mart. Finally, it offers filters, mostly in the form of search and a multilevel category structure, to help buyers find what they're looking for.

The range of products for which the eBay model has proven to work has exceeded anyone's expectation. It now does far more than clear the nation's attics. It's also America's largest used-car dealer and largest seller of automotive parts. It's among the largest sports equipment sellers and is one of the largest computer dealers. With its purchases of Half.com (overstock items) and Shopping.com (an online superstore selling new goods), it now extends from head to tail, selling both the newest blockbuster products and the most narrow niche goods and one-offs.

More than 724,000 Americans report that eBay is their primary or secondary source of income, according to an ACNielsen study in 2005. In the UK, Nielsen found that more than 68,000 cottage industries, from CD shops to sculptors, depend on the site for at least a quarter of their income. On average, each eBay-based business employs nine staffers, and almost half of those businesses earn more than three-quarters of their income through the site. It's the ultimate small-business aggregator.

But eBay is not the perfect Long Tail marketplace, for a reason that I and the team of Stanford Business School students who worked with me on an eBay case study discovered early in our research. One of the questions we asked is why eBay did not have Amazon-like recommendations, product reviews, ranking by price and ratings, and other sophisticated filters. The answer is that eBay, surprisingly, often doesn't know what's being sold on its site.

It knows *who* is selling and who is buying, but because the product listings are created by the sellers themselves and each seller describes things differently, there is nothing like the standard "shelf-keeping unit," or SKU, designation (a unique product number) that most retailers use to track their inventory. (There are exceptions in categories such as CDs and cars, where eBay has encouraged sellers to use standard categories and nomenclature in their listings.) Without this product-level information, eBay can't offer many of the powerful filter technologies, such as recommendation engines, that drive demand so effectively at other Long Tail retailers. And because sellers can list their products in so many different ways, including misspelling them, it's even hard for buyers to know if they have indeed found all the examples of what they're looking for.

This represents a significant vulnerability in eBay's otherwise remarkable marketplace. Most of eBay's sales volume comes not from grannies selling old Beanie Babies, but from nearly 400,000 small- and medium-sized merchants worldwide who use eBay as a storefront. But most of them have their own Web sites, too, and Google's Froogle, Yahoo! Shopping, and other aggregators are finding smarter and smarter ways to extract the necessary information from these hundreds of thousands of merchants and create a virtual marketplace that can offer product-comparison features eBay cannot. The challenge for eBay will be to do the same within its own service, keeping competitors at bay by providing better filters to help customers find what they want and buy with confidence, not just in the seller but in the product.

KITCHENAID

You might not think that there's a Long Tail of kitchen mixers, but there is, and it's all about color. KitchenAid is known for the quality of its high-end kitchen appliances, but even more so for the range of colors they come in. Indeed, KitchenAid is considered one of the world's trend-setters in color variety.

If you go to a big-box retailer such as Target, you'll typically find three colors of KitchenAid mixers on display: white, black, and one other. That other one is typically an exclusive color, such as cobalt blue, that KitchenAid has negotiated with the retailer in exchange for the extra display space for not two mixer colors, but three. This tiny amount of variety not only distinguishes KitchenAid among the other mixers and increases its overall sales, but the company has found that adding a third color actually improves the sales of white. The reason, KitchenAid suspects, is that the colorful display attracts people to the KitchenAid shelves in the retailer's housewares section, and the range of colors confers a brand distinctiveness that consumers value. Once pulled in by the bright variety, however, many customers, on reflection, realize that they have a renewed appreciation for classic, timeless white, and that's what they eventually buy.

So far, so good. But what third color should each retailer pick? And which colors should KitchenAid offer? It has a staff of colorists and other experts to decide, but as with other "pre-filters," there's an element of guesswork involved. And once the decisions are made and the products put out on the shelves, it's hard to know why they do or don't sell, given the compounding variables such as display conditions and competitors' products. Until recently, that was pretty much the end of it: KitchenAid could offer retailers any number of colors, but each year the only ones available to consumers were the six to seven that the retailers actually chose.

But between 2001 and 2003, KitchenAid built a system to offer *all* of its colors—typically more than fifty between its different models—online. If you shop for mixers on Amazon or KitchenAid.com, you can now pick any of those colors from a drop-down menu. These include the regular staples along with bolder colors that are Web-only: pistachio, tangerine, cranberry, grape, crystal blue, sienna, lemon, and others.

What's interesting is that when customers are allowed to pick from all of the fifty KitchenAid colors, they don't just stop at the half dozen available in traditional retail. Instead, a Long Tail emerges. Of course white and black remain the best-selling colors, along with most of the others available in regular stores. But all the others sell, too—every one. And each year, somewhere in the top ten, there is a color that nobody expected to be popular.

In 2005, that color happened to be tangerine. No bricks-and-mortar retailer had picked that color to carry, and, to be honest, KitchenAid is not quite sure *why* it is popular. Things that can affect color choice include items seen on the sets of popular TV shows, color used by influential trendsetters such as Martha Stewart, or just random seasonal variations. But until KitchenAid had an online channel that allowed customers to pick from its full range of products, it had no way of knowing that there was latent consumer demand that it hadn't previously tapped.

LEGO

If you just know LEGO from kids' birthday parties and the display shelves of a toy store, you've only seen half of the company. The other half is the LEGO that caters to enthusiasts, ranging from kids who want more than the stock kits to adults who have turned to bricks as the ultimate prototyper's tool kit.

It all starts with LEGO's mail-order business, which began as a traditional shop-at-home catalog and is now increasingly organized around the company's Web site. In a typical toy store, LEGO may have a few dozen products. In its online store, it has nearly a thousand, ranging from bags of roof tiles to a $300 Deathstar. If you want to see how different the online market is from the traditional retail market for LEGO, check out their top-sellers list. Only a few of those products are even available in stores, such as a $140 *Star Wars* sandcrawler and a big bag of minifigures for $43.

It's worth pausing here and considering the Long Tail implications of this. At least 90 percent of LEGO's products are not available in traditional retail outlets. They're only available in the catalogs and online, where the economics of inventory and distribution are far friendlier to niche products. Overall, those non-retail parts of the business represent 10 to 15 percent of LEGO's annual $1.1 billion in sales. But the margins on these products are higher than on the kits sold through Toys "R" Us, thanks to not having to share the revenues with the retailer. And because the virtual store can carry products for *all* LEGO fans, from kids to adult enthusiasts (not just the sweet spot of nine-year-old boys), the range of prices can be far greater online, from $1 bricks to the aforementioned $300 *Star Wars* kit.

The next level of LEGO obsession is joining its Brickmaster club for $40 a year. This brings a bigger magazine with a lot of DIY projects, five exclusive kits that show up at your door, and a ticket to LEGOland. This is LEGO's way of segmenting its customers, ranging from casual to fanatic, and finding ways to move beyond the one-size-fits-all market of the retail shelf.

After that, it's time to start getting serious about your own creations. LEGO has a long history of offering tools online to encourage model trading and other collaborative peer production. In 2000, its "My Own Creation" project led to a contest for the best user-created model. The winner was a blacksmith shop that LEGO licensed from its creator and offered for a while as a commercial kit. Later, it offered LEGO Mosaic, which let users upload images that were then converted into 2D LEGO brick patterns, downloadable by all.

In 2005, LEGO launched its most ambitious peer-production effort to date, LEGO Factory. This virtual fab lets you download software to design your own models, then upload them to the LEGO site. A week or so later, you get a kit with all your specified bricks and other parts delivered in a box with an image of your creation on the front. What's especially cool is that others can buy your kit, too, and there's a nice selection of user-created models available for purchase. More than 100,000 models have been designed this way, and some of the best of them get released as official LEGO products. LEGO even pays the creators a small royalty.

However, all is not what it could be in Factory land. Mass customization is cool, but when you have 7,000 possible parts in seventy-five possible colors (that's more than a half million possibilities), the fulfillment challenge of offering users full freedom quickly becomes overwhelming. So LEGO limits choice in two ways. First, each model can be built only from a single brick palette, such as "car parts." Second, those parts come in prepackaged bags of a fixed number of bricks, so you'll likely get more than you need. If you're not careful, a simple vehicle that might cost less than $10 in a retail store can turn out to cost nearly $100 in LEGO Factory simply because it uses those bags of parts inefficiently.

Fortunately, there's a work-around. LEGO enthusiasts compiled a database of what bags are in each palette and also created software to help builders use those bags more efficiently, sparing them the curse of an expensive bag of parts for a single brick. And to its credit, LEGO has encouraged this. But that's still too hard and limiting for most people (including me), so LEGO is now considering how to improve the experience, starting with easier-to-use design software.

I asked Michael McNally, LEGO's senior brand-relations manager, whether LEGO saw parallels in any other company's approach to catering to niche markets and encouraging peer production. Interestingly, he gave Apple's iTunes as an analogy. ITunes lets you download individual songs, not just albums. You can also make your own playlists and share them with other users, which is a bit like a custom LEGO creation from standard parts. "What iTunes does for music, LEGO Factory is doing for people who like to build," McNally said. Welcome to the Long Tail of plastic bricks.

SALESFORCE.COM

As 2005 opened, Mark Benioff found himself in a tricky position. His company, Salesforce.com, had brought an innovative approach to the otherwise pretty boring world of selling software for salespeople. Rather than offer his contact management package as a set of discs to be installed on a company's computers as other companies did, he ran the software on his own servers and offered customers access to it through a standard Web browser for a subscription fee. Effectively he'd turned software into a service, something that particularly appealed to small- and medium-sized businesses that didn't want the hassle of maintaining their own software. This worked all too well: By 2005 Salesforce.com had grown so quickly that it had attracted the attention of the big corporate software vendors, such as Oracle and SAP, which were setting out to match his offerings and destroy him.

The usual defense would be to try to get bigger, adding more and more functionality to Salesforce.com's offerings to match the features of the big competitors. And that is indeed what Benioff did, initially. But then it occurred to him that he could grow the other way, too. His method of offering software online could also allow hundreds of smaller developers, many of them in low-cost places such as India, to reach those same customers. Typically, companies are loath to work with small developers for fear the software will be buggy and poorly supported and will fail to evolve. By shielding his subscribers from the complexities of installing and maintaining software and instead providing it remotely through a Web browser, Benioff also created a platform through which others could do the same.

What he was doing was applying the Long Tail theory to the software business. And it fit remarkably well. As in other industries, there is a head and tail of software, with Microsoft on one end and millions of individual programmers, many of them in India and China, on the other. In between is the work of a huge number of small groups of developers, most of whom have few good ways to reach customers around the world. But it's still a very top-heavy distribution: Microsoft's quasi-monopoly is the ultimate hit-dominated market.

But just as in media and entertainment, three forces are working to change the economics of the software industry. The costs of writing software, which fell dramatically with the spread of powerful PCs, are now falling even faster as the Internet introduces millions of cheap and talented programmers in India and China to the rest of the world. The cost of delivering that software is also falling, as the CD-ROM gives way to the download. And the cost of finding the best software for your specific needs has never been lower, thanks to the hugely connected groups of users online who collectively provide better recommendations (and support) than most high-priced consultants. The ability to offer software through a Web browser, running remotely without any risk to your own computers, has further lowered all these costs—both real and psychic.

There has always been a market for niche software, starting with shareware traded online and try-before-you-buy demoware. But it wasn't a huge market, mostly because of the usual problems of risk, complexity, and standards that come with software that has to run on a PC and work with its operating system. The hosted software model offers an opportunity to break through that, by letting professionals deal with most of the complexity and using the Web browser as a universal user interface and shield from the operating system.

In late 2005, Salesforce was the first to launch a Long Tail software marketplace on its platform. Third-party developers could write a targeted niche application (focused on performance reviews or recruiting, for example) and it would run on Salesforce's servers, integrating with Salesforce's other software. The hope was that hundreds or even thousands of small developers would meet all the specialized needs of Salesforce's customers, allowing Salesforce to concentrate on the more common needs. In other words, the tail would reinforce the head. By early 2006, there were more than two hundred applications selling on the marketplace, and Benioff confirms that the shape of the sales curves is just as predicted. "Even I was stunned," he says. "It's a perfect Long Tail. Textbook!"

SAP soon followed with its own online platform strategy, as did several smaller companies with similar models. All the usual Long Tail conventions applied. Such companies aggregate niche software on their respective platforms and provide filter mechanisms (ranging from best-seller lists within categories to user reviews). This helps people move with confidence down the curve into niche applications that may suit their needs better than the monolithic one-size-fits-all software that has dominated the market to date. This model neatly connects head to tail.

It's too early to say how well these new software markets will work, but they are yet another example of how lowering the costs of reaching niches can change the game. As Joe Kraus, CEO of JotSpot (another software company attempting to apply this strategy), puts it, "Up until now, the focus has been on dozens of markets of millions, instead of millions of markets of dozens." He, like a growing number of others, is now betting on the rise of the latter.

GOOGLE

The traditional advertising market is a classic, hit-centric industry where high costs enforce a focus on the biggest sellers and buyers. The way it works is that an advertiser, say General Motors, has a marketing budget. GM commissions an advertising firm to create some ads and then a media buyer to place those ads in television, radio, and print and online.

Meanwhile on the other side, those ad-driven media have their own ad sales forces. They pitch the advertisers and their media buyers on the virtues of their advertising vehicles. If all goes well, millions of dollars change hands. All of it is labor-intensive and made even more costly by the expensive schmoozing that's required in businesses where a lack of trusted performance metrics makes salesmanship and personal relationships key to winning business.

Most ads, whether they run in the Yellow Pages or during the Super Bowl, are actively sold phone call by phone call, visit by visit. Very few just appear because somebody decided to advertise. These days salespeople don't just twist arms, they also serve as advertising consultants, informing advertisers about the most effective ways to use a given medium or brainstorming creative new approaches to getting the advertisers' message out. That works well enough, but because it's expensive, it imposes a subtle cost: a focus on just the largest and most lucrative of potential advertisers. In other words, the system is biased toward the head of the advertising curve.

As with every other market we've looked at, that head is just a tiny fraction of the potential market. But because it's so expensive to sell advertising the traditional way, the smaller potential advertisers have been left to their own devices, mostly picking up a phone and placing a classified ad or sending some homemade display copy to the local newspaper.

That's pretty much how advertising has worked for most of the past century. But in 2001, a two-year-old Google, the fastest-growing search engine on the planet, started looking for a proper business model. And just as it had done search differently from its predecessors, it decided to do advertising differently, too. Borrowing a model pioneered a few years earlier by Bill Gross, the entrepreneur who started Overture, Google built what would become the most effective Long Tail advertising machine the world has ever seen.

What Google realized is that if it could take most of the cost out of both selling and buying advertising, it could dramatically increase the pool of potential ad buyers and sellers. Software could do almost all the work, thereby lowering the economic barrier to entry and reaching a much larger market.

Google's advertising model has three important Long Tail characteristics. First, it is based on search keywords, rather than banner images, and as we've already seen, there is a virtually infinite Long Tail of words and word combinations. Search terms work the same way—here's a chart of search terms (circa 2001) provided by Joe Kraus, the cofounder of the Excite search engine:

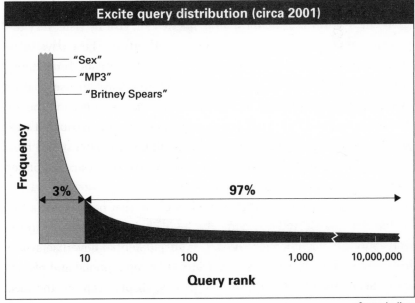

Source: Joe Kraus

The top ten words account for just 3 percent of all searches. The rest are spread between tens of millions of other search terms. What Google realized is that each one of those unique search terms is an equally unique advertising opportunity: tens of millions of expressions of interest and intent, each of which could be converted into a highly targeted advertising opportunity if the ad placement were determined by exactly the same PageRank algorithms as those that return Google's search results.

But how to sell tens of millions of unique ads? There was only one answer: Let software do it. Thus Google's second Long Tail technique—dramatically lowering the cost of reaching the market. Its technique is based on a simple and very cheap self-service model. Anybody can become a Google advertiser by buying a keyword in an automated auction process where the minimum bid is just $0.05 per click.

Not only is it cheaper for both Google and an advertiser to use the self-service model, but it also results in more effective ads. Google provides tools to customize and test ads to achieve the highest "click-throughs" (when a consumer clicks on the ad and goes to the advertiser's site), and it's not uncommon for advertisers to obsessively tweak their keywords and ad copy until they get the results they want. After all, who knows their businesses better than they do?

The effect of this model has been to extend Google's advertising business farther down the tail than any company ever has. Today, there are thousands of small Google advertisers who had never advertised anywhere before. Because of the self-service model, the measurable performance, the low cost of entry, and the ability to constantly tweak and improve the ads, advertisers are flocking to this new marketplace. They don't have to have their arms twisted; no human at Google need ever contact them at all. The result: fewer employees and a model that is as efficient in the tail as it is in the head.

Finally, Google did the same for publishers. Traditionally, there were only two significant ways for Web publishers to make money from advertising. They could either hire their own ad sales forces and court likely advertisers, or they could join an ad network and take whatever they were given at rock-bottom prices. Google's insight was that the same relevance-finding technology that could match the right ad with a keyword search could also put the right ad on a third-party content site.

Today, whether you're the *New York Times* or a blog, you can put a couple lines of HTML code on your site and it will display Google ads—targeted to whatever content you're providing. Again, it's self-service: no permission or phone call required. Every time an ad is clicked on, the advertiser pays Google, and Google passes some of the money on to you.

Google doesn't care whether you're a professional or an amateur, or how narrow or broad your content may be. If the ads aren't working, Google will automatically replace them with different ads to see if they work better. Because the pages ("inventory") cost Google nothing, it can afford to wastefully run ads that no one ever clicks on—the "opportunity costs" of the lost potential revenues are borne by the third-party publisher. It's a remarkable way to extend the advertising market down the Long Tail of publishing, which includes hundreds of thousands of blogs.

At Google's first shareholders meeting, CEO Eric Schmidt elaborated on why he describes Google's mission as "serving the Long Tail."

He started by showing a slide of a powerlaw with dollars on the vertical axis and people on the horizontal one. Wal-Mart was at the very head. The number "6 billion" was at the end of the tail. Schmidt explained:

> We took a look at our market last year and asked ourselves: "How are we doing?" If you look at the advertiser, the market we're in from the largest companies—Wal-Mart—in the world, all the way down to the smallest companies in the world, the single individual. We call this The Long Tail. A lot of people have been talking about it—it's a very interesting idea.
>
> We looked at this and we said, "We've been doing really well up until now in the middle part of this—well-run, mid-sized businesses, smart people solving interesting problems. But how well do we do against the problems of the very largest customers?" So last year we brought out a whole suite of tools for very large advertisers who can use our services in all of their divisions to generate lots and

lots of revenues because, of course, in our model the advertising drives predictability, it drives conversions, and so forth.

And what about the individual contributor, the small business, the company where Joe or Bob is the CEO, the CIO, the CFO and the worker and the support person—a one-person company, a two-person company, a three-person company? We built a whole bunch of small, self-service tools which allowed them to almost automatically use this service.

So [we went] in both directions. By going to the bottom with self-service, we were able to reach advertisers who fell below the threshold of traditional advertising. And by going all the way to the top, we were able to capture very large and historically undeserved businesses as well as a whole new area that never had access to these kinds of online services.

Schmidt later explained to me how these millions of small to mid-sized customers represent a huge new Long Tail ad market:

The surprising thing about the Long Tail is just how long the Tail is, and how many businesses haven't been served by traditional advertising sales. The recognition that businesses such as ours show a Pareto distribution appears to be a much deeper insight than anyone realized. It's something that scientists have known for a long time, but it's never gotten any attention. When we looked at our business, we concluded that we built a model that works particularly well in the middle of the curve. After reading the [original *Wired*] article, we looked at the Tail and asked ourselves, "How are we doing against this opportunity?"

Take a Pareto curve of the world's businesses, ranked by revenue. Number one is Wal-Mart. So what is the last entry? It turns out it's a person in India with a basket selling something they made. The area under that curve, which includes about a billion people, is essentially the world's GDP. So start at the bottom and move up the curve until you've got people with an Internet connection. They're reasonably educated, they're a small business, and they want to market their goods. And we ask ourselves, "What benefit can our model bring them to increase their revenues?" And the answer is that if we let them do business outside their own villages, they're reaching a larger market, have got more suppliers, better price competition, and so on.

There are a lot of reasons why this is slow to happen, mostly having to do with infrastructure. So let's say for the purpose of argument that we don't focus on 90 percent of the people. That still leaves 100 million people. The numbers are so large that you can lop off a large chunk and it's still a huge market.

Google now has revenues of more than $5 billion a year, and that's doubling every nine months. Although most of its revenues come from the head of the curve, most of its customers are somewhere in the tail, which suggests that this is where much of its growth will come in the future. And Google's just getting started.

One of the interesting things about Google is how many ways it plays the Long Tail game. As discussed, it's an advertising aggregator, creating a market where the Long Tail of advertisers can reach the Long Tail of ad-driven publishers. But Google is even better known as an information aggregator, and as such it has shown some interesting techniques in evolving away from a one-size-fits-all model.

One of the problems with Apple's iTunes music aggregator is the limited way it displays very different genres of music. The same challenge exists with information—it may all start with words, but they can appear in many different contexts. Google realized that different contexts need different presentations. So if you're searching for a place, you probably want a map view. If you're searching for an image, you probably want a visual view. If you're searching for video, you probably want a video view. Again, one size doesn't fit all—even in the case of a search. Google now offers different styles of "vertical search" (search just within a single category): Google Local, Google Scholar (academic papers), Google Maps, Froogle (products), Google News, Google Book Search, Google Video, and so on.

Now that Google has been joined by Yahoo!, Microsoft, and others, the rise of the vertical search market is simply a case of slicing aggregation into niches, optimized for different needs. Each of Google's search products has a unique presentation and pulls from a subset of the information universe that gives the most appropriate and useful results. In other words, it customizes the display of searches in a way that's meaningful for each particular medium.

The virtue of this is that if you know at least the kind of thing you're looking for, and if you use a focused, fine-sliced aggregator rather than a generalized aggregator, you'll get better results. And the better the result, the more likely people are to continue digging deeper, barreling down the Long Tail of everything.

14

LONG TAIL RULES

HOW TO CREATE A CONSUMER PARADISE

The secret to creating a thriving Long Tail business can be summarized in two imperatives:

1. Make everything available.
2. Help me find it.

The first is easier said than done. Fewer than a dozen of the 6,000 films submitted to the Sundance Film Festival each year are picked up for distribution, but most of the rest of them cannot be legally shown outside of a festival because their music rights have not been cleared. Likewise for most TV programming in the networks' archives: It's too expensive to clear the DVD or streaming distribution rights to the music.

Similar rights issues also keep classic music and video games under lock and key. Until we have some way to clear the rights to *all* the titles in *all* the back catalogs—thoughtlessly, automatically, and at industrial scale—legal restrictions will continue to be the primary barrier to growing the Long Tail.

The second necessary element is moving more quickly. From collaborative filtering to user ratings, smart aggregators are using recommendations to drive demand down the Long Tail. This is the difference between push and pull, between broadcast and personalized taste. Long Tail businesses treat consumers as individuals, offering mass customization as an alternative to mass-market fare.

For the entertainment industry, recommendations are a remarkably efficient form of marketing, allowing smaller films and less mainstream music to find an audience. For consumers, the simplified choice that comes from following a good recommendation encourages exploration and can reawaken passions for music and film, potentially creating a far larger entertainment market overall. (The average Netflix customer rents seven DVDs a month, three times the rate of the bricks-and-mortar faithful.) The collateral cultural benefit is much more diversity, reversing the blanding effects of a century of distribution scarcity and ending the tyranny of the hit.

Now that you've got the big picture, here are nine rules of successful Long Tail aggregators:

LOWER YOUR COSTS

Rule 1: Move inventory way in . . . or way out.

Sears blazed the trail. It achieved its first big efficiencies with the old mail-order advantage of large, centralized warehouses. Today, the online sides of Wal-Mart, Best Buy, Target, and many others are using their existing warehouse networks to offer far more variety online than they do in their stores, because centralized inventory is so much more efficient than putting products on shelves in hundreds of stores.

To offer even more variety, companies such as Amazon have expanded to "virtual inventory"—products physically located in a partner's warehouse but displayed and sold on Amazon's site. Today, its Marketplace program aggregates such distributed inventory, products held at the very edge of the network by thousands of small merchants. Cost to Amazon: zero.

Digital inventory—think iTunes—is the cheapest of all. We've already seen the effect the switch from shipping plastic discs to streaming megabits has had on the music industry; soon the same will come to movies, video games, and TV shows. News has left the paper age, podcasting is challenging radio, and who knows, you may already be reading this book on a screen. Eliminating atoms or the constraints of the broadcast spectrum is a powerful way to reduce costs, enabling entirely new markets of niches.

Rule 2: Let customers do the work.

"Peer-production" created eBay, Wikipedia, Craigslist, MySpace, and provided Netflix with hundreds of thousands of movie reviews. At the same time, self-service enabled Google to sell advertising for a nickel a click and Skype to sign up 60 million users in two-and-a-half years. Both are examples where users happily do for free what companies would otherwise have to pay employees to do. It's not outsourcing, it's "crowdsourcing."

The advantage of crowdsourcing is not just economic; customers can do a better job, too. User-submitted reviews are often well-informed, articulate, and most important, trusted by other users. Collectively, customers have virtually unlimited time and energy; only peer production has the capacity to extend as far as the Long Tail can go. And in the case of self-service, the work is being done by the people who care most about it, and best know their own needs.

THINK NICHE

Rule 3: One distribution method doesn't fit all.

Some customers want to go to stores. Some customers want to shop online. Some customers want to research online, then buy in stores. Some customers want to browse in stores, then buy online. Some want it now; others can wait. Some customers are near stores; others are scattered to the winds. Some products have concentrated demand; others have distributed demand. If you focus on distributing to just one customer group, you risk losing the others.

It may sound like metaphysics, but the best Long Tail markets transcend time and space. They're not constrained by any geographic boundaries, nor do they make any assumptions about when people want what they want. ITunes' advantage comes primarily from its huge variety and convenient downloads, but being open 24/7 doesn't hurt either.

Today, you can get *CSI* on broadcast TV, video-on-demand, iTunes download, DVD (purchase or rent), and TiVo season pass, and watch it on any device from a plasma screen to a Sony PSP. Likewise for some NPR radio shows, which you can get via terrestrial broadcast (real time and delayed), satellite broadcast, Web streaming, podcast, and, if you like, an emailed transcript. Multiple distribution channels are the only way to reach the biggest potential market.

Rule 4: One product doesn't fit all.

Once upon a time, there was one way to buy music: the CD album (so few CD singles were sold that many artists didn't bother offering them). Now consider the choice you have online: album, individual track, ringtone, free thirty-second sample, music video, remix, sample of somebody *else's* remix, streamed or downloaded, all in any number of formats and sampling rates.

Umair Haque calls this "microchunking." Increasingly, the winning strategy is to separate content into its component parts ("microchunks"), so that people can consume it the way they want, as well as remix it with other content to create something new. Newspapers are microchunked into individual articles, which are in turn linked to by more specialist sites that create a different, often more focused, product out of content from multiple sources—the blogger as DJ, remixing the news to create something new.

We've seen this before in the form of product and brand segmentation—a dozen different kinds of spaghetti sauce for a dozen distinct palates. Now that trend is being extended to everything from individual video-game characters and levels (mix your own game) to selling cookbook chunks one recipe at a time. Each recombination taps a different distribution network and reaches a different audience. One size fits one; many sizes fit many.

Rule 5: One price doesn't fit all.

One of the best understood principles of microeconomics is the power of elastic pricing. Different people are willing to pay different prices for any number of reasons, from how much money they have to how much time they have. But just as there's often room for just one version of a product in traditional markets, there's often room for only one price, or at least one price at a time. In markets with room for abundant variety, however, variable pricing can be a powerful technique to maximize the value of a product and the size of the market.

EBay, for instance, offers auctions (typically lower prices, but at the cost of greater hassle and uncertainty) or "Buy It Now" (higher prices). Even iTunes, which has stuck with a single price of $0.99 per track for simplicity's sake, will give you a lower price if you buy the tracks as part of an album. Rhapsody has gone even farther, experimenting with track prices from $0.79 to $0.49, and finding that cutting the price in half roughly triples sales.

The natural model for music and anything else where the marginal costs of manufacturing and distribution are close to zero is variable pricing. Retailers can charge more for the most popular items and less for the less popular. Why hasn't that happened already? Because the labels typically charge a fixed wholesale price of around $0.70 per track, largely to avoid "channel conflict" with CDs, which still produce the bulk of the music business revenues. Someday the labels will see the light and pricing will become more fluid, allowing retailers to draw consumers down the Tail with lower prices.

LOSE CONTROL

Rule 6: Share information.

The difference between an overwhelming shelf of look-alike products and the bliss of "rank by best-selling" is information. In one case, the store knows what sells best but doesn't tell its customers. In the other, it does. So too for "rank by price," "rank by review," and "sort by manufacturer." All that data already exists; the question is how best to share it with customers. More information is better, but only when it's presented in a way that helps order choice, not confuse it further.

Likewise, information about buying patterns, when transformed into recommendations, can be a powerful marketing tool. Deep information about products, from reviews to specifications, can answer questions that would have otherwise halted a purchase. Explaining why a consumer is getting a certain set of recommendations builds confidence in the system, and helps consumers use it better. Transparency can build trust at no cost.

Rule 7: Think "and," not "or."

One of the symptoms of scarcity thinking is assuming that markets are zero-sum. In other words, the mistake of assuming that everything is an either/or choice. Release this version *or* that version. Sell this color *or* that color. On shelves or broadcast channels, that's natural enough: There really is room for only one product in any single slot. But in markets with infinite capacity, the right strategy is almost always to offer it *all*.

The problem with choosing is that it requires discrimination, and the process of discrimination requires time, resources, and guesswork. Someone must decide, on the basis of some criteria, that one thing is likely to be more successful than another. They may be right at the macrolevel, but such a decision almost always gets it wrong at the microlevel. Consider the phenomenon of the "alternative ending" on DVD movies. Even if most people like the standard ending best, there are always some who prefer the alternative one. Now they can have both. Extend that to the foreign language option, the choice of standard or widescreen, and even the variety of cuts for various ratings (PG, PG-13, R, and uncensored)—each option has an audience, even if it's not as big as the primary audience.

All those "extras" are enabled by the abundant capacity of the DVD, allowing directors to "waste" storage with content that they could not have included in a more scarce medium, such as a theatrical screen or a videotape. So, too, for any digital market online, where the falling price and rising capacity of storage ensure that whatever capacity you want, it's only a matter of time before it's virtually free. The more abundant the storage and distribution, the less discriminating you have to be in how you use it. "And" is a far easier decision than "or."

Rule 8: Trust the market to do your job.

In scarce markets, you've got to guess at what will sell. In abundant markets, you can simply throw everything out there and see what happens, letting the market sort it out. The difference between "pre-filtering" and "post-filtering" is predicting versus measuring, and the latter is invariably more accurate. Online markets are nothing if not highly efficient measures of the wisdom of crowds. Because they're information-rich, it's relatively easy for people to compare goods, and spread the word about what they like.

Collaborative filters, for instance, are a market-based way to do product promotion. Popularity rankings are another voice of the market, amplified by the positive-feedback loop of word-of-mouth. And ratings are collective opinion, quantified in ways that make it easy to compare across products and sort them. All of these tools can order variety in ways that make sense to consumers, without some retailer having to guess at what will work. The lesson: Don't predict; measure and respond.

Rule 9: Understand the power of free.

Free gets a bad rap, evoking piracy and other such evaporations of value. But one of the most powerful features of digital markets is that they put free within reach; because their costs are near zero, their prices can be, too. Already, one of the most common business models on the Internet, from Skype to Yahoo! Mail, is to attract lots of users with a free service and convince some of them to upgrade to a subscription-based "premium" one that adds higher quality or better features. Because digital services are so cheap to offer, the free customers cost the company so little that it can afford to convert only a tiny fraction of them to paying customers.

Samples, from thirty-second music clips to video previews, are possible because the cost of delivering bits on broadband pipes is so low. Video-game makers routinely distribute demos with a few free levels; if you like them, you can pay to unlock the others. In 2005, Universal released the first nine minutes of *Serenity* (a sci-fi film) online, free and uncut. Why? Because it could. The cost of delivering nearly 10 percent of a movie to anyone who wanted to watch it online was trivial compared to the marketing value of pulling an audience into the plot and leaving them with a cliffhanger, an itch that only a paid trip to the movie theater could scratch.

Most television is already free and advertising-supported. Yet the networks still want to find ways to charge for it online, even though the production costs are paid for by broadcast, and online distribution costs are low. Why not give it away online as well, bookending (rather than interrupting) it with ads or just finding a bigger audience for the product placement, which can be neither stripped out nor fast-forwarded past? Ultimately, in abundant markets with loads of competition, prices tend to follow costs. And thanks to the power of digital economics, costs just get lower.

CODA: TOMORROW'S TAIL

For around $30,000, you can now buy a machine called a Solidscape T66 3D printer for your home. It's a beautiful piece of desktop engineering, although still a bit expensive. But the price is falling fast, and it's the sort of radical technology that can set the imagination soaring. Remember the LEGO Factory story, in which you could design models, upload them, and have the kits delivered a week or two later? Well, you can now take out the waiting for delivery part. A 3D printer is a domestic factory, capable of manufacturing almost anything in lot sizes of one. Someday, they may be as common as inkjets and not much more expensive. Just think what that might enable.

Today's 3D printers come in various types, but a common one uses a laser to turn a bath of liquid polymer or powder into hard plastic in any shape you desire. Feed it a 3-D object file, such as the output of a CAD program or even the screen-captured polygon file of a character from a video game, and the laser will get to work tracing it out. Layer by layer, a perfect plastic reproduction of the object emerges out of the bath. It's like magic. The Solidscape 3D printer can turn bits into atoms in your own home. It's the ultimate manufacturing technology for the Long Tail of things.

As 3D printing technology extends beyond brittle plastic to a range of materials, from metals to synthetic fabrics, we may be able to self-manufacture spare parts, toys, perhaps even entire machines that we've downloaded from some virtual retailer. We already have that power for digital goods: Today you can choose to have Amazon ship you tax software in a box in ten days or simply download it and run it right now. Other services offer you the same choice for music: a CD next week or the digital tracks now. But someday that may also extend to physical goods. Today you print your own photographs at home; tomorrow you may print the frame, too.

You can get a glimpse of this already. Will Wright, the legendary video-game designer, is putting the finishing touches on his next game, Spore. In it, you'll be able to evolve your own creature, imbuing it with traits and characteristics of your own design. If you like your work, you'll be able to upload the creation to the Spore servers. And then, for about $20, you can have it 3D printed into a real action figure—colors, texture, and all. Each one is unique and will show up at your front door in a matter of a week or two. Think of it as the Long Tail of merchandising, and a mind-blowing glimpse of what's still to come.

Like everything else, tomorrow's Long Tail of Things will be aggregated, efficiently stored as bits, and then delivered to your home via optical fiber. Only then will it be materialized, coming full circle to atoms again at the point of consumption. It sounds like science fiction, but then again so did having an entire music library in your pocket just a decade ago.

In the worlds of entertainment and information, we've already lost the capacity constraints of shelf space and channels, along with their one-size-fits-all demands. Soon we may lose the capacity constraints of mass production, too. The explosion of variety we've seen in our culture thanks to digital efficiencies will extend to every other part of our lives. The question tomorrow will not be whether more choice is better, but rather what do we really want? On the infinite aisle, everything is possible.

NOTES ON SOURCES
AND FURTHER READING

This book is the result of nearly two years of research and interviews, from business executives to academic economists. It's also the result of a good deal of original data analysis of proprietary sales and usage data from companies that are building Long Tail markets, from Netflix to eBay. (My eternal thanks to the executives who supported this project and made the data available.) And finally, it builds on the work of many other researchers, thinkers, and writers whose ideas and conclusions influenced my own thinking, many of whom I've quoted in the text.

The notes below indicate primary sources, along with additional information, explanations, and suggestions for further reading. In many cases the primary material is on the Web, in which case I give a simplified URL. But URLs can change, so in most cases I aim to also give enough unique identifying information so that it can be found with a search engine.

INTRODUCTION

2 *Most of the top fifty*: Hit album data comes from the Recording Industry Association of America (www.riaa.org), which has an excellent searchable database of albums that have sold Gold (500,000 units), Platinum (1 million), Multiplatinum, and Diamond (10 million or more). Hollywood box office data is from www.boxofficemojo.com.

2 *Every year network TV*: Television data, both current and historic, is from Nielsen Media Research.

7 *Which is what I was doing*: Vann-Adibé left Ecast in 2005.

1. THE LONG TAIL

20 *On Rhapsody, the top 4,500*: This conversion requires some explanation. The offline (Wal-Mart) market is a CD market, which is to say that almost all music is sold as part of an album. Online, at services such as iTunes and Rhapsody, songs can be downloaded individually, and most are. To convert from an album market to a singles market is not as simple as multiplying by 14, which is the average number of tracks per album, since some tracks on an album are more popular than others. So to derive a better conversion rate, we analyzed the top 100,000 tracks on Rhapsody. We found that they were drawn

from about 22,000 albums, for an average of about 4.5 tracks per album. To account for the less popular tracks that were beyond the top 100,000, we gave the average album an equivalency score of 5.5 tracks. Therefore, Wal-Mart's 4,500 unique albums are equivalent to 25,000 Rhapsody tracks.

22 *What's truly amazing*: Comparing book superstores and Amazon is equally fraught. Amazon has not released its title-level sales data, so we were forced to reverse-engineer it from what was available. That consists mostly of Amazon's listed sales rank figures for each title, and third-party data on absolute sales figures for various sets of books. The earliest work on this was by MIT's Erik Brynjolfsson, along with Carnegie Mellon's Michael Smith and Purdue's Jeffrey Hu. In "Consumer Surplus in the Digital Economy: Estimating the Value of Increased Product Variety at Online Booksellers" (2003), they estimated Amazon's sales curve based on a large-scale analysis of its sales rank data. They concluded that sales of titles beyond the top 100,000 (the typical inventory of a traditional book superstore) amounted to 40 percent of Amazon's sales.

In subsequent discussion with Amazon and others in the book industry, we concluded that this was an overstatement, most likely due to problems with Amazon's sales rank algorithms and a tendency for this sort of full-curve analysis to undercount the top 100 titles. We have subsequently re-fined the analysis by calibrating the relative rank numbers with known sales figures that we obtained directly from publishers. We then checked that with analyst estimates of Amazon's overall book sales revenues. We now estimate that sales of titles beyond the top 100,000 account for somewhere between 20 percent and 30 percent of Amazon's total book sales, and have used 25 percent as a median figure.

2. THE RISE AND FALL OF THE HIT

28 *The rise of such powerful*: Benjamin's essay is "The Work of Art in the Age of Mechanical Reproduction," 1936.

3. A SHORT HISTORY OF THE LONG TAIL

48 *"I was sorting through"*: Bezos was speaking at the Churchill Club in February 2005.

50 *Finally, to give an idea*: Robb's Web site is at globalguerrillas.typepad.com. The post is dated March 18, 2005.

5. THE NEW PRODUCERS

65 *In January 2001*: For the Wikipedia background, I relied heavily on "The Book Stops Here" by Daniel Pink, which we published in *Wired* in March 2005.

69 *Author Paul Graham*: www.paulgraham.com/web20.html.

78 *South Korea's*: The source is the World Economic Forum's *Global Agenda* magazine, 2006.

80 *Soon more videos*: I am indebted to Xeni Jardin's excellent article in *Wired* magazine, December 2005, for the details in this passage.

83 *A team at the University*: Ryan Shaw and his colleagues at the Media Streams Metadata Exchange at the School of Information Science and Management.

6. THE NEW MARKETS

86 *Publishers ensure*: Source: www.nacs.org.

87 *It made that database*: Source: www.bisg.org.

7. THE NEW TASTEMAKERS

109 *"Historically Blockbuster"*: Hastings was speaking at the Lehman Brothers Small Cap Conference in November 2005.

8. LONG TAIL ECONOMICS

126 *In other words*: I've used the term "powerlaw" loosely here to refer to distributions in the form of $y = ax^k$. In the empirical data used in this book, y is typically absolute sales or popularity and x is the corresponding sales or popularity rank of unique products. The a term is a constant for a large x, and k is the power to which x is raised, called the "powerlaw exponent." In fact, there are many variations of these kinds of exponentials, and different markets that at first glance look like powerlaws may actually be "lognormal" distributions or other statistical cousins. It's not within the scope of this book to explore these differences, but I am indebted to Hal Varian of the University of California, Berkeley (and Google), for pointing out this subtlety.

128 *Sadly, here's*: Source: www.film-festival.org.

130 *The same is true*: The statistics here for Barnes & Noble, PRX, and rediff.com all come directly from personal correspondence with their executives.

135 *A 2005 study*: This study has not yet been published and was provided in draft form; as a result some of these figures are subject to change in the final version.

137 *Another way to look*: The contrast between online and offline markets is striking. The differences between the sales distribution of the markets are shown in table form on the next page.

PERCENTAGE OF TOTAL SALES

Title Rank	Wal-Mart*	Rhapsody	Blockbuster*	Netflix
1–100	65%	47%	68%	38%
101 and up	36%	53%	32%	62%

*Wal-Mart and Blockbuster sales are actually figures from Nielsen's SoundScan and VideoScan, which measure overall offline sales for those two retail categories. But because Wal-Mart and Blockbuster are the largest retailers in the market, it's a safe assumption that their sales patterns are very similar.

145 *"For most of human"*: Originally published in *Forbes ASAP*, this passage also appears in *Telecosm: How Infinite Bandwidth Will Revolutionize Our World*, 2000.

145 *So how to reconcile*: Personal correspondence.

9. THE SHORT HEAD

150 *"People cluster"*: *The Atlantic Monthly*, October 2005.

150 *"A store selling"*: *Discover* magazine, September 2005.

151 *"Towns and suburbs"*: *The Death and Life of Great American Cities*, originally published in 1961.

156 *Of the estimated 30,000*: Gottlieb was interviewed in the *Frontline* documentary "The Way the Music Died," 2004.

162 *In America, 20 percent*: Source: Brynjolfsson, Smith, and Hu, 2003.

10. THE PARADISE OF CHOICE

170 *He cited*: "Why Choice Is Demotivating: Can One Desire Too Much of a Good Thing?" Sheena Iyengar (Columbia) and Mark Lepper (Stanford), 2000.

176 *One of the better-known bits*: "The Lure of Choice," Nicola Brown and Barbara Summers (Leeds University Business School) and Daniel Read (London School of Economics), 2002.

176 *Francis Hamit*: Personal communication.

11. NICHE CULTURE

184 *Virginia Postrel*: *Forbes ASAP*, 1998.

12. THE INFINITE SCREEN

195 *TV produces more*: "How Much Information?" Hal Varian (UC Berkeley School of Information Management and Systems) and colleagues, 2003.

197 *Jeremy Allaire*: Source: *Streaming Media*, October 2005.

199 *Rob Reid*: Personal communication.

INDEX

Abrams Report, The, 193
abundance, 18, 19, 25, 43, 143–46, 151, 223
ad-hoc organization, 159, 160
advertising, 98, 110, 123, 143, 164, 210–11, 224
  Google and, 10, 23–24, 50, 88, 89, 139, 210–16, 219
  television, 30, 165–66
age, 142–43
aggregators, 57, 88–97, 112, 135, 148, 203, 215, 216
  DJs and, 179, 180
  hybrid retailers, 89–91, 92
  pure digital retailers, 91, 92, 96–97, 218–19
  rules for, 217–26
Alibris, 86, 87, 88
Allaire, Jeremy, 197
amateurs, 63, 73, 78, 84, 167
  in peer production, 73, 79, 219
  in Pro-Am collaborations, 60–63, 65
  Wikipedia and, 65
Amazon, 8–9, 13, 24, 57, 89, 92–95, 135, 162, 204, 218, 226
  books on, 15–16, 23, 48–49, 87, 92–93, 94–95, 138–39, 169
  Marketplace program of, 93–94, 173, 202, 218
  music on, 90–91, 155
  recommendations on, 16, 202
  searching for items on, 161
  tagging on, 161–62
  total inventory and sales of, 23
American Airlines, 109
Apple, 64
  GarageBand, 63
  iPod, 3, 34, 36, 97, 175, 190, 198
  iTunes, *see* iTunes
architecture of participation, 83–84
Arcuni, Peter, 104, 105, 106
art, 116

astronomy, 58–62
AT&T, 46
attention, 138, 143, 146, 165, 166

Baby Bells, 109
BagelRadio, 105
Barnes & Noble, 47, 49, 77, 87, 130
Barrio305, 197, 198
Basic Channel, 179–80
Bechtel, Robin, 102–3
Benioff, Mark, 207–8, 209
Benjamin, Walter, 28
Best Buy, 49, 89, 93, 133, 155, 218
Bezos, Jeff, 13, 47, 48, 49, 50, 92
BigChampagne, 33, 103
Birdmonster, 104–6
BitTorrent, 97
Black House, 168
Black Swan Problem, 120
Blockbuster, 26, 109, 134, 153, 160–61, 169
Bloglines, 88, 89
blogs, 55–57, 63, 68, 69, 75, 82, 83, 88, 89, 99, 108, 123–24, 137, 140, 185–86, 188–89, 190, 220
  music, 105, 106, 108, 123
  popularity of, 186–88
  time and, 143
  top ten, 113
BMG, 31
BoingBoing, 108
Bollywood, 17
BookQuest, 85
books, 3, 5, 9, 26, 47–49, 71, 75–76, 97, 116
  Dewey Decimal System and, 157–59, 160, 161
  in libraries, 157–60, 161
  print-on-demand, 63, 95–96
  sales data for, 121
  self-publishing of, 76–78, 82, 167
  used, 85–88

bookstores, 47, 162–63
  Amazon, 15–16, 23, 48–49, 87,
    92–93, 94–95, 138–39, 169
  Barnes & Noble, 47, 49, 77, 87, 130
  Borders, 23, 47, 169
BookSurge, 95
Borders, 23, 47, 169
Brightcove, 197
broadband, 53, 193, 198, 224
broadcast technologies, 18, 29, 147, 148,
  164, 166, 191
  see also radio; television
Brynjolfsson, Erik, 135
Business Week, 169
buzz, 164–65

cars, 169
catalog shopping, 42–44, 46–47, 49,
  135–36, 147, 164
  hybrid retailers and, 89–91, 92
categorization, 156–62, 203
CD Baby, 105, 106
CDs, 9, 17, 22, 90–91, 102, 137, 139,
  149, 155–56, 182, 220
  burning of, 33, 34, 175
  sales of, 175
celebrities, 107–8
cell phones, 36, 198
Chicago Tribune, 187
choice and variety, 53, 126, 130, 135,
  143, 148, 150, 151, 165, 167,
  168–76, 180–82, 184, 189–90, 200,
  218
  economics of, 175–76
  "either/or" vs. "and," 222–23
  fragmentation and, 181, 189–91
Chronicles of Narnia sketch, 80–81
Cinderblock, 106
cities, 149–51
citizen journalism, 78
Clear Channel, 36
consumers, see customers
Consumers Union, 153
control, 221–24
copyright, 74–75, 167, 180, 196, 217
Corante, 181
Cosgrove, Stuart, 177–78
costs
  of reaching niches, 53–57
  shelves and, 153
creation
  map of, 83–84
  motives for, 73–74, 78
Creative Commons, 75, 80

Crosbie, Vin, 181
crowdsourcing, 219
Crown Books, 47
CSI, 37, 192, 193, 194, 220
culture
  hit-driven, 38–40
  local, 27, 191
  mass, 28, 148, 181, 182, 183–84, 185,
    189, 191, 199
  massively parallel, 182–85, 191
  microcultures, 183–85
  pop, 28, 30
Culture and Society (Williams), 185
customers (consumers)
  line between producers and, 63–64,
    83–84
  Long Tail of, 163–64
  reviews by, 55, 56, 64, 99, 123, 124,
    173, 219, 222
CustomFlix, 95

DailyCandy, 108
Daily Kos, 187
Daily Me, 189
Dash, Anil, 182
Dell, 98–99
demand, 8, 9, 40, 99, 165
  cities and, 150
  curve of, 52, 53, 57, 142
  filters and, 109
  local, 17–18, 162–64, 220
  in Long Tail, 10
  Long Tail's effect on, 137–38
  natural shape of, 9, 53
  supply and, 11, 16, 24, 26, 52, 55–56,
    94
  time and, 142
democratizing of distribution, 55, 57, 81,
  84, 88, 107, 179
democratizing of production, 54, 55, 57,
  62–65, 73, 82, 84, 107, 178, 179
demographics, 169
Demos, 60, 62
Dewey Decimal System, 157–59, 160, 161
digital jukeboxes, 7–8
Diller, Barry, 79, 81, 82
distribution, 143, 180, 193, 198–99
  democratized, 55, 57, 81, 84, 88, 107,
    179
  inefficient, 16, 53, 126, 127–30, 156,
    166, 195
  multiple channels for, 219–20
diversity, 53, 184
DJs, 177–80

DVDs, 95, 97, 129–30, 133–34, 136–37, 142, 153, 169
  extras on, 222
  Netflix and, *see* Netflix
  television shows on, 9, 129, 196
DVRs, 38, 80, 193, 195–96
  TiVo, 38, 190, 193, 195

eBay, 10, 11, 12, 24, 55, 57, 88, 89, 93, 139, 169, 201–3, 219, 221
Ecast, 7–8
economics, 143–44, 145, 146
  80/20 Rule in, 7, 12, 125, 130–35, 136
  Long Tail, 125–46
  of variety, 175–76
Economist, 6
800 numbers, 46–47
80/20 Rule, 7, 12, 125, 130–35, 136
Eminem, 32
encyclopedias, 65–66, 71, 72, 73
  Britannica, 66, 67, 69, 70–71, 72, 73
  Encarta, 66
  Wikipedia, *see* Wikipedia
Ernestus, Mark, 179–80
Excite, 211
exposure culture, 74

Faxon, 85
FCC, 36
Ferris, Timothy, 60
Fey, Tina, 80
file trading, 33, 34, 74, 75, 97, 167, 175
films, *see* movies
filters, 53, 57, 108–24, 134, 135, 136, 138, 141, 148, 179, 189, 190, 223
  customer reviews, 55, 56, 64, 99, 123, 124, 173, 219, 222
  eBay and, 203
  music and, 110–12, 114–15
  post-filters, 122–24, 223
  pre-filters, 122–24, 223
  recommendations, *see* recommendations
Firefox, 50
Flickr, 108
Florida, Richard, 150
folksonomies, 162
Food Marketing Institute, 45
Fooled by Randomness (Taleb), 120
Forbes, 172
Ford, Henry, 44
fragmentation, 181, 189–91
free services, 223–24
Frog Design, 107

GarageBand, 63
geographic limitations, 17–18, 162–64, 220
German Ideology, The (Marx), 62
Gilder, George, 145–46
Gladwell, Malcolm, 176
Global Guerrillas, 50
globalization, 169
GOATSE, 182
Goldstein, Patrick, 38
Google, 55, 56, 57, 68, 69–70, 74, 89, 99, 108–9, 116, 117, 123, 137, 153, 173, 174, 182, 203
  advertising and, 10, 23–24, 50, 88, 89, 139, 210–16, 219
  categorization and, 157, 159, 161
  time and, 142–43
  Video, 89, 90, 97, 192–93, 198
Gottlieb, David, 156
Graham, Paul, 69–70
Grammy Awards, 38
Gross, Bill, 211

Hagel, John, 174–75
Half.com, 202
Halo 2, 64
Hamit, Francis, 176
Haque, Umair, 165–66, 220
Hardy, Ron, 178
Hastings, Reed, 10, 109–10
Hawk, Thomas, 194
Hayek, Friedrich, 186
Head
  offering products at both Tail and, 148
  Short, 155–56
  see also hits
Hirshberg, Peter, 140
History of House Sound of Chicago, The (Cosgrove), 177–78
hit albums, 32–33
Hitchens, Christopher, 188
hit-driven culture, 38–40, 120
hit-driven economics, 18
hits, 1–2, 3, 5, 8, 16, 18, 20, 27–40, 52, 72, 109, 120–21, 134–35, 137, 141, 147, 148, 164–67, 182
  Long Tail and, 10
  micro-, 35
  quality and, 116
  ratio of niche goods to, 53
  in Rhapsody downloads, 19, 20
  time and, 142–43
Hume, David, 120

IAC/InterActiveCorp, 79
ideas, 145
individualism, 189–90
information, 53, 89, 107, 137–38, 190, 191, 221–22
information theory, 115, 117
Instapundit, 187
InStyle, 107–8
intellectual property, 75
Interloc, 85–86
Internet, 2–6, 29, 41, 166
    distribution democratized by, 55
    growth of e-commerce on, 47–49, 147
    hybrid retailers and, 89–91, 92
Into Thin Air (Krakauer), 15–16
inventory, 132, 218–19
iPod, 3, 34, 36, 97, 175, 190, 198
iTunes, 3, 8, 9, 16, 24, 55, 57, 80, 88, 89, 90, 91, 97, 105, 106, 108, 149, 169, 175, 192, 195, 207, 215, 218, 220
    classical music on, 182
    filtering and, 111–12
    pricing of, 139, 221
Iyengar, Sheena, 172

Jacobs, Jane, 151
jam, 170–72, 173
Jarvis, Jeff, 80–81, 123
Jefferson, Thomas, 145
JibJab, 197
Jive Records, 31
Johnson, Steven, 150
Jones, Albert, 60
Jones, Norah, 32
JotSpot, 209
jukeboxes, digital, 7–8

Kamiokande II observatory, 58–59
Kelly, Kevin, 68–69
Kennedy, John F., 45
King Kullen, 44–45
KitchenAid, 203–5
"Knowing What You Like versus Discovering What You Want: The Influence of Choice Making Goals on Decision Satisfaction" (Iyengar et al.), 172
Knuckles, Frankie, 177
Koolhaas, Rem, 160
Kowalski, Richard, 61
Krakauer, Jon, 15–16
Kraus, Joe, 209–10, 211

Lagaan: Once Upon a Time in India, 17
Lankford, John, 62
LA Times, 38
LAUNCHcast, 100–102
LEGO, 205–7, 225
Letters to a Young Contrarian, 188
Levan, Larry, 178
libraries, 157–60, 161
Linux, 50
liquidity, 87, 88
local culture, 27, 191
locality, 17–18, 162–64, 220
Lonely Island, 79–81
Long Tail, 10–11, 13, 22–26
    aggregators and, *see* aggregators
    of customers, 163–64
    economics of, 125–46
    filters and, *see* filters
    history of, 41–51
    microstructure in, 139–41
    see also niches
Long Tail businesses, rules for, 217–26
lowest common denominator, 118, 147, 165
Lulu, 76–77, 82

machinima, 64
McKee, Bonnie, 99–103, 104
McNally, Michael, 207
McNaught, Robert, 60
magazines, 37, 97, 181
mail order, 42–44
    hybrid retailers and, 89–91, 92
Malthus, Thomas, 145
Mancuso, David, 178
Manley, Marty, 86
Married . . . with Children, 196
Mars, 61–62
Marx, Karl, 62, 125, 145
mashups, 33, 80
mass culture, 28, 148, 181, 182, 183–84, 185, 189, 191, 199
massively parallel culture, 182–85, 191
Mead, Carver, 144
Metallica, 74
Michaels, Lorne, 80
microchunking, 220
microcultures, 183–85
micro-hits, 35
Microsoft, 50, 70, 193, 208, 215
Minor Planet Mailing List, 61
Mintil International, 169
MIT, 135
Moore's law, 144

motives to create, 73–74, 78
movies, 3, 5, 6, 26, 28, 38–39, 97, 110, 199–200
  attention and, 165
  blockbuster, 1, 2, 79, 82, 110, 127
  Bollywood, 17
  box office revenues for, 127–29
  distribution bottlenecks and, 127–30
  documentaries, 182
  DVD extras and, 222
  indie and homemade, 57, 63, 64, 193
  machinima, 64
  Netflix and, *see* Netflix
  on-demand businesses and, 95
  pricing of, 199, 200
  rights and, 74–75, 196, 217
  in theaters, 17, 37, 151, 163, 176
  see also DVDs; video
MP3.com, 148–49
MP3s, 34, 211
  blogs for, 105, 106, 123
  iTunes and, *see* iTunes
MTV, 98, 102, 104
Murdoch, Rupert, 37
music, 1–6, 9–10, 30, 31–37, 82, 90–91, 97, 98, 99–106, 116, 136–37, 182, 226
  Amazon and, 90–91, 155
  blogs, 105, 106, 108, 123
  on CDs, *see* CDs
  classical, 182
  democratization of production of, 54, 63, 178, 179
  digital jukeboxes and, 7–8
  DJs and, 177–80
  file trading and, 33, 34, 74, 75, 97, 167, 175
  filters and, 110–12, 114–15
  hit albums, 32–33
  house, 177–80
  indie record labels and, 178–80
  iTunes and, *see* iTunes
  mashups, 33
  niche micromarkets in, 139–40
  pricing of, 139
  punk rock, 82–83
  record stores, 154–56
  Rhapsody and, *see* Rhapsody
  rights to, 74–75, 167, 180, 196, 217
  rock radio, 35–36, 98
  Wal-Mart and, 19–20, 22, 25, 26, 155–56, 169, 182
  as "want" market, 139

musical artists
  Birdmonster, 104–6
  Bonnie McKee, 99–103, 104
  My Chemical Romance, 103–4, 106
  *NSYNC, 31, 32
MusicBox, 178
Music for Robots, 105
My Chemical Romance, 103–4, 106
MySpace, 54, 89, 103, 104, 105, 106, 149, 219

Napster, 33, 175
NASA, 61–62
Nasdaq, 31
National Bureau of Economic Research, 169
Nature, 69
navigation layer, 109
NBA playoffs, 38
NBC, 80, 81
"need" vs. "want" markets, 138–39
Negroponte, Nicholas, 189
Netflix, 8, 9, 10, 13, 16, 24, 56, 57, 88, 89, 97, 109–10, 123, 130, 134, 169, 175, 190, 200, 218, 219
  documentaries on, 182
  inventory and sales of, 23, 132, 136
network effects, 126, 141, 164
neutrinos, 58–60
New Atlantic, 189
news, 142, 143, 185–89
  citizen journalism and, 78
newspapers, 185–88, 220
  declining readership of, 37
New York Times, 15, 112, 174, 182, 185–86, 188
nichebusters, 115
niche culture, 177–91, 199
niches, 3, 5–6, 8, 10, 16, 24, 26, 38, 46–47, 52, 72, 109, 134–35, 148, 166, 182, 219–21
  cities and, 150, 151
  collective impact of, 53
  costs of reaching, 53–57
  micromarkets, 139–40
  quality and, 116, 118–19
  rankings within, 114
  ratio of hits to, 53
  time and, 142–43
98 Percent Rule, 8, 9
Nintendo, 97
noise, 115–18, 119–20, 122
*NSYNC, 31, 32

Ochs, Adolph, 188
OhmyNews, 78
Oh Yeon Ho, 78
Olympics, 38
OMD, 168
ontology, 157, 161
Oracle, 208
O'Reilly, Tim, 83
organization and categorization, 156–62,
    203
Oscars, 38
Otalvaro, Noah, 197
OutKast, 32
overhead, 153
Overture, 211

Pandora, 34
Paradise Garage, 178
Paradox of Choice, The (Schwartz),
    170–71
Pareto, Vilfredo, 125, 126, 127, 130,
    131, 214
peer production, 73, 79, 219
peers, trust in, 98–99
peer-to-peer (P2P) file trading networks,
    33, 34, 74, 75, 97, 167, 175
personal computers
    production democratized by, 54,
    55
    SETI@home's use of, 61
Pink, Daniel, 66
piracy, 33, 34, 75, 223
Pitchfork Media, 108
playlist sharing, 34, 123
population spikes, 150
Posner, Richard, 185–86
Postrel, Virginia, 174, 184
powerlaw distributions, 121, 126–27,
    132, 139, 147
pricing, 138–39, 221, 222
Pro-Am collaborations, 60–63, 65
    Wikipedia, *see* Wikipedia
probabilistic systems, 68–69, 70, 71
producerism, 64
producers, 57, 58–84
    line between consumers and, 63–64,
    83–84
production, democratizing the tools of,
    54, 55, 57, 62–65, 73, 82, 84, 107,
    178, 179
PRX, 130
PureVolume, 103

quality, 71, 115–19, 126, 167, 191

radio, 1, 2, 4, 17–18, 29, 30, 100, 101,
    102–3, 104, 130, 164, 179, 195, 220
    attention and, 165
    Clear Channel and, 36
    FCC and, 36
    Internet, 34, 100–101, 105
    playlists on, 112
    rock, 35–36, 98
    Telecommunications Act and, 36
RealNetworks, 19
recommendations, 16, 53, 55–57, 107–8,
    110, 111, 115, 119, 122–24, 134,
    135, 153, 173, 174, 190, 217–18,
    222
    eBay and, 202–3
Reid, Rob, 109, 199–200
rent, 153
Reprise, 99–100, 101, 102, 103, 104
Republic.com (Sunstein), 189
reputation, 74, 141
reviews, customer, 55, 56, 64, 99, 123,
    124, 173, 219, 222
Reynolds, Glenn, 187
Rhapsody, 9, 13, 16, 19–22, 24, 57, 72,
    88, 91, 97, 106, 109, 175
    genres and filtering in, 35, 110–11,
    114, 140
    graphs of downloads from, 19, 21
    inventory and sales of, 23, 132,
    136
    popularity of titles on, 25
    pricing of, 221
    top ten artists on, 114
Rice to Riches, 168
Riggio, Steve, 77–78
ringtones, 130
Rise of the Creative Class, The (Florida),
    150
Robb, John, 50–51
Robertson, Michael, 148
Rocketboom, 193
Roebuck, Alvah C., 42
Rosen, Christine, 189–90

Salesforce.com, 207–10
Samberg, Andy, 79
samples, 135, 223–24
SAP, 208
Saturday Night Live, 80–81
scarcity, 223
    of information, 53
    mindset of, 167, 198–99, 222
    of products, 8, 9, 18, 23, 40, 116, 122,
    143–44, 145, 156, 165

Schaffer, Akiva, 79
Schaffer, Micah, 79
Schmidt, Eric, 213–15
Schonfeld, Erick, 115
Schwartz, Barry, 170–71
searches, 108, 119, 122, 154, 159, 160, 161, 172, 174, 211–12, 215–16
    costs of, 56, 135, 136
    on Google, 55, 56; *see also* Google
    vertical, 215
Searls, Doc, 64
Sears, Richard, 42
Sears, Roebuck and Co., 42–44, 164, 218
Seeing in the Dark (Ferris), 60
Seigenthaler, John, Sr., 67
Seinfeld, Jerry, 188
SETI@home, 61
Shelton, Ian, 59–60
shelves, 93–94, 96, 116–17, 122, 151–64
    categorization on, 156–62
    costs of selling products on, 153
    locality and, 17–18, 162–64, 20
    space on, 49, 53, 123, 126, 134, 136, 143, 144, 195
    wastefulness of, 152–53
Shirky, Clay, 158–59
Shopping.com, 202
signal-to-noise ratio, 115–18, 119–20, 122
Simpson, Joe, 15–16
Sims, 64
Sirius Radio, 36
SixApart, 182
Sky & Telescope, 62
Skype, 219, 223
Smith, Adam, 68, 144
SNOCAP, 90
software, 50, 62, 208–9
    Salesforce.com and, 207–10
Solidscape printer, 225–26
SoundScan, 136
South Korea, 78
spaghetti sauce, 176, 220
Spears, Britney, 32, 211
Spiradellis, Gregg, 197
Spore, 226
sports, 198
Sports Illustrated, 187
Starbucks, 168
Stern, Howard, 36

Stewart, Jon, 192, 193
Sturgeon's Law, 116
Sundance Film Festival, 217
Sunstein, Cass, 189
supermarkets, 44–46, 151, 153–54, 160, 173
Supernova 1987A, 59–60
supply, 123
    abundance and, 18, 19, 25, 43, 143–46, 151, 223
    demand and, 11, 16, 24, 26, 52, 55–56, 94
    scarcity and, *see* scarcity
Surowiecki, James, 68

Taccone, Jorma, 79
Taleb, Nassim, 120
Target, 93, 203–4, 218
tastemakers, 106–8
taxonomies, 156–62
Technorati, 113, 140, 186–87
Telecommunications Act, 36
television, 1, 2, 3, 4, 18, 26, 29–30, 81, 82, 97, 137, 164, 166, 181, 191, 194–96, 224
    advertising on, 30, 165–66
    attention and, 138, 146, 165
    DVDs, 9, 129, 196
    falling ratings in, 37–38
    golden age of, 29–30
    produced vs. available content on, 195–96
    programming conventions of, 198–99
    Web-only, 196–97, 198
textbooks, used, 86, 87
3D printers, 225–26
Tiki Bar TV, 193
time, 142–43
TiVo, 38, 190, 193, 195
toll-free 800 numbers, 46–47
top ten lists, 112–15
Touching the Void (Simpson), 15–16
Toys "R" Us, 93, 205
tribes of interest, 184
Triplets of Belleville, The, 17
TV Guide, 109
Twister, 142

USA Today, 67

Vann-Adibé, Robbie, 7–8
Varian, Hal, 12
variety, *see* choice and variety

VCRs, 199, 200
video(s), 79–82, 97, 192–200
  Chronicles of Narnia sketch, 80–81
  Google, 89, 90, 97, 192–93, 198
  Internet, 129–30, 196–97
  viral, 82
video games, 2, 3, 4, 50, 63, 64, 97, 217, 224
video rentals, 163, 199–200
  Blockbuster, 26, 109, 153, 160–61, 169
  Netflix, *see* Netflix
viral marketing, 34, 43
Von Oswald, Moritz, 179–80

Wales, Jimmy, 65, 66, 67, 71
Wallace, David Foster, 192
Wal-Mart, 44, 49, 55, 133, 201, 218
  music sold at, 19–20, 22, 25, 26, 155–56, 169, 182
"want" vs. "need" markets, 138–39
Warehouse, 177
warehouses, 41–42, 43, 46, 90, 218
waste, 145–46
Weatherford, Richard, 85–86, 87

Weblogs, Inc., 107
wedding planners, 174
West End Records, 178
White House, 168
White Store, 168
Wikipedia, 65–68, 69, 70, 71–73, 88, 89, 143, 191, 219
  Tail of, 72–73
Williams, Raymond, 185
Wired, 6, 10, 104, 124
Wisdom of Crowds, The (Surowiecki), 68
WKRP in Cincinnati, 196
World Series, 38
Wright, Will, 226
Wu, Tim, 74

Xbox, 50, 193

Yahoo!, 89, 193, 203, 215, 223
  LAUNCHcast, 100–102
Yeltsin, Boris, 45

Zipf, George, 125–26, 130
Zúñiga, Moulitsas, 187